LANFORD WILSON

LANFORD WILSON
The Talley Trilogy

CONTEMPORARY PLAYWRIGHTS SERIES

SK
A Smith and Kraus Book

A Smith and Kraus Book
Published by Smith and Kraus, Inc.
PO Box 127, Lyme, NH 03768

First Edition: March 1999
10 9 8 7 6 5 4 3 2 1

Fifth of July, Talley & Son, and *Talley's Folly*
reprinted by permission of Hill and Wang, a division of Farrar, Straus & Giroux, Inc.

Fifth of July ©1979 by Lanford Wilson, revised ©1982 by Lanford Wilson.
Talley's Folly ©1979 by Lanford Wilson.
Talley & Son ©1986 by Lanford Wilson, revised ©1995 by Lanford Wilson.
A Tale Told ©1981 by Lanford Wilson.

Book design by Julia Hill Gignoux, Freedom Hill Design

The Library of Congress Cataloging-In-Publication Data
Wilson, Lanford, 1937–
[Plays. Selections]
Lanford Wilson: the Talley trilogy. —1st ed.
p. cm. —(Contemporary playwrights series, ISSN 1067-9510)
Contents: Fifth of July—Talley & Son—Talley's Folly—A Tale Told.
ISBN 1-57525-133-7 (paper) ISBN 1-57525-069-1 (cloth)
I. Title. II. Series.
PS3573.I458A6   1996
812'.54—dc20   96-1909
CIP

CONTENTS

THE TALLEYS

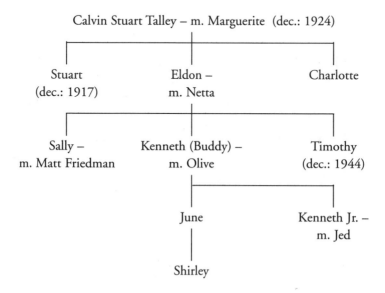

Calvin Stuart Talley – m. Marguerite (dec.: 1924)

Stuart (dec.: 1917)   Eldon – m. Netta   Charlotte

Sally – m. Matt Friedman   Kenneth (Buddy) – m. Olive   Timothy (dec.: 1944)

June   Kenneth Jr. – m. Jed

Shirley

FIFTH OF JULY

For Frank Anderson

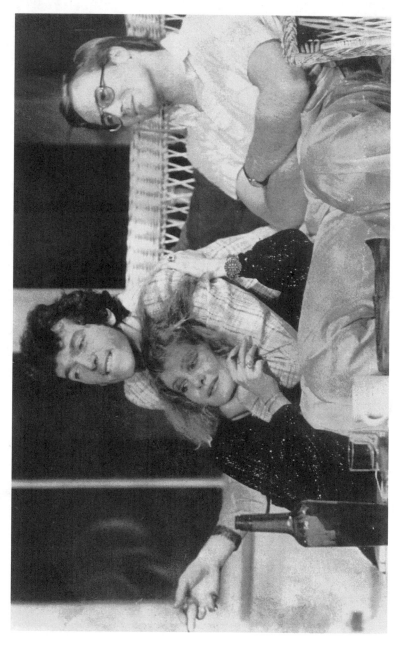

Nancy Snyder, Jonathan Hogan and William Hurt in the Circle Repertory Company production of *Fifth of July*. Photograph ©1980 by Gerry Goodstein.

INTRODUCTION

The genesis of *Fifth of July*, and what would develop into the Talley plays, occurred in about the same flurry of disorganized frustration as a distressingly large proportion of my work. In other words I was floundering, looking for any idea that would drive a wedge into this solid block of anger and dismay and alarm and, well, *frustration* I was experiencing at the complacent state of the country after the activism of the 60s and early 70s. For years soldiers had been returning from Vietnam to join the peace movement and tell us just how bad it was over there. The entire student body of the country, every artist I knew, had been either protesting or fleeing. And finally the war was over. It seemed to take years but America had finally finished pulling our troops the hell out of there. It was finally the admission of a tragic, immoral error. Statesmen, missing the point magnificently, tried to call our signing of a cease fire agreement a victory. We knew exactly what it was and didn't care as long as it was over. But then what often happens in defeat: The country seemed willing to forgive in order to forget and the war was all but forgotten, pushed under the rug. Our soldiers returned, many of them years later, from hospitals, to a cold shoulder and a psychiatrist, to group therapy and silence. Student protesters shut up, graduated, and started looking for good jobs. The air skillfully had been let out of the bell-bottomed balloon and it had sunk behind some hill, unnoticed. One almost had to admire the beautifully finessed betrayal of the peace movement. America has a way of turning something fine into bunk—or more likely into a buck. If African-Americans, finally in union, cry, "Black is beautiful," within a week it will be a new shade of lipstick. We had been singing "We Will Overcome" for years, but we had not overcome, we had been overcome, and I didn't know quite how it had been achieved.

To illustrate just how far we've traveled from meaningful activism, notice how quaint, old-hat, tiresome, and retrograde all that sounds now.

I was as content personally as I had been in a long time. I had a decent love life, the house I had bought and started to restore five years earlier was almost habitable, my work was being seen all over the country and still I felt—what? mislead, deceived. The life we had envisioned after the war had been degraded, dismissed; the well had been tainted. We had gone from Kennedy to Johnson to Nixon, through Watergate, to "I'm not a Lincoln, I'm a Ford." It's weird to be almost perfectly content and still seething. Oh, well...

One beautiful night my lover and I were walking around Washington Square Park. Maybe we had come from dinner or were on our way. He had been reading a book of Eskimo myths. (He was like that.) He was very serious as he told me, straight-faced, the story of an Arctic Hero who had saved the food supply of his family by a means so vile they couldn't eat it and so they had all starved to death. The story, if you look at it right, is hilarious. It is also perfectly ironic. And it occurred to me that night that it was also an apt metaphor for our involvement in that damn war. I wrote just that scene: the telling of the Eskimo myth. The impudent comments that are interpolated into Weston's telling of the story are roughly my thoughts as the myth was related to me that night. I had no characters, just the teller of the story and the listeners' rude remarks, about a three-page scene. I carried the notebook around for weeks. It also contained a scene that eighteen years later became scene two of *Sympathetic Magic*. I thought maybe the Eskimo scene took place in the friendly confines of the art department of an advertising agency I had worked for in Chicago. I believe I changed the locale because I thought John Lee Beatty, Circle Rep's brilliant set designer, would be completely uninterested in designing an art department. Now I almost wish I hadn't changed it, he would have designed a wonderful art department. The locale changed to Long Island; I had wanted to write something that took place there since I first saw the place. Maybe one of those big old houses. The characters (I still didn't know who they were) would be restoring the place, as I was restoring my house. I certainly knew about that. They would be building a garden, working on the land. The play would be one of restoration and commitment. Something the country sorely needed. I was almost surprised when I realized that the play had to be set in my hometown of Lebanon, Missouri. This had to be about the heartland. The house would not necessarily be in disrepair, but Jed would be a botanist and would be building a garden.

That summer I accepted the job of teaching a playwrighting course at Southampton College. I am not a teacher. The reason I write about teachers so often must be that I admire them enormously and think good teachers are the heroes of our time. There have been four who certainly were central to my life's path. I should have asked someone how to teach or at least had the sense to make a syllabus. On the first day I told the class everything I knew about playwrighting. And there was still half an hour left in the period. I don't know how I stuttered through that summer semester but I'm pretty sure I didn't fool anyone.

Among my students was a stunningly handsome man who had had both legs blown off AK (above the knee) in Vietnam. He walked with two aluminum crutches, clattering like a crab across the room. He was always late because it took him longer to get from class to class, and (maddeningly) he always took a seat by the windows—across the room from the door. The class was silent as he clanged cheerfully to his chair, hips flying out akimbo with each step, and sat with a great crash. Then he breathed a deep, exhausted sigh of relief and said, self-deprecatingly, describing what he must look like to the class, "Cha cha cha." He had a wonderful sense of humor and was a pretty darn good writer. The majority of the class was actually very talented. The only thing I felt bad about was their teacher.

One day I was given a lift home by a sweet, beautiful, tiny, infuriating pest of a girl who drove me crazy, usually standing at the back of the class:

> Teacher: Carey, would you care to sit down?
> Student: I can't I got this really bitchy rash on my
>   ass that's killing me.
> Teacher: Well, you're driving me crazy fidgeting
>   around back there.
> Student: That's your problem.

She was so flip and uninterested, staring out the window, chewing gum, playing with her hair, that I should have expected that her play, three pages, torn from a spiral notebook, written in faint pencil, would be the best work the class did all summer. Anyway, she drove me home. In the course of conversation, discussing the class, I said that David (I'll call him) was really a remarkably good-looking man. "Really?" she replied, "I've never looked at him. I don't think people like that like to be looked at."

That chilling remark was the beginning of *Fifth of July*. That was the wedge that finally split open the knot of all I had been feeling and had not known how to approach. Almost everything in the play can be traced to that ride home.

I took David out for coffee. I told him I wanted to write a play about someone who had come home injured. David had had his legs blown off in a land mine accident—those devices our government currently maintains are essential to its security. He said the only other person who had asked him how he had been injured was a nurse in the hospital where he was stationed in England. They had been married now three years and were expecting their first child.

I told him I was thinking of making my character gay. He said, "Well, don't make him a downer, I'm so sick of angry, depressed, bitter vets in plays." I said I was sick of depressed gays in plays (one of them my own) and was thinking of the play as a comedy. One where the character's homosexuality was hardly mentioned, and was certainly not an issue. I promised to give him a lover as supportive and gorgeous as David's wife.

It had first been my intention to make the character of Kenneth quite effeminate: gestures so huge and sweeping that he was forever losing his balance and falling over. But in the writing it wouldn't happen. David's steady sense of humor and dignity and proportion kept asserting itself on my character. And one of the things he said frightened him the most was falling over backwards. "You're completely helpless and it's a bitch to get back up. You have to crawl to a big heavy chair for support, and it still isn't easy."

This play was written when Circle Rep was at its most glorious. Actors were in the office all the time; I almost never left. Much of the play was written with actors blabbing away in the room, all but looking over my shoulder. Everything seemed to feed the play, not just the energy of the office, and of people coming from one of Marshall's rehearsals, but when writing is going well, everything seems to pertain to your work. One of our board members was an accountant. He came to a meeting early, exhausted, saying what a weekend he'd had. His dad (also an accountant) had died three years ago and his mother had been carrying the ashes around ever since. They had finally gotten her to dump them in the lake. On the way back from the lake, walking to the car, she had a stroke. Not a big one, just a mild little stroke, but she'd been at the doctor's office all day. That went into the play that night and was the initiation of a nice offstage character named Matt Friedman (an accountant).

I wrote for specific actors in the company. Helen Stenborg, of course, and several I hadn't worked with before. My vet would be a newcomer to the company, Bill Hurt; his lover would be Jeff Daniels who had been so brilliant in *The Farm* the year before. Danton Stone had a moment, only a second, in *Mrs. Murry's Farm,* where he was momentarily confused. That had suggested someone I met in Woodstock; the guy was an actor but I met so many musicians there that I made my confused, bemused, character a composer. In the first draft I didn't have names for the characters. They were called Bill and Jeff and Danton and John—I never did come up with another name for the John Hogan character.

The first reading of the script was thrilling. The actors had known their characters for months, just waiting for me to finish the script. I had written Shirley for Amy Wright, an actress I had just talked to on the street, not a member of the company. She introduced herself and said she had played The Girl in *Hot L* the year before. I asked how she had been in it. She said she had been brilliant of course. She was so vibrant and exciting I knew I wanted her in my plays. She was probably twenty-two and Shirley was fourteen, but what the hell. All the other actors were deeply into their characters and playing the devil out of them on the first reading—Marshall had encouraged them not to try to act unless an impulse came to them and if that happened for God's sake go with it. Amy just read—dull words. I was watching her very closely as I was the only one in the company who knew her. Toward the end of the first act she looked around and seemed to realize that she wasn't showing Marshall (who didn't know her from Eve) or anyone else—anything. So she took a deep breath, glared daggers at me, cut loose, and just amazed everyone. She was so convincing in the part I'm afraid it cursed her with playing teenagers till she was well into her thirties. The part of Gwen had been written for Trish Hawkins. I wanted Trish in every play I wrote. I was crushed when she couldn't do it. Marshall and I thought we would have to go out of the company to replace her. We held auditions within the company first, but with low expectations. Nancy Snyder blew us totally away. She gave one of those auditions where the only thing to say is you've got the part, we don't need to read anyone else. We've been lucky with that role. When Nancy couldn't move to Broadway she was replaced by Swoozie Kurtz who won the Tony that year (deservedly) for best supporting actress.

All during rehearsals I kept working on the script. The focus was slightly off—Gwen was running away with the show, and I couldn't seem to tame her. It didn't matter; the play opened in late April and was repeatedly extended to run through the summer.

Almost two years later, more than a year after the play had been published, Gordon Davidson, Artistic Director of the Mark Taper Forum in Los Angeles, saw *Talley's Folly* and said he wanted to produce both the plays in rotating rep. He asked if there were any changes I wanted to make in *Fifth of July*. I first said no, but when I reread the play I realized immediately how to refocus it more toward Kenny, and to what I had been trying to say all along. Some of Gwen's funniest lines had to be sacrificed (a killer, that), but in the end it's closer now to what I was trying to say.

After every opening night at Circle Rep a crew cleared away the chairs and we had a party. A loud, dancing, lots-of-food-and-wine, party. One of our party regulars was the excellent director and critic Harold Clurman. Being a theater man and fond of the company, he felt nothing of partying with us all night then ripping our heads off in print. He always had a collection of girls around him who prompted him to tell fanciful stories and give impromptu lectures on aspects of the theater and art in general. On one of these openings Harold was talking about commitment. One of the girls said, "Lanford is writing a play about commitment." Harold said, "Oh, I don't care what a play is about, just so long as it's joyous!" A few months later, at another opening, I told him I was just about finished with my "joyous" play, but I wasn't certain how it would end. "It must end joyously!" he said, then grabbed my arm, and growled very seriously, "But what happened to the play you were writing about commitment?"

What a fine man he was, and what an inspiration. I promised myself the next comedy, the next "joyous" play I wrote, I would dedicate to Harold Clurman.

ORIGINAL PRODUCTION

Fifth of July was first presented by the Circle Repertory Company in New York City, on April 27, 1978. It was directed by Marshall W. Mason; the setting was by John Lee Beatty; costumes were by Laura Crow; lighting was by Marc. B. Weiss; the original song was by Jonathan Hogan; sound was by Chuck London. The cast, in order of appearance, was as follows:

Kenneth Talley, Jr.	William Hurt
John Landis	Jonathan Hogan
Gwen Landis	Nancy Snyder
Jed Jenkins	Jeff Daniels
June Talley	Joyce Reehling
Shirley Talley	Amy Wright
Sally Friedman	Helen Stenborg
Weston Hurley	Danton Stone

(*Fifth of July* ran at Circle Repertory Company for 168 performances. For the last fourteen weeks Ken was played by Timothy Shelton.)

Fifth of July was subsequently presented by Jerry Arrow, Robert Lussier and Warner Productions, Inc. at the New Apollo Theatre, in New York City, on November 5, 1980. It was again directed by Marshall W. Mason; the setting was by John Lee Beatty; costumes were by Laura Crow; lighting was by Dennis Parichy; the sound by Chuck London; and the production stage manager was Fred Reinglas. The cast, in order of appearance, was as follows:

Kenneth Talley, Jr.	Christopher Reeve*
Jed Jenkins	Jeff Daniels
John Landis	Jonathan Hogan
Gwen Landis	Swoosie Kurtz
June Talley	Joyce Reehling
Shirley Talley	Amy Wright
Sally Friedman	Mary Carver
Weston Hurley	Danton Stone

later succeeded by Richard Thomas

CHARACTERS

KENNETH TALLEY, JR., had both legs blown off seven years ago in the Vietnam War. He is 32, strong, good-looking and a touch cynical, but not deeply.

JED JENKINS, 25, his lover. Larger, stronger; an almost silent listener.

JUNE TALLEY, 34, Ken's sister.

SHIRLEY TALLEY, 14, her daughter.

JOHN LANDIS, 33, childhood friend of the Talleys.

GWEN LANDIS, 33, his wife. Racy.

WESTON HURLEY, 25, composer friend of Gwen and John. Listens late.

SALLY FRIEDMAN, 64, Ken and June's Aunt. Not really batty; preoccupied.

SCENE

The Talley place, a farm near Lebanon, Missouri

TIME

Act I: Early evening, Independence Day, 1977
Act II: The following morning

Fifth of July

ACT ONE

The set is the large sun porch/family room of a prosperous southern Missouri farmhouse built around 1865.

We see the wide doors to a hallway upstage, and a stairway going up. At one side, doors open to a porch that wraps around most or all of the house.

The room is furnished with two matching armchairs, tables, a desk. Ken sits at the desk. He is very hung over, and in this state tends to be blandly cynical.

He is listening to a small portable tape recording. The recording is of a boy who speaks with great hesitation, mangling words so badly nothing is intelligible to us. Ken listens, makes notes, rubs his eyes and head. There is the sound of distant firecrackers. Followed by dogs barking. Ken turns off the recording, realizes what the noise is, looks back to the recording, rewinds a bit of it, turns it on again.

Jed comes up onto the porch.

JED. Light's going, I'm about half blind.

KEN. *(Turning the recording off.)* What say?

JED. Don't stop. I have to go back down. I said the light's going; can't see a thing down there.

KEN. Where have you been hiding all afternoon?

JED. Aw, the stupid herb garden is going rank. The lavender's all other the thyme, the angelica's flopping all over the germander. Where are your two friends? *(Jed enters house.)*

KEN. John is showing Gwen his hometown, which should take about ten minutes.

JED. They came down to see me this afternoon. John was bragging about their garden in Carmel. It really pissed me off. I was throwing that lavender over my back, the whole garden smells like an English bathhouse. Check it out early. It'll be grown over by noon. *(Kisses him.)*

KEN. Holy God, you smell terrific.

JED. Come on, under that fragrance I'm as rank as a goat. You look like you're in great shape.

KEN. Oh, I'm fine. On a scale of one to ten, I'm about to show up on the chart any minute now.

JED. How much did you drink last night?

KEN. Much. You have no idea how little you missed by going to bed.

JED. That was the point.

KEN. You made that clear.

JED. I tried.

KEN. We wake you?

JED. Not me.

KEN. Even you. Even the dead. The little people in the wood. I didn't get to bed till five-thirty. All the birds were having fits. "Get the hell off that nest, get down into the garden and get me a bug." Got up at ten, that's six-thirty, seven-thirty—

JED. Four and a half. Did you eat?

KEN. I had coffee, I didn't even recognize it.

JED. You take your pills?

KEN. After last night my system would go into shock if I sent down one more chemical. *(Jed gets up.)* Yes, yes. I took my vitamins, I took my minerals, I took my protein and I took my birth control pill— Now, if only I had something to start it all moving. I've been up almost twelve hours, my heart hasn't beaten more than five times.

JED. You still feeling sorry for yourself?

KEN. *(Pause. Level.)* I wouldn't put it quite like that.

JED. How would you put it? *(Pause.)* It's been two weeks. You've had time to recover by now.

KEN. The incident to which you refer merely served as an illustration of something of which I've been aware for some time. *(They look at each other, mild Mexican standoff.)*

JED. You get testy you start sounding like a bad textbook.

KEN. I'm not testy.

JED. What are you?

GWEN. *(Off.)* Honey, did you call that prick in Nashville?

JOHN. *(Off.)* Negative, we're taking dinner with him tomorrow at eight.

KEN. Did he say "negative"? Dear God.

JED. I'll close the door.

KEN. We'll talk tomorrow after they've gone.

JED. Could I have that in writing?

JOHN. *(Enters.)* Hey, Teacher. Oh, hi, Jed—you should have stayed up. We had a party last night.

JED. *(Still looking at Ken.)* So I hear.

GWEN. *(Dead stop on porch.)* Oh, God! I have never been at such peace in my life!

JOHN. We've been everywhere.

GWEN. *(Entering.)* I want you to know this afternoon I have set your town on its ass.

JOHN. Don't kid yourself. Lebanon, Missouri, has been on its ass for a hundred and fifty years.

GWEN. I love the way you people live. *(Kisses Jed.)*

JOHN. We brought back munchies for everybody.

JED. I have to go turn off the water. *(Sits on sofa, puts on shoes and socks.)*

GWEN. *(As she hands out burgers and fries.)* Hey, I forgot to ask: What are the little red flags?

JED. What little red flags?

JOHN. What little red flags?

GWEN. These sweet little red flags that are in rows all over the hill.

KEN. Oh, God! That's were Jed has planted his—hedges.

GWEN. Hedges.

JED. That's O.K. In five years you'll be able to see the plants.

GWEN. Honey, you think you've explained something to me, don't you? It's not that I'm slow; I'm just not horticultural.

KEN. He's making an English garden.

GWEN. *(To Jed.)* You tell me.

JED. Each flag is where I planted a cutting.

GWEN. Yeah?

JED. A row of cuttings will grow into a hedge. The hedges will divide the garden into rooms.

GWEN. Rooms.

JED. Eventually the hedges will be held at seven feet tall; dividing the garden into different-sized spaces that are called rooms. And each room is treated differently—a pool or an herb garden, a rose garden, etc.

GWEN. And you're starting seven foot walls with plants I can't even see? You couldn't buy grown plants?

JED. Not the variety I want. I have to go turn off the water.

KEN. He baby-sat the cuttings all winter. Turned this sun porch into a greenhouse. He closed off the rest of the house, just lived in this room and the kitchen.

GWEN. You guys spent the winter here?

JED. I was here this winter. Ken was in St. Louis.

GWEN. Wait a minute. What am I hearing? What's the dirt?

KEN. I came down here three or four times.

JED. Twice.

KEN. Jed came up to St. Louis three or four times.

JED. Five. I'll be right back. *(Exits.)*

GWEN. What kind of lover sits down here alone all winter rooting hedges?

KEN. A botanical lover.

JOHN. Broke your heart, right? Don't forget we know you.

KEN. *(Flattering himself.)* No...no, come on. I'm not as wild as we used to be.

GWEN. Oh, sure. Alone in St. Louis all winter.

KEN. Listen—Gwen—stop flying around. *(They do rather.)* I've been thinking since you called. How serious are you about buying a place down here for your new studio?

GWEN. Oh, man, we have gotta have our own studio.

JOHN. The studios in Nashville bleed you dry. You wouldn't believe it.

KEN. I may have a proposition for you. If we could talk about this before Jed gets back up here.

JOHN. What's on your mind?

KEN. I know this place is a wreck, but actually any place you find would have to be completely rebuilt before you could use it for a recording studio wouldn't it?

JUNE. *(Entering room from upstairs. Carries purse.)* I thought I heard you come back. So Kenny, are we doing this?

GWEN. Oh great. You haven't gone yet. I really made John burn rubber.

KEN. Gone where?

GWEN. You know. The funeral down by the river—Nommy yo-ho; Krisna yommy yommy—

KEN. No, no, soon.

GWEN. Good, because I'm coming along.

JUNE. Oh, sweetheart. You don't want to do that, really.

GWEN. Listen, Matt Friedman was very important to me too; I mean he really straightened me out. He was like a leveling influence. Like he told me not to take flying lessons. He kept trying to impress on me that I have a grave responsibility.

KEN. He didn't mean his, Gwen.

GWEN. You're quick. He was really pissed because Schwartzkoff, the bastard, appointed his wife's nephew to handle the trust. And if that's not nepotism, like by definition, I don't know what is.

KEN. *(To Gwen.)* Oh, that reminds me. You have a stack of phone calls. "While you were out."

JOHN. *(Crosses to Gwen.)* Later. Later. Honey, we got to get dressed if we're going to this shindig.

KEN. It's hardly a shindig.

JUNE. There's no reason for you two to—

GWEN. *(Looking out.)* Would you look at that fuckin' sunset! *(Wes enters from kitchen, exits upstairs.)*

KEN. Guaranteed every night.

JUNE. Aunt Sally doesn't show it, but she's really upset—

KEN. There's no reason for you to come.

JUNE. There's no ceremony.

JOHN. No, Gwen's got a real bug up her ass. She's been talking about it all afternoon.

GWEN. No Shit. Like I feel a responsibility, you know? *(Heads for stairs.)*

JUNE. There's no reason—

GWEN. *(Leaving, singing.)* Rock of Ages. Cleft—cleft for me. Let me hide. *(John gooses her. Gwen screams. Laughs. Shirley appears, sneaking after them. Yelps and runs off when she sees June.)*

JUNE. Shirley! Shirley! *(Gives up, gets pills out of purse.)* Why didn't you tell me those two were coming down here?

KEN. I believe I did.

JUNE. Don't get cute. *(Takes pill with wine.)*

KEN. They'll be gone tomorrow.

JUNE. I should have taken Shirley somewhere. Down to Branson for a couple of days.

KEN. How often do you see them?

JUNE. Every single year for the last five years they've showed up—always just happening to arrive on Shirley's birthday. Loaded down with presents.

KEN. Very subtle.

JUNE. Very cute.

KEN. Be thankful he doesn't come on Father's Day.

JUNE. *(Shirley might overhear.)* Shhh! The walls have ears. She's playing Mata Hari today. *(Pause.)* Oh, to hell with him. At least you've finally straightened yourself out.

KEN. Certainly not.

JUNE. In St. Louis you were never home when I called.

KEN. You don't have to look out for me any more, sis. I'm a big boy.

JUNE. Oh, sure. Running to every bar in town. I don't know what the hell you thought you were doing to yourself last winter.

KEN. Don't you?

JUNE. Oh, can the bitter and wise pose; I can't bear it. You're a lot better off back down here with Jed.

KEN. You were here two weeks ago. I think we all had a very graphic demonstration of the total fiasco it would be for me to stay here.

JUNE. *(Beat.)* I beg your pardon?

KEN. There are a number of options open to me.

JUNE. Kenny, it is all settled.

KEN. Very well. It's all settled.

JUNE. You signed a contract. This is your life, Ken; this is one thing you're not going to crap out on.

JOHN. *(Entering from upstairs.)* Yeah, babe. You said somebody called? Hey, babe. Look alive. I only have a sec.

KEN. What? Oh. Ah—what do you want first? A plasterer called. An Arthur Schwartzkoff called at eleven.

JOHN. What in the hell does he think he's doing? The man is crazy. You talked to him?

KEN. Not very coherently, I'm afraid.

JOHN. Damn. I told him not to call. If he did call not to leave his— *(Dialing.)* Hey. I wheeled Gwen by the high school to see where you'll be teaching this winter.

JUNE. We were just talking about that.

JOHN. How about that new building? That's what we were campaigning for, remember? Ten years ago.

KEN. Fifteen, but who's counting?

JUNE. The old building collapsed.

JOHN. You're shittin' me. That finally fell in?

KEN. Unfortunately nobody was in it at the time.

JOHN. *(Phone.)* Operator, sorry to wake you up, doll— This is a credit card call. Card number 072-691-3037L. L…as in Love your lovely voice. Thank *you. (June crosses to sofa and sits. John notices them.)* Is this the only phone?

KEN. Sorry.

JOHN. *(Phone.)* Yeah, doll. This is Jack, he in? Goddamn, we are really missing each other today. Sure, have him call, but person-to-person. Right. *(Hangs up.)*

JUNE. Boy, you're really becoming quite a magnate.

JOHN. Naw, naw, this is nothing. Leg work, busy work. It's nothing.

JUNE. Consisting mainly of keeping your wife at arm's length from the board of directors of her company.

JOHN. No, no, Gwen's cool. She just gets a little too enthusiastic sometimes.

JUNE. Then why all the clandestine phone calls?

GWEN. *(Off.)* Hey, John, what the hell's up?

JUNE. *(Yelling.)* Funny you should ask!

JOHN. Come on, lighten up. What are you doing?

JUNE. Well, I don't like it. We can see what's going on.

JOHN. There was only one thing I did that you ever liked.

GWEN. *(Off.)* Hey, John. What the hell's up.

JOHN. *(Sotto voce.)* Funny you should ask. *(Yelling.)* Comin', doll. *(Jed comes up on the porch.)* You said you had a scheme you wanted to talk over?

KEN. Uh…later.

JOHN. What's on your mind? 'Cause if it's what I think it is, we're definitely interested. We pulled up in front of the house, Gwen said this is the only place in the county that has the sort of layout we—

KEN. We'll talk, we'll talk. Good.

GWEN. *(Off.)* John, Goddamn it, shake a leg.

JOHN. Right with you, babe.

KEN. Later, okay?

JOHN. Sure, listen, we'll talk—I like it. *(Exits upstairs.)*

KEN. You ok?

JUNE. Yeah, I'm fine. *(Shirley enters and creeps up the stairs.)* Shirley!

KEN. Shirley, your mother is talking to you.

JUNE. Shirley, your uncle is talking to you. *(To Ken.)* What options?

KEN. I beg your pardon?

JUNE. You said you had a number of options open to you instead of staying down here to teach. As I recall you signed a contract. *(Jed enters.)*

KEN. Contracts are made to be broken, as is everything. *(To Jed, for June's benefit.)* There's no hurry, Jed. Gwen has decided she's coming with us.

JED. *(Entering.)* Oh, great.

KEN. They went up to change. I suppose into something black.

JED. You told them it wasn't formal?

KEN. I wouldn't presume.

JUNE. I saw them down in the garden with you this afternoon.

JED. Yeah. Gwen even pulled up what she thought was a weed.

JUNE. What did you think of John?

JED. He looks fine.

JUNE. Isn't he amazing? Somewhere there's a portrait of him that's really going to hell. You know he's running the whole copper business from your phone.

KEN. Behind Gwen's back.

JUNE. You can bet this new singing career he has her hyped on is just diversionary tactics.

KEN. Oh, I'm sure. That's all just so much...stardust.

JED. Smoke gets in your eyes.

KEN. I think given my choice between them now, I'd take her.

JED. Given my choice, I'd take hemlock.

JUNE. Oh, to hell with them both. Where's Aunt Sally? Is she ready at least?

KEN. Maybe not ready and willing, but probably able.

JUNE. I love being the villain in this. I'm really crazy about that. *(Off in the direction Shirley was last seen.)* Shirley! *(Shirley immediately sneaks on downstairs, out the door.)*

KEN. I'm going to bite that toe.

JED. What toe?

KEN. That toe. That toe. The big dirty one.

JED. *(Beat.)* They're only going to be here another twenty-one hours. I can hang in there if you can.

KEN. How could I ever have had the energy to live with those two?

JED. And June.

KEN. No, Gwen moved in, June moved out. Six months pregnant, big as a whale. Oh boy...all the old Berkeley days came back to wreck us last night. Reminiscences, and camaraderie, and everyone had an awful lot of "medicine." Snow rained like...snow. We called each other "man" and "cat," you would have vomited. I'll bet I said "dig it" five hundred times. It's a damned wonder we weren't down in the garden singing, "We Shall Overcome."

JED. I thought snow was heroin.

KEN. Oh, probably by now it is, but when we were very tired, we were very merry, we rode back and forth all night on the Sausalito ferry, snorting snow, snow was cocaine. And very dear even then.

JED. What does that matter to Gwen. She probably owns Peru or wherever it comes from.

KEN. She does not own Peru. She owns Montana and Colorado. Colorado owns Peru.

SALLY. *(Sally enters from downstairs carrying a macrame basket and a dried rose. She is looking for something.)* All right, you wretch. I know you're in there somewhere. This is fair warning.

KEN. Nothing has run through here in the last five minutes—unless you're looking for Shirley or June or Gwen or John...

SALLY. You haven't seen a roll of copper wire? The beast is being very difficult this evening. *(Hands rose to Ken.)* What does that feel like? Is that dry? I think that's perfectly dry.

KEN. Yes, that is perfectly dry and perfectly hideous-looking.

SALLY. The magazine said it would retain its color...

KEN. What color was it? *(Weston enters from upstairs, strumming his guitar.)*

SALLY. *(To Jed.)* Have you seen a roll of copper wire? *(Sees Wes.)* You haven't seen a roll of copper wire?

KEN. Darling, don't start anything now. We'll be leaving any minute.

SALLY. You're Wes Hurley, aren't you?

JED. Gwen's composer friend.

KEN. You met him last night, darling.

SALLY. I remember last night perfectly.

JUNE. *(Entering from upstairs, to Weston.)* Are they changing? *(Weston stares at each in turn.)* Gwen and John. Are they changing?

WESTON. Gwen and John.

KEN. Are they changing?

WESTON. How...do you mean...changing?

KEN. Clothes.

WESTON. Oh, wow, I had this whole metamorphosis thing going... I was reading this book about Kafka...

KEN. Gwen insists on coming with us tonight, so we are presumably waiting on them.

WESTON. I don't know. They shut the door. *(He goes out to the porch.)*

KEN. That means that they're going at it. Every day in every way I'm getting stronger and stronger.

SALLY. How long are you all staying, Wes?

JED. Twenty-one hours.

SALLY. What kind of a visit is that?

KEN. This isn't a visit, it's a business trip—they're looking for a house down here.

SALLY. Oh, They aren't serious about a place in Missouri. Gwen could buy any house in the country.

KEN. Darling, if they think they're interested in a place down here, it's no business of ours.

JUNE. They want their own recording studio. Away from Nashville.

KEN. And God knows Lebanon is away from almost anything you could think of.

SALLY. I can't believe Gwen is seriously interested in a singing career.

KEN. Can you believe that John is interested in Gwen having a singing career?

SALLY. Oh, that is perfectly apparent. Well, everything changes, everyone's moving; I can't say I'm looking forward to it.

JUNE. You won't be alone; Mom and Dad are right next door.

SALLY. You remember how well we've always gotten along. Oh, I don't know why I let your father talk me into moving to some senior citizens enclave in California. Matt and I always hated retirement communities. Imagine choosing to live in the only neighborhood in the country that has a full one hundred percent unemployment.

JUNE. Mom and Dad love it.

SALLY. Well, I'm sorry. All those women in their ballet classes and craft classes, getting tangled up in their macrame. Even your mother. Did you get a basket from Olive for Christmas?

KEN. Ummmm.

SALLY. Yes, so did I. That sort of thing should really be left to the Indians. And I don't like the house.

KEN. You've hardly seen the house.

SALLY. No, it's too...big.

JUNE. Why are you buying it?

SALLY. Well, Buddy swears I'm lonely now that Matt's gone. Really he and Olive are just afraid of who might move in next to them.

KEN. This is undeniably true.

SALLY. But I don't love St. Louis any more, no one does.

KEN. There's nothing wrong with St. Louis.

JED. There's nothing right with it.

SALLY. The mayor on TV looks like he'd rather be the mayor of any other place on earth. And you aren't going to get anywhere with Shirley while I'm around.

JUNE. *(Overlap.)* Don't let that worry you.

SALLY. No, now, the two of you should be on your own. *(Spots spool of tape.)* Is that you? No, you're the green tape. I'll need you, too. How can people ever organize a hobby? It's just exhausting. Is it going to rain? I suppose they'll cancel the dance and the fireworks. Probably they'll move it to the Community Hall.

KEN. A fireworks display in the Community Hall?

JED. That'll be nice.

SALLY. I never liked fireworks. The smell of sulfur makes me sick. I wouldn't look very patriotic throwing up.

KEN. Oh, any honest reaction, I think. *(Weston, on the porch, is playing a soft melody on the guitar.)*

SALLY. *(At the screen door.)* It's gonna rain on Harley Campbell's funeral tomorrow. It must have rained every vacation we came down here. I don't know why Matt loved it. Everyone hated him. If it rained, he went fishing. Never caught a fish. I don't think he baited his hook. Loved every minute of it. Hated catching fish. Didn't want the responsibility. Sat in the rain and laughed like a moron. They all must have thought he was mad.

KEN. Don't be absurd; he was as sane as you.

JUNE. I really don't see any point in waiting for those two.

SALLY. *(Looking out the door.)* Where have they got to now? They came back from town.

KEN. They went into their room, shut the door, and are, we presume, going at it.

SALLY. Again? He certainly does try very hard to keep her occupied, doesn't he?

KEN. John has always known what side he was buttered on.

SALLY. You get the feeling the moment they're alone if she opens her mouth and doesn't sing, he sticks something in it. Was he like that when you lived with them?

JUNE. I didn't live with them, Kenny lived with them, and yes, he was like that.

KEN. June moved out; if you can't stand the heat, get out of the kitchen.

JUNE. The heat didn't bother me; it was the smell of all those burning cookies. *(Ken starts the tape recorder, the mangled words are heard again.)* I've been meaning to tell you that's really my favorite thing to listen to.

SALLY. Is there a moon tonight?

JED. Yeah, later.

JUNE. I think that and Mahler are in a class by themselves.

SALLY. He loved swimming naked.

KEN. Mahler? Loved swimming naked?

SALLY. Your Uncle Matt, darling.

KEN. This kid's name is Johnny Young. He's at the junior high. Wouldn't be in my class for years. And don't smirk, he's got an IQ of about 200. At noon tomorrow I'm supposed to tell this kid what I thought of his story.

JUNE. That's a story? I could tell you now.

KEN. It's kind of amazing. He's into the future.

JUNE. God, that entire Young family scared me to death. I'd walk a mile out of my way not to pass that house.

SALLY. Who did?

JUNE. You remember the Young brood. The church was always taking food baskets to them.

KEN. That they promptly sold.

JUNE. Four hundred white-haired children. All beautiful. All vacant as a jar. A snaggle-toothed old crone out in the back yard, literally stirring a bubbling caldron. Grinning through the steam, cackling like a hen.

SALLY. She was making soap.

JUNE. Ummm... Sure, she was making soap. But out of what?

KEN. Oh, he's impossible.

JUNE. He certainly is. (Ken turns it off. He gets up, taking a crutch in each hand, and crosses to another chair.)

KEN. He's more than likely a mathematical prodigy. No one here is qualified to judge. He communicates with scribbled messages. Half his problem is just tension. Fear of being anticipated. Everyone has cut him off as soon as they get the gist of what he's trying to say for so long that—

JUNE. Okay, okay.

KEN. (He glares. She smiles.) He had almost no control over his entire vocal apparatus when we started. Nothing more than tension, really. He was simply terrified.

JED. Pissed his pants.

KEN. Not since that first time, actually.

JUNE. Oh, fine.

KEN. Entirely my fault. I couldn't understand the son-of-a-bitch was asking for permission to go to the john.

JUNE. You're terrific.

KEN. The patience of Job.

JUNE. (Exiting upstairs.) What a mother you would have been.

KEN. Was Job a good mother?

SALLY. June is being an awful tart, isn't she?

KEN. June is even more impossible with a straight man in the house than she is without one.

SALLY. I don't know why she had to come down here with me.

KEN. Oh, don't you. Three weeks ago as soon as she heard John was coming…

SALLY. That's over long ago, surely.

KEN. You know that, and I know that…

SALLY. But where would that get her?

KEN. Nevertheless.

SALLY. Well, it gives her focus. Poor June. You were always so bright and so popular, June was always rather "The Cheese Stands Alone."

KEN. *(To Jed.)* Is that the pest book?

JED. Mildew.

SALLY. Mildew? Not on the roses.

JED. Sally, bite your tongue.

SALLY. How to you know so much about gardening? Did you grow up on a farm?

KEN. No, darling, he has a Master's in botany.

JED. And no botanist has ever known anything at all about gardening, or there wouldn't be mildew on the phlox.

SALLY. Mildew on the phlox…What's the name of that novel?

GWEN. *(Off.)* No, I love it!

JOHN. *(Off.)* I'll kill her; you kidding me? *(Entering, elated.)* Hey, you sneak! Where is she? Hey, you know in Europe you could have your eyes poked out for something like that? Caught the little twerp at the window. You're really going to get it. She was up a tree looking in the—

SHIRLEY. *(Appearing at the door.)* I certainly hope you aren't addressing me.

JOHN. How's that for innocence?

SHIRLEY. I have no idea—*(June enters down stairs, on landing.)*

SHIRLEY. —what you are making such a disturbance about, but if you are alluding to me, there are any number of low and sniggling people who might do something of that kind.

JOHN. You little sneak. You peeper. If you don't watch out, I'll tell it all. You could get yourself in a pack of trouble. That wasn't just snorting coke and smoking dope like last night.

SHIRLEY. I have no memory of last night and I am a minor and not responsible for the delinquency that so-called majors are leading me into.

KEN. What are you got up as?

JUNE. She makes about as good a drag as you would.

KEN. Anything is possible with a little taste and charm.

SHIRLEY. This is a beautiful gown that my great-grandmother wore when—

JUNE. She's been at Grandma's trunk in the attic. *(Gwen enters, wearing only a sheet.)*

SHIRLEY. And you are a degenerate, is what you are. Yes, I was looking in the window and I was smoking a cigarette and I have never seen anything so disgusting in my entire life. He didn't even have his shoes off! He didn't even have his pants down! He was fully dressed and Gwen was fully naked! And he was performing cunnilingus all over her and his face was all over mucus and it was the most disgusting thing I've ever seen in my life. And worse, worse, worse, she was moaning and groaning and he—he—he—was reaching down with his own hand and masturbating his own thing at the same time. Himself! I have never seen anything so unnatural and warped in my young life! Ever!

JOHN. You are too much; and she was also smoking a cigarette weren't you? When did you start that? And she was spying on a private act, weren't you? I think you ought to learn a lesson. I think you should learn a thing or two...You better watch it. You're asking for it... You watch it. You better just watch it. You're gonna get it now. That's it. You've had it. *(He continues.)*

GWEN. Oh, I was! It was fantastic! Oh, God, we were caught in the act! It was too fantastic! I looked back and saw this face at the window. Oh, shit, spies. No, audience! Oh, God, how fabulous. And like, wow, I really hit the moon. I mean I came like a flash! I've never come like that in such a flash in my life. I just went flash! Flash! All my blood, like, just went flash! All through my body. You were terrific! Shirley, you gotta always be there!

(John has continued saying "I'll get you for this. You just see. I'm gonna really get you for this.")

SHIRLEY. You just try it. You keep your dirty hands off me. *(Yells when he would touch her.)*

JUNE. *(Overlapping.)* John, Shirley, Shirley. You are going to rip that dress that does not belong to you. And you are forgetting that this evening is rather a sober occasion for some people if it isn't for you. Try for one night to respect Aunt Sally and Uncle Matt.

GWEN. Oh, shit. I forgot! I've got to dress. Don't anybody leave without me. *(Runs off upstairs.)*

SALLY. If he's waited over a year, he can wait a little longer.

JUNE. Sally, it cannot wait any longer.

SHIRLEY. I have just seen something that will warp my young mind and all you can think of is death and ashes. And I love Aunt Sally, whom I consider my mother, and Uncle Matt, who was the only father I ever had, a good deal more than—

JUNE. I'm gonna bust your ass for you, too, honey, if you try to dump that guilt trip on me.

SHIRLEY. I will not be a party to casting my dear granduncle's ashes into some filthy swimming hole, because I have more respect for his memory than that.

JUNE. I'm going to dump you in the river, which is something I should have done when I had the chance.

JOHN. You better watch that one. She's gettin' a little big for her pants, ain't you? How old are you now? How old are you?

JUNE. You wouldn't know, of course.

SHIRLEY. Age is the most irrelevant judge of character or maturity that—

JOHN. Yeah, yeah, how old are you?

JUNE. She's thirteen.

SHIRLEY. *(To June.)* I am eighteen years old, *(To John.)* and it is none of your business…

JUNE. She's thirteen.

SHIRLEY. If you must know, I'm seventeen.

JUNE. You are not seventeen, you cretin.

SHIRLEY. I am fifteen years old!

JUNE. She's fourteen. *(John picks Shirley up and carries her over his shoulder to the porch and slams the door on her. All through this, she is screaming: "Put me down, put me down, Rhett Butler, put me down.")*

JOHN. *(Smiles, turns back to the bedroom.)* Yeah? You better watch that one. *(Exits to the bedroom upstairs.)*

SHIRLEY. *(Comes back in, follows him to steps.)* I happen to, am going to be an artist, and an artist has no age and must force himself to see everything, no matter how disgusting and how low! *(Door slams offstage.)*

WESTON. *(Pause.)* Far out.

KEN. *(Pause.)* I'm terribly sorry, Wes, what is it that's far out?

WESTON. The dude's been dead over a year?

SALLY. Oh, I know, I just don't get things done.

KEN. It isn't as though he'd spoil.

SALLY. No, the dear, he won't spoil.

SHIRLEY. Oh, God. Oh, my God!

JUNE. Will you please get out of that dress and stop trying to be the center of attention…*(Indicates bedroom.)* That was cute. Wasn't he cute?

KEN. We always thought so.

WESTON. He wanted you to scatter his ashes on the water?

JUNE. He said flush them down the toilet.

SALLY. Matt's wishes were never expressed.

JUNE. But we're taking him to the river. Better late than never.

KEN. It's hardly the Ganges, but you go with what you've got…

WESTON. Sure.

SALLY. *(To June.)* All he said was don't keep my ashes in a goddamned urn.

SHIRLEY. Oh, Jesus, God, I—ughh. *(Lights a cigarette in a long holder.)*

SALLY. But one thing and another…

WESTON. Far out.

SHIRLEY. I cannot bear it. I am a spiritual person. I happen to…

JUNE. If you please…*(Takes cigarette from holder, stubs it out.)*

SALLY. Well, of course the funeral home gave him to me in an enormous, blue, hermetically sealed urn with MATT FRIEDMAN in gold Old English lettering. I certainly took him out of that and put him in a box.

WESTON. Sure.

SHIRLEY. I cannot bear mature people calmly talking about cremation and death and ashes in a box. I cannot bear it.

SALLY. I open it up every day and give him a little air.

WESTON. Sure.

JUNE. Wes, don't start her off.

SHIRLEY. I cannot bear it.

SALLY. I dried a rose in him last week. Dried it very nicely, too. You know, Jed discovered this lost rose.

JED. Slater's Crimson China.

SALLY. Matt made a very good drying agent, too.

JUNE. He would have had a fit.

KEN. Actually, he might be put to better use spread around the rosebushes as fertilizer.

JED. Potash, absolutely. Prevents dieback.

KEN. Or John's ashes should be good for a quantity of potash, if you think about it...

JED. You cremate John and I'll happily spread his ashes.

SHIRLEY. I will absolutely *scream* if anyone says "ashes" one more time.

KEN. She will, too.

SALLY. I'm not at all happy about dumping him down at the boathouse. It looks too much like a shrine and Matt would hate that. But—we made love there the first time.

JUNE. Do we have to wait for those two?

SALLY. There's something wrong about it.

SHIRLEY. That's where they saw the UFO from.

SALLY. No, it was not. We were standing right on that porch when we saw the UFO.

WESTON. You've sighted UFOs here? I read this book about flying saucers.

JUNE. Don't start her...Wes, you read too much, concentrate on your music.

SALLY. We went out onto the porch. This was only our second date, mind.

WESTON. Sure.

SALLY. And we saw this silver flying thing...rise straight up from the river down there. Very slowly, till it was just over the trees. Just this huge lit-up top. And then it went off sideways—phettt! and was gone—just like nothing.

WESTON. Did it go "phettt!"?

SALLY. No. I went "phettt!" It didn't go anything.

JUNE. A marriage made in heaven, right?

WESTON. There's a saucer-shaped one and a cigar-shaped one. Only they think the cigar-shaped one is just the saucer-shaped one seen on an ellipse, like. Did it have a tail?

SALLY. No, no tail.

WESTON. Some of them have tails.

SALLY. This one didn't have a tail.

WESTON. Some of them don't have tails.

SALLY. This was one of the ones that didn't have a tail.

WESTON. Some of them don't have tails.

SALLY. Well, I mean to tell you, I wet my pants.

WESTON. Sure.

JUNE. You were lucky.

SALLY. I did. I wet my pants. Of course, we thought we were being invaded by the Japanese.

WESTON. Sure.

SALLY. We got on the telephone to the Civil Defense and they said to stay away from the area, don't go down there. Of course, we were down there in a minute.

WESTON. Sure.

SALLY. And, well, all the weeds and brush all along our riverbank were burned away. The place was still smoldering.

WESTON. Sure.

SHIRLEY. Probably they were burned by all kinds of radiation.

KEN. That would explain a good deal.

SALLY. And we ran all up and down the river, looking for spies, and listening, because that's what we thought it was. That they had landed Jap—Japanese troops.

WESTON. Sure.

SALLY. And by the time we had gone all the way to the boathouse we had to rest, and we talked and looked at the moon, and I'm afraid we got all involved with each other and forgot about the Japanese.

KEN. With wet pants? I'm sorry.

SALLY. Isn't that funny? I completely forget what I did about that. Of course, we had no idea what we had seen. It was years before anyone started talking about UFOs.

WESTON. Sure.

SALLY. But every time we came down here, every year after that, we went out to watch for them.

SHIRLEY. That's probably why Uncle Matt kept coming back down here instead of some place nice.

JUNE. Shirley, are you going to go or are you going to stay, because you can't go looking like that.

SHIRLEY. I have said repeatedly that I was staying here, and the sooner we get back to St. Louis and you stop acting like a mother the happier I'll be.

JUNE. Just a simple decision, we don't need the production number.

SHIRLEY. Unlike either of you, I do not have a single memory of the boyfriends I dated during the war in this one-horse burg.

JUNE. Where do you get the way you talk? I did not have "boyfriends," we did not go on "dates"; haven't you learned anything? She spends twenty-four hours a day in the queer movie house, watching Betty Grable reruns.

SHIRLEY. Betty Grable is the greatest star Missouri ever produced.

KEN. Oh, God. I'll bet that's true.

SHIRLEY. I would think one would know better than to proclaim her chastity to her illegitimate daughter.

JUNE. There is a world of difference between making love and teasing some basketball player after the junior prom.

KEN. June certainly never teased anyone. *(Gwen enters, dressed flamboyantly.)* Holy God.

JUNE. Oh, Good Lord! *(Over.)*

GWEN. I decided, if Shirley is wearing that, I'd let her set the tone.

JUNE. She isn't going, and she certainly isn't wearing that.

JED. *(To Ken.)* Be a minute; hold down the fort. *(Exits to upstairs.)*

SALLY. *(Overlapping.)* Now, where did you get to? You were here last night, and what did I do with you? It was hot—I know that.

KEN. *(Overlapping.)* Has anybody seen Aunt Sally's roll of copper wire?

GWEN. What brand? Copper's my business.

SALLY. What? Oh, yes, but no, darling, Uncle Matt. I can't seem to remember what I've done with his box of ashes.

KEN. *(Ken and June at the same time, overlapping.)* Don't say it!

JUNE. Please don't! *(Shirley screams.)*

WESTON. *(Pause.)* Far out.

GWEN. Oh, God, that's so great. I'd be a new person if I could do that. Ever since my shrink told me I should scream, I haven't been able to.

JUNE. Don't pay any attention to her. She's only trying to be the center of— oh, God, I sound exactly like Dad, don't I?

KEN. His voice was higher.

JUNE. Men and women aren't strong enough to have children. Trees should have children.

KEN. I'm afraid I can't help you, Aunt Sally. I haven't seen them.

SALLY. *(Overlapping.)* I only have to concentrate a moment. I had them last night, when it was so warm, and I took them up the bedroom, but I don't remember bringing him down this morning. I remember it was so hot.

KEN. *(Yelling upstairs.)* Jed! Hey, Jed!

GWEN. That's so wonderful.

JED. *(Off. Yelling.)* Yo!

GWEN. Jed is really butch, isn't he? Don't you love him?

KEN. *(Yelling.)* Listen…!

GWEN. I mean he's dull as dishwater, but he's so butch!

KEN. *(Yelling.)* Bring down Uncle Matt from Aunt Sally's bedroom when you come!

SALLY. No, darling, something tells me I didn't leave him up there. It was so warm, I was worried—

JED. *(Off.)* He's in the refrigerator.

SALLY. Oh, of course he is.

WESTON. Wow, that's really—

JUNE. Don't say it. One word.

WESTON. *(Mouth open, can't close it.)* I been reading this book about the Bermuda Triangle.

SHIRLEY. Oh, the Bermuda Triangle.

GWEN. Listen, forget it; it's a total rip-off. We went down there to try to disappear. Like we did everything you could think of to make ourselves conspicuous, you know? Not a fuckin' thing happened to us. Two solid months.

SHIRLEY. How long are you going to be in Nashville?

GWEN. Just a couple of weeks to line up a band. You want to come?

SHIRLEY. Yes! *(June starts to leave the room, to kitchen.)*

SALLY. Where are you going?

JUNE. I'm…going to…the loo. You want to come?

SALLY. Just leave Matt in the refrigerator. He's fine there. *(June stops, stares.)*

JUNE. *(To Ken.)* I'm only asking if we're doing this or not.

KEN. Don't push, don't force it.

JUNE. You're the original Will o' the Wisp.

SHIRLEY. The only place I've ever been for a vacation is Lebanon.

GWEN. Oh, shit. That's probably the pits, right? We were in Egypt, the guide stands in front of the Sphinx; he says, "For five thousand years the Sphinx had not given up her secret. Command her to speak but she remains silent." I said, you gotta be runnin' that up my ass, right?

KEN. Lebanon, Missouri.

SHIRLEY. *(Overlapping.)* Here; you're there now.

GWEN. Oh, listen, no, this is the greatest place I've ever been. We walked down to the river, we were up on the hill; I've never seen such peace in my life.

SHIRLEY. Every place I've ever been has been peaceful.

GWEN. No shit; we're gonna move here.

SALLY. Oh, you are not.

KEN. Aunt Sally, darling.

GWEN. Hell yes, the whole bit; back to the land, it's John's hometown.

SALLY. John's dad moved to Miami ten years ago.

GWEN. He has great feelings for the place, though—and we got to have our own studio, see. Hey, John, damn it, come down here.

JOHN. *(Off.)* What say, babe?

GWEN. Come down here. Hey Ken, how many rooms have you got?

JUNE. Nineteen, why? *(John enters from upstairs.)*

GWEN. Woo! You look great.

JOHN. Okay, I'm clean.

SHIRLEY. Don't touch me, I don't care.

JOHN. She's gonna really get it.

GWEN. *(To Ken.)* We were talking about your proposition—

JOHN. Not now, doll—

GWEN. Oh, sure. We got to have our own place to record, see, 'cause the studios bleed you dry. You wouldn't believe it.

WESTON. Oh, wow, and she's...

JOHN. Gwen's got a little problem; we're working on... It runs into a lot of bread.

WESTON. She gets blocks.

JUNE. She gets what?

WESTON. Blocks. You know, like mental blocks.

JOHN. No, it all goes fine until they turn on the mikes.

KEN. Beautiful.

GWEN. Fuck it, it's not that bad.

JOHN. Listen, I thought it was cool.

WESTON. She freezes.

JOHN. It's nothing. She freezes. Her jaws clench up.

WESTON. You can't even pry them open with your fingers. We tried. It's really a bitch.

GWEN. Just to cut two sides I'm probably the only singer ever spent more money on the shrink than we did on the band.

JOHN. The band was really great, though.

GWEN. 'Cause they had decided I was just this rich bitch, you know, but like when we finally got it together and cut the tape they really flipped.

WESTON. But like she won't even listen to the demo.

GWEN. I don't want to hear it.

WESTON. Like she's got this real pain in her voice.

GWEN. Well, let's face it, like if I don't have pain in my voice, who would?

JOHN. There had to have been something to impress Jimmy King.

GWEN. Who's like the top manager in the business. They don't know Jimmy King.

JOHN. He wants to sign them both.

GWEN. Only thing he said I really should concentrate on this one thing.

JUNE. I'll bet.

GWEN. And like what happens to the copper business?

JOHN. One thing at a time, one thing at a time.

GWEN. Only I'm never sure which time to take what thing.

JOHN. You gotta learn to think about yourself.

GWEN. But wouldn't that be far out to have this really major career after you're already thirty-three years old and burned out?

JOHN. Nobody says you're burned—

GWEN. Everybody says I'm burned out. How can you take that many drugs and go through what I've gone through and not have your brains fried?

SHIRLEY. You are thirty-three years old?

GWEN. Isn't that gross?

SHIRLEY. How did you get burned out?

GWEN. Listen, I'm a real case, no shit. Like a year doesn't go by without me getting something terminal wrong with me.

WESTON. She's got this history of like medical milestone operations—

SHIRLEY. On, no.

GWEN. It's really crazy; I mean, I'm this fuckin' shell. They took everything out by the time I was twenty-five. You know, not all at once, one or two things at a time.

SHIRLEY. Oh, Lord…Can't you have children?

GWEN. Oh, please, that was like the first thing to go. If I didn't have this history of longevity in my family, I'd've been dead before I was ten.

WESTON. But like nobody in her family ever dies.

GWEN. Like you got to kill us off. Daddy's been like paralyzed, you know, for the last four years, with all these tubes and wires and all, but—I mean, like he's a Brussels sprout, but he's alive. It'd be really tragic, but you can't think about it without laughing, 'cause you know he had this stroke—

SHIRLEY. Oh. I cannot bear it.

GWEN. No, listen, it's far out. His face is all paralyzed, you know, but it's stuck in this real weird comic position. I mean even Arthur J. Schwartzkoff, who's like the most serious person I know, had to leave the room to keep from cracking up.

WESTON. She's got this real tragic history.

GWEN. Ask Wes.

WESTON. Her mother and her brother were killed in an airplane crash.

GWEN. Ronny, it was too bad; Mom was a bitch. *(Pause.)* I don't want to be a down or anything. *(Ken is pouring a glass of wine.)*

JUNE. *(Takes bottle.)* Hey, don't start that again tonight.

KEN. You're right. *(Drinks.)*

JUNE. This idiot was up to St. Louis all winter trying to kill himself—drinking himself blind—trying to prove what a swinger he is—till finally he managed to collapse in the street and wound up in the hospital. And now he's back in physical therapy.

KEN. I only go twice a week.

GWEN. Yeah, and—?

KEN. This nice dyke nurse tries to kill me. It's this game we play.

JOHN. I thought you were finished with all that.

GWEN. Why are you back in muscular therapy, creep?

KEN. Good God, no reason. Apparently I was walking wrong. I was walking with my arms instead of my stomach. *(Shirley presses the recorder.)*

GWEN. Oh, God, I was gonna tell you. That's really weird to make love to.

KEN. Sorry, but it's really fascinating—

JOHN. You've got your work cut out for you, if this is one of your English students.

KEN. No, no. When I was in rehabilitation learning to walk, I worked with a couple of boys who had lost their ability to speak. Mac McConnell wanted me to work with this kid privately to see if I could help him.

JUNE. Johnny Young. Remember the Young brood?

JOHN. Jesus, forget I mentioned it.

KEN. He's too shy to talk to me. I gave him a tape recorder so he could tell me about himself, but instead he's filled the entire cassette with this amazing science fiction story about the future.

JOHN. When do you start back again?

JUNE. School starts the first Monday after Labor Day.

KEN. Start what?

GWEN. I think that is so far out to return to the fold like that. I mean it's parochial as hell, but it's so far out.

KEN. Oh, hardly. The profession has done very nicely without me for six years, I think it will survive a while longer.

JUNE. What the hell are you talking about?

GWEN. I thought that's what you were down here for. You were going back to your old high school.

KEN. I was never that interested in teaching.

SALLY. Oh, you were so.

GWEN. *(Overlapping Sally.)* You used to scream about it all the time.

JOHN. Hell you weren't, that was your mission, I thought.

JUNE. Kenny, it is quite settled.

JOHN. That guy said you were the best teacher Oakland ever had.

KEN. *(Suddenly unleashing his pent-up tension.)* Well once again Superfag's plans fail to materialize. Yes, I was quite happy leaving our cozy abode in Oakland each morning and walking briskly into the Theodore Roosevelt High School. Very "Good Morning, Miss Dove"; very "Good-bye, Mr. Chips." And—by prancing and dancing and sleight of hand, I actually managed to keep their little minds off sex for one hour a day. They became quite fascinated by trochees, thrilled by *Cyrano de Bergerac.* But now I'm afraid my prancing would be quite embarrassing to them.

JUNE. There was a little incident two weeks ago that has him running like a rabbit.

KEN. *(Almost angry.)* It is merely that as I slowly realized no accredited English Department was interested in my stunningly overqualified application, except the notoriously parochial hometown—

JUNE. Fine, that's where you belong.

KEN. —I became aware that what everyone was trying to tell me was—that teaching impressionable teenagers in my present state, I could only expect to leave quite the wrong impression. You have no idea how much noise I make falling down.

JOHN. Oh, bull. A big-deal war hero. They'd love you.

KEN. I don't think so. And though it seems incredible to us, they don't even know where Vietnam is.

JUNE. Why don't you just admit you're vain and terrified and face it instead of—

KEN. I have simply developed an overpowering distaste for chalk.

JUNE. Well, fine, teaching is the only thing you're prepared to do with your life, you obviously don't think that agrees with you anymore. What the hell do you see for yourself? Huh? What you got in mind to do with your life?

KEN. Just pack that away, all right? *(Yelling.)* Jed! come on. Let's go!

JUNE. What are you going to do down here then? 'Cause you sure as hell aren't going back to St. Louis this winter.

KEN. Jed and I might go to Greece; we might move to Spain. What the hell difference is it to you?

JUNE. Jed would love that. Have you dropped this on him?

KEN. *Not one word* about school to Jed! We will deal with that privately. Now that's it—no more!

GWEN. Well, listen, John and I were talking about your proposition, you know? The only thing was where would you and Jed go. Hell, if you're not going to be here, there's no hang-up is there?

KEN. *(Over a bit.)* Not now, doll, not now.

JOHN. *(Over.)* Later, babe.

GWEN. Why the hell is everyone being so circumspect? They'll have to know eventually— We haven't even talked price; hell, it may all be academic!

JOHN. *(To Wes.)* Come on, off your butt, we're gonna travel.

WESTON. Goin' where?

JOHN. We're gonna do the Matt Friedman gig; then we're gonna see my hometown's Fourth of July bash.

WESTON. No way.

GWEN. Honey…?

JOHN. Big deal, get off your butt, get some air.

WESTON. I been getting air all day— I've never seen so much air in my life.

KEN. They don't have air in New Jersey?

WESTON. They got something, but it ain't air.

JOHN. He hasn't been home in two years.

GWEN. Honey, maybe I should stay here, 'cause Wes and me have to work, you know.

JOHN. No, we'll all go; we'll go on to the fireworks. You know if you don't go you'll be disappointed later.

GWEN. I just came here to see Kenny, I didn't bargain for funerals.

JUNE. It won't be like that at all.

JOHN. When you chicken out, you're always sorry later—

GWEN. Come on, I can't do it. I thought I could 'cause he was so nice, but I'm going to freak out. I just keep thinking about my daddy and my brother and I'm gonna freak. Tell me it isn't ashes. Tell me it's something else.

KEN. It's something else.

GWEN. No, no, you know, Johnny. Tell me it's something else. Make it better.

JOHN. Baby, you're thinking about your old man. You can't think about him. He's fine. The last time I saw him, he was—

GWEN. No, no, no, you're trying to change the subject; it's not gonna work to change the subject. You've gotta tell me it's something else.

JUNE. It's pickled peaches. We're going down to the river, we're going to have a picnic, we'll—

GWEN. —No, no, God, no, not something to eat! Tell me—oh, God, I'm going to freak out. I'm really gonna freak.

JOHN. Baby, you don't have to do a thing you don't want to.

KEN. Gwen. I do not know why you are carrying on. Have you seen that box? Have you seen it?

GWEN. No.

KEN. Well, you know while I was in the hospital I got all these presents from people who don't go to hospitals—you know that.

GWEN. People are such creeps! People are so candy-ass.

KEN. Well, you remember all the chocolates I got—

GWEN. We brought you a pound of peyote buttons, we didn't bring you—

KEN. But others, granted, less enterprising. You remember all those chocolates?

GWEN. Yeah, we sat on your bed and punched the bottoms out of them.

KEN. And half of them were something vile like—what was it you don't like?

GWEN. …maple.

KEN. I hate jelly chocolates.

GWEN. Oh, God, I hate jelly chocolates.

KEN. Well, that box is filled to the top with a six-year supply of jelly chocolates with their bottoms pushed in. And we are finally going to feed that crap to the fish.

GWEN. I hate it.

KEN. The fish will love it.

GWEN. Why don't you just throw them in the garbage?

KEN. It's against the law.

GWEN. Fuck 'em. Throw it in the garbage. *(Jed enters, from upstairs, in a suit.)*

JOHN. We thought we'd make a party of it.

GWEN. So you go on to the party and Wes and I'll stay here. *(Screams when she sees Jed.)*

JOHN. That's just Jed with clothes on and his hair combed. You know I'm not going to leave you. We go or we stay, I don't care.

GWEN. You come back for us after you've dumped the candy.

JUNE. Fine, now. Aunt Sally, can we do this?

SALLY. I'll go, June. Kenny said don't push me. You always push. *(Exits kitchen. June follows her Off.)*

JOHN. They don't need this friction, honey, they're having a little problem.

GWEN. Well, I'm having a little problem, too. I don't believe for a minute it's candy in that box; I know perfectly well who's in there. *(Shirley enters from upstairs, wearing a different dress.)* Oh, that's fabulous.

SHIRLEY. I had it made for me in Paris. *(Phone rings. Jed gets up to answer it.)*

KEN. That's long distance.

JOHN. I'll get it, it's gonna be for us.

JED. *(Has picked up the phone.)* Please do.

JOHN. No, no, please.

JED. Hello? It's person-to-person. *(Hands phone to John, goes outside to the porch.)*

JOHN. *(On phone.)* Yeah, hello. *(June re-enters from kitchen.)*

JUNE. *(To Ken.)* She's talking to him, for God's sake.

KEN. Well, why not? Wouldn't you?

JUNE. She's talking into the refrigerator.

GWEN. *(Going to John.)* If that's the prick in Nashville, I want to talk with him.

JOHN. I've got it, I've got it. It's cool. Soon as I'm finished.

GWEN. Five fuckin' seconds.

JOHN. It's cool, it's cool.

GWEN. Well, Jesus, break my arm. *(Pause.)* Does anybody want a Quaalude? I'm really freaking out.

KEN. Darling, the town of Lebanon is not ready for you freaking out at their Independence Day celebration. That independent they aren't.

GWEN. Bullshit; if they can take you, they can take anything.

JUNE. *(To Ken.)* I don't know if Aunt Sally's going to do this tonight or not.

GWEN. You want me to talk to her?

KEN. No! *(To June.)* It's all up to her.

JUNE. You're the only person I know who can say "I'm not involved" in forty-five languages.

KEN. Seven or eight.

GWEN. *(To Shirley, who has Gwen's pillbox.)* Honey, you better not take one of those.

JUNE. Oh, let her have one.

SHIRLEY. I was merely trying to examine the pillbox.

GWEN. Yeah, but like one day you're trying to look at the box and the next day you're burned out and your hair won't hold a permanent. *(John hangs up the phone.)* You didn't hang up? I wanted to talk to him.

JOHN. No, it was just the engineer, checking our schedule.

GWEN. You haven't talked to Schwartzkoff, have you?

JOHN. Honey, it's the Fourth of July.

GWEN. Have you talked to Schwartzkoff?

JOHN. Everyone will be back to work tomorrow.

GWEN. Yeah, the creep. Every time I leave L.A., he calls the board. The last time I went to the hospital, I was having like my spleen stripped—

KEN. Hardly that—

GWEN. Well, who remembers, the son of a bitch called a meeting of the board to stab me in the back. He votes Daddy's stock, I can't vote it.

SHIRLEY. Stripped spleen?

KEN. Cassandra had it easy, you don't want to know.

GWEN. Cassandra? Oh, shit, don't you wish you knew all those myths? Like way down in some primordial place I've got this intuition that it's all in the myths, all the answers, if we could just get it together right.

WESTON. I was up in Canada, I got this book of Eskimo folk tales.

JUNE. Do you think we could go now, while nobody's freaking out?

JOHN. The Eskimos are in Alaska.

WESTON. No, they're both; they're in Canada, too. Did you know igloos aren't warm inside?

KEN. I hadn't thought about it before, but it makes sense.

WESTON. They're below freezing.

KEN. If it were above freezing, igloos would melt, wouldn't they?

WESTON. They have these blubber oil lamps and these fur blankets and each other to keep themselves warm, and that's all.

JUNE. I'm sorry, I don't find that romantic at all.

GWEN. What's an Eskimo myth about?

WESTON. They're mostly about blubber. They're really these strange people. Like, they think very different from the way we think.

JOHN. I don't think I've ever been interested in the Eskimos, have you?

KEN. I don't think I have.

WESTON. There's this one folk story about this family. They had all this caribou meat stacked outside their igloo. Frozen, see. But it got so cold that their whole winter's supply of meat was frozen in one solid block of ice and none of the family could get at it. And they were all starving 'cause no one could break off any of this meat. So in a kind of last-ditch heroic effort this young Eskimo warrior goes outside and lets off this tremendous, powerful fart.

SHIRLEY. Oh, God.

WESTON. And thaws all the meat.

JUNE. That is very gross.

WESTON. But it stank so bad none of the family could eat it. And they all starved to death.

SHIRLEY. Oh, God.

KEN. This isn't, I hope, the basis for one of your songs.

JOHN. What kind of story is that supposed to be?

GWEN. I never heard that. Where did you hear that?

JUNE. That is gross.

WESTON. Isn't that gross?

JOHN. I mean, what kind of story is that?

WESTON. It's a folk story. I read it in this book.

JUNE. Even for an Eskimo.

JOHN. That isn't a folktale. Talley, have you ever heard a folktale like that?

KEN. Never. And I never wanted to.

WESTON. It is. That story has been handed down from father to son, generation to generation, verbally, for hundreds of years.

SHIRLEY. Oh, God.

KEN. That isn't a folktale, because there's no—

JOHN. What's the moral? There's no moral.

KEN. Exactly.

JOHN. Folktales have morals. There's no moral. There's no point...

WESTON. They couldn't eat the meat, so they starved to death.

JOHN. They were starving to death before he farted on the damn caribou meat.

WESTON. Well, then the moral is that that isn't the way to thaw caribou meat.

JOHN. No one could. It couldn't happen.

KEN. And if it could, it is not particularly beneficial.

JOHN. Heroic actions must have saving results.

WESTON. Who says?

KEN. It is the law of folktales.

JOHN. It's the law of heroes.

WESTON. Saving results for whom?

JOHN. For everybody. Like the little Dutch boy, for God's sake.

WESTON. Well, maybe these people are more realistic than the Greeks or the Dutch.

JOHN. It isn't realistic. It couldn't happen.

JUNE. And it's gross.

JOHN. And if it could happen, what do we learn from it? We have to learn something from a folktale.

KEN. That's a fable, but for the sake of argument.

WESTON. We learn that that isn't the way to thaw caribou meat.

JOHN. Who cares how to thaw caribou meat?

WESTON. The Eskimo cares! It's his staple diet!

JUNE. You are certifiable, you know that?

WESTON. I said it was this alien mind.

JOHN. This is the sort of thing you read in your own time.

KEN. Where did you find him, anyway?

WESTON. Skip it.

JOHN. No, you brought it up. I think it's very interesting. I mean the story is ridiculous, but the fact that you read it I find very interesting.

KEN. And retained it.

WESTON. Skip it. You obviously don't have the sensitivity to appreciate—

SHIRLEY. I have nothing but sensitivity and even I don't understand it.

WESTON. I thought it was a funny story to have been handed down from generation—

JOHN. I didn't find it funny at all. I see it as a tragedy. The entire family dies in the snow of starvation.

WESTON. They were dying already.

JOHN. That's what I said. It is a pointless, vulgar—

KEN. Scatological—

JOHN. —scatological story.

WESTON. I only thought it was interesting because it is a completely different culture.

JOHN. Wes, that isn't culture. That's hardship.

WESTON. No, no, it is. It's an alien culture. Like they call themselves *"The People"* and everybody else is *"The Other People."*

KEN. Wes, every people call themselves "The People," and everyone else is the other people.

WESTON. They have fifty different words for snow! *(Pause.)* You don't think that shows a subtle mind?

KEN. *(Pause.)* Wes, of course they have fifty different words for snow.

JOHN. *(Pause.)* Their winters are fourteen months long.

KEN. They have nothing else to talk about.

JOHN. Snow is all there is.

KEN. They have to find some way to make it interesting.

JOHN. The Bedouins probably have fifty different words for sand.

WESTON. They probably do. They're a very interesting people. *(He slams out to the porch. Jed enters from porch.)*

KEN. They call themselves "The People" and...

JOHN. *(Yelling after him.)* Wes, you know why you're not going to make a successful songwriter? Because you have too many interests.

GWEN. There's a song about syphilis, though; songs can be about anything.

SHIRLEY. You are so depressing. *(Jed hands Ken pill case, points to his watch.)*

GWEN. What are you taking?

KEN. We get these special little birth-control pills. In my condition we can't take chances.

JED. It's Percodan. (*Pours a glass of water from his watering can.*)

GWEN. That's like a horse-size painkiller.

KEN. We try to spice up our lives, what we can.

GWEN. Listen, when we heard that you were wounded, Kenny, I'll bet I never told you this—I called up, (I had to go right to the head of the damn Naval Hospital in Philadelphia). I didn't get off the phone till he told me Kenny's sexual performance would be in no way impaired.

KEN. Depends on what I'm expected to perform.

GWEN. Don't screw around, you know what I mean, your sexual performance…

KEN. …was absolutely in no way impaired; though we have had to cut out one show a night.

GWEN. I was so thankful, I went to church and actually lit a candle.

KEN. Appropriately.

SHIRLEY. I never intend to have sex in my life.

GWEN. Honey, it's not what you intend.

SHIRLEY. I am going to devote my life to art. The way Marie Curie devoted her life to science.

GWEN. Oh, science. I did that. I did.

JUNE. Darling, you didn't devote your life to science. You donated your body to science.

GWEN. Are those fireflies?

JUNE. Lightning bugs. (*Gwen runs out to garden.*)

JOHN. Who's Marie Curie?

SHIRLEY. She was only the only person to ever receive two Nobel Prizes for science.

JUNE. (*With Shirley.*) Two Nobel Prizes.

SHIRLEY. She was only the greatest scientist who ever lived.

JOHN. Okay, okay…

JUNE. Aunt Sally, can we go now?

JOHN. Sure, let's go. Gwen can stay with Wes and Shirley.

KEN. You don't have to stay with Gwen?

JED. No, he got his call from California. He doesn't have to hang around waiting for it any more.

SHIRLEY. I thought it was the engineer calling from Nashville.

JOHN. Come on, let's go. Before the squirt starts up again.

SHIRLEY. I am not starting up. I said I was going to be a great artist, which I have said repeatedly for the past solid year.

JUNE. With the emphasis on repeatedly.

SHIRLEY. And I am not a squirt!

JUNE. If I had it to do over again, I wouldn't give her to Aunt Sally. You live with a bat, you fly like a bat.

JOHN. You might have thought of that at the time.

SHIRLEY. I'm glad I was reared by Uncle Matt and Aunt Sally who had a true political and spiritual awareness and—

JUNE. Forget it. They did fine, you're doing fine; I'm doing fine.

JOHN. Yeah, but Matt's gone and Sally's going to California. You're gonna have her on your own, now. She's getting to that age when they start costing a lot of bread; a decent school, private tutors—

JUNE. Well, she'll just have to get along without the Sorbonne. Where was that bright idea ten years ago?

JOHN. You were out making a revolution, who could find you.

JUNE. I damn well did what I damn well had to do.

SHIRLEY. I don't think she was militant at all. I think you were just cross and angry.

GWEN. Are you kidding me? She was sensational.

JUNE. *(Shaken.)* You have no idea of the life we led.

GWEN. Really.

JUNE. *(With difficulty controlling herself.)* You've no idea of the country we almost made for you. The fact that I think it's all a crock now does not take away from what we almost achieved. *(Pause; then she runs upstairs; exits.)*

GWEN. *(To Shirley.)* Baby, you shouldn't—I mean, I think you're great, but you really don't tell someone that they aren't what they think they are. What's the profit?

SHIRLEY. Who?

GWEN. June was really something else. You would have been proud. It was her mom and dad made her send you to Sally.

SHIRLEY. I consider myself extremely lucky to have been raised by Sally and Matt.

GWEN. June was ready to carry you around like a flag. I mean, she was like Ma Barker or Belle Starr. She was really dangerous.

KEN. Mostly to herself.

GWEN. No, you don't know! Like they used to hitchhike to these rallies. I couldn't cut it. I couldn't bear the rejection. The first car passed me up,

I was destroyed. I used to fly ahead and meet them. Also, I couldn't march 'cause I've never had a pair of shoes that were really comfortable.

JOHN. You were pretty good. She helped fire-bomb Pacific Gypsum, and it's her own company.

GWEN. One cocktail in the doorway of the building, broke about six windows.

SHIRLEY. And it was your own company?

GWEN. Oh, please, I was stoned. Who knew what we were doing? We were on TV, we were on the cover of *Time* magazine, it was a blast. Also it was such a crock, really. You go to an antiwar, end-the-war rally, right? You march to the White House.

JOHN. You take a taxi.

KEN. But nonetheless.

GWEN. Anyway. You get there. Five hundred thousand people, speaker's platforms, signs thick as a convention, everybody's high, we're bombed, the place is mobbed, everybody's on the lawn with their shirts off, boys, girls; they're eating chicken and tacos, the signs say: End the War, Ban the Bomb, Black Power and Gay Power and Women's Lib; the Nazi Party's there, the unions, demanding jobs, they got Chicano Power and Free the POWs and Free the Migrants, Allen Ginsberg is chanting Ommm over the loudspeakers, Coretta King is there: Jesus! How straight do you have to be to see that nothing is going to come from it? But don't knock your mother, 'cause she really believed that "Power to the People" song, and that hurts.

JOHN. It's all right, baby.

SHIRLEY. *(Quietly determined.)* I'm going to be the greatest artist Missouri has ever produced.

JOHN. Would that be so difficult?

SHIRLEY. The entire Midwest. What do you mean? There have been famous people—world-famous people from—Tennessee Williams grew up in—

JOHN. Tennessee Williams is from Mississippi.

SHIRLEY. He may have been born there, but he grew up—

JOHN. And his people were from Tennessee, that's why—

SHIRLEY. He grew up not three blocks from where I live now! All his formative years!

JOHN. Okay, what do I know.

SHIRLEY. And Mark Twain. And Dreiser! And Vincent Price and Harry Truman! And Betty Grable! *(Gwen, Ken and John say "Grable" with her.)*

But me! Oh, God! Me! Me! Me! Me! I am going to be so great! Unqualified! The greatest single artist the Midwest has ever known!

JOHN. Yes, yes, doing what?

SHIRLEY. Something astonishing! Just astonishing!

JOHN. *(Overlapping.)* In what field? What are you going to be?

SHIRLEY. A painter. Or a sculptor. Or a dancer! A writer! A conductor! A composer! An actress! One of the arts! People will die. Certain people will literally have cardiac arrest at the magnitude of my achievements.

JOHN. If you're going to be a dancer or a composer, you might matriculate into some school before too much—

SHIRLEY. I will have you know that I intend to study for ten years, and then I will burst forth on the world. And people will be abashed!

KEN. I don't doubt it for a minute.

SHIRLEY. Amazed!

GWEN. I think you're terrific.

SHIRLEY. Astonished! At my magnitude. Oh, God! Look! Is that she? Is that SHE? *Is that she? Is it?* IT IS! IT IS SHE! IT IS SHE! AHHHHHHH-HHHHHHHHHHHHH! *(She collapses on the floor. June enters from upstairs to landing.)*

JOHN. She recognized herself on the street and fainted.

SHIRLEY. *(Slowly getting to a sitting position; with great dignity.)* She died dead of cardiac arrest and astonishment at the magnificence of my achievement in my chosen field. Only Shakespeare, Michelangelo, Beethoven, and Frank Lloyd Wright have risen to my heights before me.

JOHN. And Madame Curie.

SHIRLEY. Marie! Marie! She had a name of her own. Not Madame! Marie!

JUNE. *(Almost admiring.)* You are something else.

SHIRLEY. *(To John.)* And when I first achieved my first achievements I was eleven years younger than you are now. *(She sweeps to the front door and out to the porch. Sally enters from kitchen with an enormous chocolates box.)*

GWEN. Boy, if I had been like that.

SHIRLEY. Weston…

JUNE. Well, we're all here now.

KEN. Shhhh. *(They listen.)*

SHIRLEY. *(On the porch to Wes.)* As we'll be traveling to Nashville together, I don't want you to think I haven't noticed the way you look at me. But I believe in putting everything on the line, and I could never seriously consider marrying you, Weston Hurley. All her life until she was thirty-one and married Matthew Friedman, my Aunt Sally lived with the impossible handicap of being named Sally Talley. And if I married you, I'd be Shirley Hurley. *(She runs Off into the garden.)*

KEN. Aunt Sally, I see you've got Uncle Matt there in your lap. I don't think we should put this off.

SALLY. *(Long pause.)* They all hated him because he was a Jew. Your mother, your father, my folks, the whole damn town hated him.

JUNE. He kept coming back down here.

SALLY. Oh, nothing bothered him except when it bothered me. And if it didn't bother him, it didn't bother me. He liked young people. Shirley was a joy. He was terribly concerned about Gwen. He was very upset with Kenny for going to Vietnam and getting your legs blown off. But I know he was glad when you met Jed. People said he didn't love this country because he wasn't afraid to speak his mind.

JOHN. They say a lot.

SALLY. I think they were right. I don't think he loved this country a bit. He loved the countryside. *(Weston is heard on porch strumming "Anytime.")* No, I'm sorry. I know you all liked him, and you don't mean to push, but I'm not going to dump Matt's ashes down in that rotting boathouse: We'd probably all break our necks anyway. Matt fell through those boards more than thirty years ago.

KEN. It doesn't really matter where, does it? Matt said he didn't want you to keep them, you know why—

SALLY. Kenny, I know what you're planning. Well, do it: The place belongs to you for what you can get from it, but I want you to know I'm damned angry with you. And if that's your scheme, then Matt doesn't belong here.

JUNE. *(To Sally.)* Darling, if you don't go tonight, you'll think of some reason to wait the whole year again.

KEN. Sally, it makes no difference to me, but Matt would—

SALLY. Altogether too many things make no difference to you all of a sudden, Kenny.

JED. A scheme?

SALLY. Exactly. And now he thinks he isn't interested in teaching anymore— He's talking about Spain and Greece—

KEN. Sally, damn it—

JED. That's okay, let him fantasize.

SALLY. *(To Jed.)* After all these people have gone to the dance, I want to talk to you. Now everybody go on.

JUNE. Sally, you can't take that box to California. They won't let you into the state.

SALLY. I don't want you to badger me. You people go dance. I'm going to get ready for bed. *(She exits to her bedroom.)*

JUNE. Well, to hell with it.

GWEN. Is Sally a little—I mean, not that everybody isn't.

JED. She's all right.

JUNE. I don't intend to come here every year waiting for—I told Dad I'd get her to dump the damn ashes before she came out there, if I had to dump them myself. *(She storms outside to the porch.)*

KEN. June!

JED. What scheme?

KEN. Nothing, nothing, we'll talk tomorrow.

JED. There's getting to be a pretty long list of things we're going to talk about tomorrow.

KEN. I know. *Later.*

JOHN. Hey, come on, the Lebanon band must be starting to boogie down across the river.

JED. I'm going to change if It's off for tonight.

KEN. Might as well.

GWEN. Oh, listen, about your place.

KEN. Darling...

GWEN. Well, Sally blew it, didn't she? Jed, if we put in an airstrip up on the hill, we wouldn't fuck up your garden, would we?

JED. No, not at all. But it takes twenty years for a garden to mature into any-thing; we only started three years ago; you don't have to follow through with it—do anything you want. *(Exits upstairs.)*

GWEN. Hell, no, we can hire gardeners.

JOHN. Write down what you got in mind. We'll do it.

KEN. Hey, we'll talk.

JOHN. Hey, June. *(Jed is gone; June returns.)*

JOHN. What say we check out the fairgrounds. The band's already started. Hey, look at this. Just the four of us. How about that.

JUNE. Son-of-a-bitch; together again.

GWEN. Oh, Jesus, I loved the four of us. That was like the greatest period of my life.

JUNE. Let's don't rerun that again. I couldn't take it.

GWEN. You should have stayed with us; we had like our own little commune...

Then Kenny chickened out. John and I ended up by ourselves on that fucking European tour just like—not what we'd planned at all.

JOHN. Let's go celebrate. Come on.

JUNE. You three go on.

KEN. Not tonight. I've got to turn in. I've got to work tomorrow afternoon. I haven't exercised today. Not tonight.

GWEN. This is the last night we're here.

JOHN. I bet that really rips them up.

KEN. No, I'm just beat.

JOHN. Come on, June, let's go.

JUNE. You go on.

JOHN. *(To Gwen.)* Come on, babe, I want to show you the nightlife around here.

KEN. Crickets,

JUNE. Frogs,

KEN. Chiggers,

JUNE. Owls.

JOHN. You need a sweater, need a coat?

GWEN. No, I'm fine.

JOHN. You sure, now?

GWEN. I'm sure.

JUNE. We'll see you in the morning.

GWEN. Yeah, see you tomorrow.

JOHN. Hey, Wes, we're gone. *(Gwen and John exit.)*

JUNE. Those two exhaust me.

KEN. Get over it.

JUNE. Easy said. *(Looks at Ken for a long moment. Then gets up and turns off the light on Ken's desk. Sally reappears on porch, dressed in her nightgown and robe.)*

WESTON. Hey, Sally, what's happening?

SALLY. It didn't rain. There's even going to be a moon. Look at that sky.

JUNE. I'll see you in the morning. *(She goes upstairs.)*

KEN. Good night.

SALLY. You haven't seen anything?

WESTON. Wasn't really lookin'.

SALLY. *(To the sky.)* We know you're up there. We won't hurt you. We want to see you.

WESTON. We'd like to talk with you.

SALLY. You can trust us.

WESTON. No shit.

KEN. *(Gets up. Picks up his crutches.)* With the stomach, not the arms. *(Moves to the Center of the room.)* Cha-cha-cha.

SALLY. Please show yourself to us again. We won't tell a soul! *(Painfully Ken gets into a sitting position in the middle of the floor. He stretches out on his back to rest a moment. Then begins sit-ups. Jed enters from upstairs. Pause.)* No. Not tonight. *(To Weston.)* Good night. *(To Ken.)* Good night, in there.

KEN. *(Who has heard her.)* Night doll; go to bed.

JED. Good night Sally.

SALLY. *(To the sky.)* Good night. *(She goes off into the garden. Weston continues to play. Ken is punting very hard.)*

KEN. *(Exhausted.)* Oh, God...I'm just knocked out. I really...have done myself...in.

JED. So what do we do? You want to sell the house and run?

KEN. I can't teach those kids, Jed...We can't stay here... I can't walk into a classroom again...*(Jed picks him up, holding him in his arms. Leaning his head against him.)* I really have knocked myself out. *(Jed holds him for a moment, then carries him upstairs.)*

JED. Hang in there. *(Weston continues to play for a moment.)*

CURTAIN

END OF ACT ONE

ACT II

The porch. Jed is sitting in the sunshine, referring back and forth between two books, trying to compose a letter on a legal-size yellow pad. A bell tolls in the distance, five seconds between each deep, heavy stroke.

Shirley enters. She enjoys being alone with Jed for a moment. She looks out over the garden, quite forgetting that Jed does not see her there. She notices the bell.

SHIRLEY. Oh! Listen!

JED. *(Jumps a foot.)* Oh, God.

SHIRLEY. "Ask not for whom the bell tolls... It tolls for..."

JED. *(Overlap.)* It tolls for Harley Campbell.

SHIRLEY. Who?

JED. Your Aunt Sally went to the funeral. They ring the bell before the service and after the service.

SHIRLEY. Oh. Oh, God, now it sounds horrible. Oh, God, that's mournful.

JED. If the man made more than a hundred thousand a year and left a widow, they ring it all during the service as well.

SHIRLEY. We, of course, are the first.

JED. First?

SHIRLEY. To arise this morning.

JED. You're the last. You're up in time for brunch.

GWEN. *(Inside, on phone.)* What the fuck for, dial one?

SHIRLEY. Gwen is up?

JED. Yeah. And on the phone.

SHIRLEY. Uncle Kenny's up?

JED. Yeah, Sally and I had breakfast at seven and did a few things.

SHIRLEY. Like what?

JED. Never mind. And I drove her to church, woke up Ken, and we made an herbal anti-fungus concoction guaranteed to fail, and sprayed thirty-five phlox plants. With Wes's, uh…supervision.

SHIRLEY. *(Adjusts.)* Oh. Yes…I slept…fitfully. I tossed, I…

JED. Turned?

SHIRLEY. I had this really weird dream. I was being chased by a deer. All through the woods, over bridges, this huge deer. What does a dream like that mean?

JED. Did he have antlers?

SHIRLEY. I don't remember. Why? *(Jed goes back to his books.)*

JED. If you happen to dream about seven fat cows and seven lean cows, I know what that one means.

SHIRLEY. I would never dream of a cow.

JED. Not a feisty young heifer? Jumping fences, trying to get into the corn?

SHIRLEY. Oh, please. I certainly hope you don't think of me like that! I am not a common cow! I am a…flower, Jed. Slowly and frighteningly opening her petals onto the spring morning. A trimu-a-timulus, a timu—an opening bud.

JED. A mimulus. You're probably a mimulus.

SHIRLEY. What's a mimulus?

JED. Mimulus is a wildflower. Pinkish-yellow, the monkey flower, they call—

SHIRLEY. No, not that one. Not a monkey flower! I am a…

JED. What?

SHIRLEY. Well not—I don't know. And it's important, too. But…I can *see* it. A nearly white, small, single…

JED. What about an apple blossom? The first tree of spring to—

SHIRLEY. No, oh, God, no. And grow into an apple. A fat, hard, red, bloated, tasteless apple? For some crone to bake in a pie for her ditchdigger husband to eat without even knowing it? Oh, God. Never. I'm more than likely the daughter of Che Guevaro or Lawrence Ferlenghetti. My mother was very promiscuous.

JED. So I've heard.

SHIRLEY. *(Thinks.)* I am a blossom that opens for one day only…and I fall. I am not pollinated. It's too early for the bees. They don't find me. And I fade. Dropping my petals one by… What kind of flower is that? *(He thinks a moment.)* A wild rose?

JED. No, you wouldn't flower till May at the earliest. There'd be bees lined up around the block.

SHIRLEY. Well, *what?* Daisies are when?

JED. No.

SHIRLEY. Peony?

JED. There are some anemones…that bloom in March.

SHIRLEY. An anemone…

JED. The original ones are from Greece, so they're all claimed by heroes who fell in battle and their blood seeped into the ground and anemones sprang up, but I think they've found one or two somewhere else that haven't been claimed yet.

SHIRLEY. Do you have a picture of it?

JED. It's around; I'll look it up.

SHIRLEY. *(Hand on sleeve.)* Jed. Thank you. This is, you know, very important to me.

JED. *(Mock seriousness.)* Shirley. It's important to us all.

SHIRLEY. I know.

JED. We don't dwell on it because we try to spare you the pressure of all our expectations. We multitudes.

SHIRLEY. I know. But don't. Don't spare me. It makes me strong.

GWEN. *(Off, on phone.)* Yea, well screw you, too. I don't like the way you're handling this whole thing. *(Slams phone down.)*

KEN. *(Coming out.)* She hasn't been off the phone all morning. Your mother was up at the crack of ten and is baking bath buns.

JED. Bath buns?

SHIRLEY. Believe me, you don't want to know. God, when she gets domestic, there's no hope.

KEN. She speaks not with forked tongue.

JED. I'm no good at this; you'd better reconsider.

KEN. No way, do it yourself.

SHIRLEY. What are you doing?

JED. I'm trying to answer a letter.

KEN. I think there's a harpy in the bottom of our garden. *(Yelling.)* Yo! Aunt Sally!

SALLY. *(Offstage.)* I see you, I see you. Don't rush me.

KEN. She's at the roses again.

SHIRLEY. I retired late, of course, I was packing.

JED. Thought you were here for another two weeks.

SHIRLEY. I will probably return after only a few days; I can't imagine Nashville to hold anything of real interest.

KEN. I'm quite sure the City of Nashville is not ready for you.

JUNE. *(Offstage.)* Outside, everyone outside. This is just the first batch.

KEN. *(To Sally.)* I thought you were going to Old Man Campbell's funeral…

SALLY. *(Entering.)* Oh, fine. Old Man Campbell. Imagine Harley Campbell being Old Man Campbell. No, no, I couldn't do it. That's the hottest place I've ever been in my life. The minister is mad at the whole congregation. They voted down a new air conditioner, so he shut the old one off and told them it broke. He's trying to sweat them out. They'll never give in. A good battle, especially if it's over money, brings out the stoic in them.

JUNE. *(In and out.)* This is just the first batch; another coming.

SHIRLEY. Gird your loins; Mom's making bath buns.

SALLY. Oh, dear. That's quite a walk.

KEN. Looks like it's done you in.

SALLY. Don't look at me.

KEN. Why didn't you call someone to pick you up?

JED. *(Overlapping.)* I could have—

SALLY. *(To Jed.)* I walked that road to school before even your mother was born.

KEN. You didn't know his mother. She could have been fifty. He might have been the—what's the expression?

JED. Last fruit on the tree.

KEN. I wasn't going to say that.

SALLY. I'm afraid I've done something very stupid, Jed.

JED. How's that?

SALLY. Never mind.

KEN. What are you two plotting?

SALLY. Never mind. What terrible houses they've built along the road. Windows right out to the street. I'd feel naked as a jay. Oh, dear.

KEN. Don't walk that again. There's always someone here to drive you.

SHIRLEY. *(With a letter Jed has received.)* That's very impressive. "Sissinghurst Castle. Property of the National Trust."

JED. Come on.

KEN. The lucky bastards.

SHIRLEY. Have you been there?

JED. Huh? Yeah.

KEN. Before we laid out the garden, we took a tour of the competition.

SHIRLEY. Is it fabulous?

JED. It's fabulous.

SHIRLEY. "Jed Jenkins, Esquire…"

JED. In other words, not Sir or Lord.

SHIRLEY. "First of all, we are writing to confirm the identification of your rediscovery of the Slater's Crimson China rose…"

KEN. Thank you so very much, though actually we did know that from the Royal Horticultural Society.

SHIRLEY. It's very exciting to have discovered a rose everyone thought was lost ages ago. How did it get here?

KEN. We assume someone planted it.

SHIRLEY. "Which bloomed in our test garden this summer and will be moved to a prominent position in the rose garden this autumn."

KEN. Do you love it? Only the greatest rose garden in the world.

SHIRLEY. How did they get it?

KEN. We sent it to them.

JED. They asked us for it.

SHIRLEY. "And second—" Should that be "second of all?"

KEN. Certainly not. Never.

SHIRLEY. "Second we would like to inform you that—"

GWEN. *(Entering, followed by Weston.)* Oh, God, would you feel that fuckin' sun? Don't let me fall asleep. I fry like a starfish. *(Flops down in the sun.)*

SHIRLEY. "Second we would like to inform you that the Phyle-Hastings Nursery has—"

GWEN. I read that letter and they're so full of it.

SHIRLEY. If you please.

GWEN. Sorry. Hand me a cup.

SHIRLEY. "…Nursery has requested the honor of adding this rose to their catalogue so it can once again be propagated and grown as it deserves. You of course will be credited with this important rediscovery…"

JED. *(Embarrassed.)* Blah, blah, blah, blah.

GWEN. *(Overlapping.)* They are so full of it. No way, baby—

SHIRLEY. *(Overlapping.)* He rediscovered it, I don't know why not.

GWEN. You check with a lawyer before you sign anything. The limeys would as soon rip you off as look at you.

KEN. They did raise it, after all.

GWEN. Right, and lost it. Fuck 'em. They want it so bad they can pay for it. Not without a commission. Have you got Sweet 'n' Low? Oh, forget it.

SHIRLEY. How was the celebration?

GWEN. When?

SHIRLEY. The fireworks you went to last night?

GWEN. Oh, hey, I wanted to come back and get you. It was great. There—

SHIRLEY. They were pretty?

GWEN. —were these really—what? The fireworks? You've never seen anything so lame in your life.

KEN. Present company always excepted.

GWEN. There were these—*(Slaps him.)*—field hands—

KEN. *(Overlapping.)* You would strike a crippled fairy.

GWEN. These really randy, country Republican high school juniors drinking beer out of a paper sack.

SALLY. I remember.

GWEN. You've never seen a hornier—

SHIRLEY. I would not have been interested.

GWEN. ...collection of male brawniness in—oh, God, it was John and Kenny when we were in Berkeley. They were exactly the same randy farmhands when we first met.

KEN. Me? A farmhand? Son of my father who never farmed a day in his life?

GWEN. Yeah, and John's father was a dentist! They even look like you looked then. They still have long hair.

KEN. John and I moved in quite a different circle from your—

GWEN. You're such a snob.

KEN. We were quite a different social stratum from the horny river trash you're trying to associate with us.

GWEN. Horny. River. Trash! That's exactly what they were. And you were exactly like that. *(Hits his leg.)* Ouch!

KEN. Fiberglass! Light but strong.

GWEN. —You can't tell me you didn't drink beer out of a sack. You jerked off behind the same bushes they do.

KEN. I profess to have no memory of the bushes I jerked off behind.

JED. Very fickle.

KEN. Well, I warned you. *(John enters.)*

GWEN. Honey, good, tell them. There was one blond stud—what was his name, you said you knew him.

JOHN. Jim Pendergast's little brother. Only he's assumed a very sinister style.

KEN. Decidedly unstable family.

GWEN. I don't care, he was gorgeous. Shirley would have loved him.

SHIRLEY. I don't think about men physically. I never have. I think about all people spiritually.

GWEN. I know, but you gotta get over that real quick. *(To John.)* Oh, baby, at noon our time you gotta call Schwartzkoff, because they're really screwing up. I don't care if we have to fly back to L.A. tonight, we have to straighten him out.

JOHN. He called here? Why didn't I hear—

GWEN. I called him, 'cause we hadn't heard from him and when he's silent for three days it means he's got something up—

JOHN. Honey, we got a recording session—

GWEN. I don't care. I have to think about one thing at a time. They aren't going to do what we want unless we really lean on him.

JOHN. He just panics. I told you it'll be all right. I'll worry about that. You worry about Nashville.

GWEN. *(Backing down a bit.)* No lie, though, he started in on the inner politics of Tasmania and the state wages precedent, and the whole song all over again. He's really not listening to us at all. *(June comes in with breakfast.)*

JUNE. Here it is.

JOHN. I know. I'll talk to him. You worry about you.

GWEN. Lean on the son of a bitch. He doesn't have a leg to stand on.

KEN. Begging my pardon.

JOHN. *(To Ken.)* Hey, your name's going to be mud, too.

KEN. Why's that? Not that I mind. Kenneth Mudd.

JOHN. Mudd Talley, I think. We talked to Mac. Boy, he never changes.

GWEN. Oh, yeah, we talked to your boss. What a prick.

JUNE. Wouldn't you know he'd be there.

SHIRLEY. Who's Mac? *(Jed gestures inside. Sally shakes her head.)*

JUNE. Mac McConnell; principal of the high school.

KEN. Superintendent, now.

JUNE. God, I hated him almost as much as he hated me.

GWEN. No, he said he'd like to see you while you're down.

JUNE. No way.

GWEN. It was John he hated. Said he suspected him of cheating on tests.

JOHN. You believe him still harping on that after ten years?

SHIRLEY. Why is Uncle Ken's name mud?

JOHN. He still thinks you're going to be teaching there this fall.

KEN. He's very mistaken.

JOHN. You ought to call him.

JED. What did you tell him?

JOHN. I'm not going to tell him nothing. Mac thinks you're happy as a pig in shit.

SHIRLEY. Please, I'm trying to eat Mother's cooking.

GWEN. He was very excited about one of his students returning to the fold.

KEN. The prospect excites me not at all.

JUNE. Sally, scrambled eggs, hot bath buns?

SALLY. No, thanks.

GWEN. Listen, who can know anything? When did we see you in New York?

JED. Three years ago.

GWEN. Was that three years ago? That was all you were talking about. Jed was going to build this garden, you were going to teach.

KEN. Don't start on that again.

JUNE. Actually, they had a little Fete to welcome the returning Vet two weeks ago—and Kenny was taken around to meet all his classes—

KEN. *(Overlapping.)* Yes, Jed and I visited that lovely new building. Dear old Mac was a little edgy about Jed, he couldn't quite put that together—

JED. I think he was coming pretty close.

KEN. Probably be thrilled. An opportunity to exhibit his liberal tolerance. But other than that, I found him quite pleasantly condescending, didn't you.

JED. No complaints. Said he liked gardens.

JUNE. And Ken had the pleasure of being introduced to the four classes he would be teaching this fall.

JED. Well, actually only three—

KEN. *(Annoyed.)* I begged off the fourth and went back to the car.

JED. Went in full of piss and vinegar, came out white as a sheet.

KEN. I just wasn't quite ready for them; or they certainly weren't ready for me. We don't have any milk out here, I can't drink—

GWEN. What did they do?

JED. He just overreacted.

KEN. *(Overreacting.)* I did not overreact! June, could you hand me my—crutches.

JUNE. *(Overlapping.)* No one had prepared them for him—Mac has always been about as tactful—

KEN. *(Biting.)* No, I think it was more a question of a sincere lack of rapport.

GWEN. A lot of messy questions, right?

KEN. No, I was quite prepared for the messy questions. Dry urbanity; humorous self-deprecation.

JED. The kids wouldn't look at him. *(Pause. Nobody looks up.)*

KEN. Which God knows I should have been prepared for, but for some reason I was not.

JOHN. They were grossed out, for God's sake.

KEN. Well, if I had some deep-seated need to teach, trying to get at Johnny Young's speech problems will fulfill that quite nicely for a few more weeks.

GWEN. That's all too fuckin' humanitarian; I never trust that gig—it's creepy.

KEN. Not at all, the gimp leading the gimp; we form a very cozy symposium.

JOHN. So, do both.

JUNE. Came running back here.

KEN. Hardly running.

JUNE. Crawled into a closet.

KEN. Hardly a closet.

JUNE. And has been panic-stricken ever since.

WESTON. *(After a pause.)* Out of a paper sack?

GWEN. Yeah, passing these quart beer bottles in paper sacks. All very covert. None of them over seventeen. Strictly from twenty-four-hour hard-ons.

JOHN. The lucky stiffs.

KEN. Lucky now to get it up in twenty-four hours. Knock on wood. *(Hits his leg.)*

WESTON. Knock on wood? Knock on wood?

GWEN. I thought you said they were fiberglass.

KEN. A technicality.

WESTON. Oh, shit.

SHIRLEY. If you please.

GWEN. Oh, you're too much. We told you Kenny had wooden legs from his Vietnam—

KEN. "Tour," we call it.

WESTON. Oh, wow.

KEN. Heavy, huh?

WESTON. Oh, wow. I thought you meant he could drink a lot of sake.

JOHN. That would be a hollow leg.

WESTON. No shit. How come?

KEN. Well, it was either accept their kind offer of a prosthetics device or find a position as a very cumbersome basketball.

SHIRLEY. Oh, no.

KEN. And I opted for a semblance of mobility.

JUNE. Unless you could handpick both basketball teams.

KEN. No, no, I've never liked being tossed around by a bunch of sweaty ectomorphs.

JUNE. I don't know. I always thought of John as a sweaty ectomorph.

KEN. Oh, please. That was many moons ago.

JUNE. Only fifteen years.

SHIRLEY and WESTON. *Only* fifteen years?

JOHN. But those were pretty hot years back in Berkeley.

KEN. One had to move with the times. *(Jed goes into the house.)*

GWEN. It couldn't have been all that hot with Kenny. You were sleeping with June at the same time.

SHIRLEY. No! Oh, ugh! How could you. Oh, gwackk! You did it with him?

JUNE. I thought she was talking about me. *(To Shirley.)* Oh, shut up; you're too much.

JOHN. Everyone did it with June.

GWEN. Your mother was a bigger Pop-tart than I was.

KEN. Not at all, not till after you moved in and she started running with the—what do you call them?

SALLY. The wrong crowd, I think.

KEN. When we were in school here we used to sleep over and diddle each other.

JOHN. We were twelve years old.

SALLY. The two you?

JUNE. The three of us.

SHIRLEY. Oh, that's—

SALLY. It certainly is.

KEN. I'd been in love with you for years.

JOHN. You were not. That was just diddling.

KEN. Oh, yeah, remember the double date when you couldn't get Margy Majors to go all the way—

JOHN. One time. And I was drunk.

KEN. Well, I wasn't. I had planned it all week. I knew damn well you weren't going to get anywhere with Margy.

GWEN. Oh, God. Remember going all the way!

KEN. I must have been in love with you at least two years before we ran off to Berkeley. He was never out of this V-neck, sky-blue cashmere sweater, full of holes.

JOHN. Mostly from you poking your finger in them.

GWEN. He's ticklish.

JUNE. Very.

KEN. Well, then you discovered the Copper Queen.

GWEN. That would be me.

JUNE. Nobody said John didn't know a good thing when he saw it.

GWEN. Damn straight. *(Jed returns with milk and Ken's cane.)*

KEN. And they all lived happily ever after.

GWEN. Oh, I loved us then. I remember once we bought twenty dollars' worth of daffodils and your mother and I ran up and down on the Nimitz Freeway giving them to all the stalled drivers.

WESTON. Why?

GWEN. Why? June had decided they were wonderful.

JUNE. Unfortunately, they hated us. The traffic started moving; we nearly got run down.

KEN. You were decidedly before your time.

GWEN. That fuckin' war! Damn, it fucked us. It broke my heart when we weren't together. If only you'd come with us to Europe everything would have been so different. The whole idea was going off to escape from your draft thing. I'll never forgive you for chickening out on that.

KEN. I didn't chicken out; you were just afraid of the competition.

GWEN. You would never have been in Nam, you wouldn't have been injured; June wouldn't have gotten militant and estranged from us.

WESTON. I read this book. Like about war experiences in Nam? It said shock and dope were like common. In the goddamned reading room; Fairleigh Dickinson University.

KEN. *(To Shirley.)* I defy anyone to diagram that sentence.

WESTON. Really heavy.

KEN. The reading room at Fairleigh Dickinson was heavy? Vietnam was heavy or the book was heavy.

WESTON. You were there, man, I can't tell you.

KEN. Nothing was common except the American troops, and we were very common indeed.

WESTON. Like you're trying to be cool, but you still carry it around.

KEN. However awkwardly.

SALLY. Your mother was very proud that you went. I could have killed her.

KEN. Wasn't that interesting? I thought so, too. And ashamed that I came back.

SHIRLEY. Oh, that isn't true.

JUNE. The hell it ain't.   SALLY. Don't kid yourself.

WESTON. You still think about it.

KEN. I don't wake up screaming any more from visions of my buddies floating through the blue sky in pieces, if that's what you mean...

WESTON. Oh, shit.

KEN. Exactly that. The dream is more likely of some goddamned general moving down the row of beds in the hospital, handing our medals like aspirin. That's the first thing I saw when I regained consciousness.

JUNE. Beating the bushes for heroes.

SHIRLEY. Uncle Ken has five medals.

KEN. You may not be proud of that.

WESTON. What was the saving grace?

KEN. Beg pardon?

WESTON. You said a heroic action had to have a saving grace.

KEN. Silliest thing I ever heard of—

WESTON. Like with the Eskimo, you said there was no saving grace in—

KEN. Oh, Weston, doll, I'm all in favor of your Eskimo hero. I think he was a man among men. I completely blame the family. You see, if you had said that the warrior was flatulent on the walrus blubber...

WESTON. —caribou meat—

KEN. ...Be that as it may, and it stank so bad that the family could hardly eat it, but they managed and survived, we could perhaps accept that as an unpleasant but not altogether vainglorious moment in the history of the Eskimo. I thought at the time that the family was too picayune for a myth.

WESTON. Oh.

KEN. See?

WESTON. Yeah.

KEN. Yeah. The family disappointed me deeply.

WESTON. So the saving grace—

KEN. —would have been surviving. Don't choke on it, don't turn up your nose, swallow it and live, baby.

WESTON. Even if it stinks, man.

KEN. Dig it.

WESTON. Right on.

KEN. They could have forever after been known as the family who bravely ate the fart-thawed meat and went on to become...

SALLY. —vegetarians.

JOHN. Baby, we gotta pack if we're going to hit the road by three this afternoon.

JUNE. That'll get you there by when?

JOHN. Five. We're driving to Springfield, hopping a plane.

JUNE. Oh, of course you are. (*Jed begins to sing: "Hit the road, Jack."*)

SHIRLEY. I probably won't stay with you more than a few days; I can just crowd you in as it is.

GWEN. We go everywhere with an open-return ticket.

JUNE. This one is returning before she leaves.

SHIRLEY. There's nothing pressing this week.

JUNE. Can it.

SHIRLEY. What do you mean, can it?

GWEN. I thought you'd decided to let her come. Johnny, you said...

JUNE. The farthest thing from my mind. I wouldn't consider it.

GWEN. We'll take good care of her. Johnny promised me—

JUNE. No, not this time; another time.

SHIRLEY. What do you mean? You can't!

JUNE. Just cool it, because you're not going.

SHIRLEY. When have I ever had the opportunity to go some place? This could be the beginning of a whole new horizon for me.

JUNE. The one thing I can't bring myself to do is discipline the brat. I hated Mom for that.

SHIRLEY. Well, you had good reason!

JUNE. We'll discuss it some other time.

SHIRLEY. We won't discuss it at all! *(Storming out.)* I am twenty-one years old and I can do what I want to do!

WESTON. Am I going to have time to help with the cinders?

KEN. Sure.

JOHN. The what?

WESTON. Cinders. They got a problem in their garden. I'm gonna help them out.

JOHN. Yeah? Well, sorry, Jed, there goes the neighborhood. With Wes loose out there, that ought to do it.

WESTON. I helped them spray the—what was it?

JED. Phlox.

WESTON. The phlox for mold—

JED. Mildew.

WESTON. —for mildew this morning. This afternoon we got to get over to the school where Talley is going to teach...

KEN. ...is not going to teach.

WESTON. —yeah, and get a load of cinders, and spread them around the— what was it?

JED. Penstemon.

WESTON. Gonna spread them around the penstemon, so the—what was it?

JED. Slugs.

WESTON. —so the slugs can't get at them. See, they got these soft vulnerable bellies—

JOHN. The penstemon?

WESTON. No, the—

JED. *(To Weston.)* Slugs.

WESTON. The slugs. They don't like to crawl over the cinders. You spread the cinders around the plant, it keeps them off it.

JOHN. That's...ingenious.

WESTON. Yeah, well, you can laugh, but I saw the damage they done just last night. When it's wet like it's been here, the—

JOHN. Slugs?

WESTON. —the slugs become this major problem. And see, we got to get it done before tonight, see, because they come out as soon as it gets dark. They don't like the light, see.

JOHN. Really.

WESTON. Sure.

JOHN. Why don't you put a light in the garden?

JED. Then the eggplant wouldn't set flower. It requires a period of six hours unbroken dark to set—

JOHN. Jed, you're going to tell me about photosynthesis.

JED. Photoperiod.

JOHN. I don't want to know about photosynthesis.

JED. Photoperiod.

JUNE. Oh, God…

JOHN. What?

JUNE. I was just imagining having a vulnerable belly, crawling over cinders.

WESTON. No, see, you can't think like that.

GWEN. Fuck it, kill 'em. They're ruining the garden.

WESTON. Right, you gotta be like cold-blooded and ruthless. Otherwise, you won't have any—what is it?

GWEN, JUNE, and JOHN. Penstemon.

WESTON. Otherwise, you won't have any penstemon. They're really voracious. They eat six times their weight every night. I was reading one of Jed's books.

KEN. I wonder what a slug weighs.

WESTON. It didn't say.

KEN. Oh, well…

WESTON. We could catch one and weigh it.

KEN. Does anyone have something I could open a vein with?

WESTON. You know what they're trying to make here? What's the name of that garden in England? The one we didn't see.

JOHN. We didn't see any of them.

WESTON. The one we could have seen, though.

JOHN. I don't remember.

WESTON. Well, that's the one they're trying to make here.

SHIRLEY. *(Who has been standing in doorway.)* Sissinghurst Castle Gardens. They're a property of the National Trust.

WESTON. Isn't that far out?

GWEN. You know what would be even better? Just let it all go wild. Let whatever happens to grow all go wild.

JED. That would be one answer. *(The phone rings inside.)*

GWEN. Oh, shit. That's Schwartzkoff calling back because I hung up on him.

KEN. It isn't long-distance.

GWEN. Yes, it will be. John, you talk to him. He just keeps saying the same thing to me.

KEN. It isn't long—

JOHN. Honey, you don't hang up on someone who's calling from the Coast—*(He goes into house to phone.)*

GWEN. *(Yelling.)* I don't care. He was calling me capricious. I felt like showing him what capricious was. *(To them.)* I will never be able to understand why I can't do what I please with my own company.

JOHN. Ken, you or June, either one.

JUNE. I'll get it.

GWEN. It's like zero percent of the whole—conglomerate.

JOHN. We going swimming later?

JUNE. I can answer the phone all by myself.

JOHN. We've hardly had a chance to talk this whole visit.

JUNE. That really rips me up.

SHIRLEY. You own an entire company by yourself?

GWEN. Most of the like branches I own like nothing. Like six percent or fifteen percent. But Helena Copper is one hundred percent mine. Mom left it to me, damn it. I was up there. Oh, God, they loved me. I made a speech, they just went crazy. I told them what I wanted to do, no shit, they carried me around the meeting hall over their heads, like a fuckin' astronaut.

KEN. What did you promise them?

GWEN. Oh, well, see the company makes all this money, but like the Surrogate won't let me raise the—*(John is back, listening in the doorway.)* —salaries because of the labor situation in the state—

JOHN. In the industry.

GWEN. Is it the industry? Anyway, like, you remember when we read Marx? What pissed Marx off was the owners making money off the workers, just because the owners own the factory.

KEN. Exploitation of, yes—

GWEN. I may have failed economic philosophy, but I got that. Well, so I said I'd give them a bonus after the year of all the profit. But they had to divide it evenly, file clerks get as much as managers. They flipped.

SALLY. I'll bet.

KEN. Only what?

GWEN. Only Schwartzkoff, the bastard, is trying to take the profit from Helena Copper and pay for—

JOHN. Capital improvements—

GWEN. Capital improvements in the other branches and claim there aren't any profits this year.

KEN. And that surprises you?

JOHN. A hair illegal, but done all the time.

GWEN. Well, that really pisses me 'cause those people were great to us. They gave us a picnic. We had pigs' feet. Wasn't it pigs' feet, John?

JOHN. It certainly tasted like pigs' feet to me.

GWEN. Come on! They were wonderful to us.

JUNE. *(Entering.)* Hold it a second. Gwen, excuse me. *(Alarmed but very firm.)* Aunt Sally.

SALLY. He went away. I didn't know where he had gone. I got tired of waiting for him.

JUNE. He was very upset when I told him you were here. He said for you to lie down. He'll get here when he can.

SALLY. There is no reason for him to come here. And I'm fine where I am.

JUNE. *(Pause. To them.)* She passed out in church. They took her to Dr. Anderson's across the street and she sneaked out on him.

SALLY. I did not. He always tries to take care of more than he can; giving everyone five minutes. I waited as long—

JUNE. Would you please. He doesn't know. He hardly had time to examine her; she may have had a mild stroke, it might just be—

GWEN. June.

SHIRLEY. What?

SALLY. It was nothing of the kind! I merely blacked out. I do it all the time.

JUNE. When? When have you passed out before? Recently?

SALLY. When I was eleven.

JUNE. You should rest, inside. You can't tell the damage, if it was a stroke—

GWEN. June.

JUNE. Until she's been looked at.

GWEN. June.

SHIRLEY. *(Overlapping.)* Where's the doctor? Why didn't he come here?

JUNE. He'll be here as soon as he's free.

SHIRLEY. Free?

GWEN. June, you don't tell someone they have had a stroke. You say they've had a slight cerebral disturbance.

SHIRLEY. That sounds better?

GWEN. Daddy lapped it up. If they'd told him he had had a stroke, he would never have recovered.

JOHN. He didn't recover.

GWEN. John!

SALLY. It was very silly, very embarrassing. And when I woke up, I felt perfectly fine.

KEN. Don't talk. It's cooler out here. She's out of the sun.

JUNE. I don't know if she should be alone or lie down or—

SALLY. —I was sitting there listening to that stupid, vindictive Reverend Poole, and I looked over at that smug wife of his, always looking so pleased to have an occasion to show how easily she can cry. She was like that in school. You'd say, Francine, cry! And she'd burst into tears for you. And I looked at her and there were two of her. Sitting side by side. I just thought, Oh, my God, no. If there's one thing that Lebanon does not need it's another Francine Poole. And I was rubbing my eyes, trying to make one of her go away. Or both of her if possible. And I noticed that there were two Reverend Pooles giving that vacuous eulogy, and two pulpits and two caskets and it was just all too—much. And I got up to get the—hell out of there before there was two of me, and—

JUNE. She passed out in the aisle.

SALLY. Everyone must have enjoyed that. I woke up in Dr. Anderson's office, with him clucking at me, and I felt very rested. But there was only one of him. Wouldn't you know?

JED. Too bad. Town could use another Dr. Anderson.

KEN. Where's Dr. Cranefield?

JED. On vacation. Anderson's overloaded.

SALLY. Well, I wasn't going to wait all day for the man to tell me to go home. I wanted a glass of water, I still haven't had one. *(Shirley enters house to get a glass of water.)*

GWEN. Double vision is one of the symptoms of a—slight cerebral disturbance.

SALLY. I realized that while I was walking home. I had nurse's training during the war—

JUNE. Walked? You walked here from town?

SALLY. I didn't get in the least tired. No one has ever paid the slightest attention to me, so please don't now. I don't know how to cope with it. I'm sixty-one years old and I have a perfect right to have a stroke. I've suffered a trauma.

JUNE. You rest after something like that. You don't go for a five-mile hike.

SALLY. I came home slowly, June. It's only a mile and a half. I didn't go jogging.

JUNE. She's too much. I'm arguing with her. I'm killing her. *(Shirley brings Sally a glass of water. Sally takes a sip, and puts the flower she carries in the glass.)*

KEN. You really are too much.

SALLY. What a scandal to have ruined Harley's funeral. I looked for where he carved his initials on the pew, but I couldn't find it. Certainly the only mark he ever made on anything.

KEN. Would you please not talk. What do you do with her?

SALLY. We were engaged when we were kids, you know. I was certainly well out of that.

JUNE. Sally—

SALLY. His first wife and her kids and lawyer were on one side of the aisle and his second wife and her lawyer were on the other side, just glaring at each other. And both of them glaring at me. *(Laughs.)* Oh, I shouldn't enjoy it, but it's the first time I've been in that church since I was fired from teaching Sunday school thirty-six years ago. God knows what everyone was calling me. Jezebel, I'd think. Married a Jew, thrown out of town, come barging back like a brazen huzzy.

KEN. Not Jezebel. Naomi, maybe.

JUNE. You were not thrown out of town.

SALLY. I was so! I was thrown out of town. Your father said Matt was a no-good Jew and was only interested in the bank. He never forgave Matt for making more money than he did.

KEN. Aunt Sally, please don't talk.

SALLY. Well, darling, with you all acting like everything I say might be the last word I utter, I want to be sure I get it all in.

JUNE. Sally, I absolutely forbid you to enjoy this.

GWEN. What's the point if you don't get off on it?

SALLY. Pino's made Harley look very waxy.

JUNE. Who did what?

SALLY. Pino's Funeral Home. They made Harley look very waxy. You remember Mrs. Farthing?

JUNE. No.

KEN. Taught algebra.

JUNE. She couldn't possibly still be alive.

SALLY. Oh, yes. She looked at poor waxy Harley and said she supposed death was something we none of us could avoid. But she looked like she thought she might have an angle.

JUNE. How can you tell? Fool that I am, I keep listening to her to see if she sounds normal. She's never sounded normal in her life.

SALLY. Well, don't listen to me. Matt didn't believe in death and I don't either...

KEN. I beg your pardon?

SALLY. There's no such thing. It goes on and then it stops. You can't worry about the stopping, you have to worry about the going on. Is that a hummingbird? Is that a bat?

JED. Where?

SALLY. No. Gone.

JUNE. Dr. Anderson said she left a candy box in his office.

KEN. Oh, God. You left Uncle Matt in the office?

SALLY. What are you talking about?

JUNE. The candy box.

SALLY. Well, that's as good a place for it as anywhere. Tell him to keep it.

JUNE. If he brings it back, I'll kill him.

SALLY. That's all taken care of.

KEN. How is "that" all taken care of?

SALLY. That is taken care of privately. *(Pause. Phone rings offstage.)*

KEN. That one is long-distance.

JOHN. I'll get it.

GWEN. Oh, Jesus, that's going to be Nashville. I don't want to go to Nashville at all, man. I get more tense every minute.

WESTON. That won't happen again.

GWEN. No joke. Feel my back.

KEN. That won't happen; you'll relax, you'll feel fine.

GWEN. I just feel the tension creeping up my arms right to my jaws. My hands are like ice. Kenny, when could you be out, you know?

KEN. What, love?

GWEN. Like, if I'm gonna freak out till I have my own studio. Like, we could cancel this gig in Nashville, go back to L.A., and see what's eatin' Schwartzkoff while they're fixing up a place for us here and come back in August. What's it gonna cost me?

KEN. *(Overlapping.)* I've never built a recording studio, I really wouldn't—

GWEN. No, man, the place. What are you asking for it? What's your price?

I mean, I don't do it, the company does it, but I should know what you're soaking us for.

JUNE. *(Almost amused.)* What on earth are you talking about?

GWEN. *(To Ken.)* Only I want to tell you right up front, I don't bargain. So you'll rip me off, but that's nothing new. *(Pause.)* Speak, damn it—we gotta catch a plane. What are you waiting for, some Arab to buy up the whole state? Copper money is as good as oil money. Daddy used to say that, only he was talking about…Rockefeller.

KEN. Maybe we should move this inside.

GWEN. I gotta find a place, Kenny; I can't fart around.

SALLY. We know what you're doing, you don't have to hide.

JUNE. Oh, my god; I have been blind and deaf!

JOHN. *(Entering.)* Hey, baby, you're going to have to talk to King, he won't tell me what's up.

GWEN. That's King? Calling here? What does he want?

JOHN. Some deal, some record company; the man's delirious.

GWEN. What record company—

JOHN. He won't tell me, he wants to talk to you. He's got someone lined up to be at the session. Talk!

GWEN. Did you call Schwartzkoff?

JOHN. He wasn't in. Take the call; he's a busy man.

GWEN. Oh, God, I'm going to look peachy with some record company in the studio, my shrink trying to pry open my mouth with his fingers.

JOHN. Would you take the goddamned call. Come on, Wes, move your butt.

SHIRLEY. I want to hear your tape before you leave. Apparently I won't be afforded the opportunity to—

GWEN. Listen, sure, anything you want as long as I don't have to hear it. Come on, I'm serious about this house. You talk it over. And like August, September.

JOHN. I know, we will. *(Weston goes inside.)*

GWEN. No shit, it's what we been looking for. *(To John.)* Get a price. And find out when they can be out.

JOHN. I know, we will.

WESTON. *(On the phone.)* Yeah, man, what's happening.

GWEN. I got it. *(Goes into house.)*

JOHN. Uh…I been setting up this thing with Jimmy King for three months; suddenly he won't talk…

KEN. Yeah…frustrating.

JED. About your place. Gwen's really got a hair up her butt.

SHIRLEY. Oh, dear.

JOHN. You tell her what you want for it?

JUNE. No, we were just getting to that.

JOHN. So what's the bite?

JUNE. In a word, no way.

JOHN. What's say?

JUNE. I'm not talking to you. *(To Ken.)* You are going to sell the Talley place to John and Gwen Landis for a recording studio?

KEN. It is not your decision, June.

JUNE. Do you know why he's doing this?

JOHN. I don't think you have anything to say about it, do you?

JUNE. Forget it. It isn't going to happen. No sale. No sale.

JOHN. Do the two of you own it?

JUNE. It doesn't matter who—

JOHN. Is the place yours to sell? You have the title; there're no leans on it, there're no mortgages? The place does belong to you?

KEN. Yes, of course.

JUNE. I'll sit on the road with a shotgun and we'll see how fast—

JOHN. I'd think you would have learned by now that that never got any of us anything we wanted.

KEN. Okay, okay, June—fine—stay out of it; it's no business of yours.

JOHN. So what's the bite?

KEN. I'll have to get a hundred seventy-five for the place.

JOHN. Jesus H. You don't want much. I tell you what. We'll give you a hundred and a quarter.

SALLY. For the Talley place? You're joking.

JOHN. For what's left of it. It'll take that much again to make it livable.

KEN. John, I don't own Helena Copper. I have this house; I want to guarantee a future for Jed and me—

JOHN. Listen, for all we care you can live here. We wouldn't be here more than three months a year. Jed can build his goddamned English garden.

JED. No thank you.

KEN. No, come on. I'm going to sell the place and never see it again. Jed? What do we need?

JED. We'll talk later.

JOHN. A hundred and a quarter, flat out. What's the problem?

KEN. You're really putting me on the spot here. We have over a hundred lilies Jed grew from seed two years ago; going to bloom this August. Gwen is talking about moving in tomorrow almost—

JUNE. You don't even like the place—Gwen wants to grow weeds—

JOHN. I love it, I always have.

JED. Yeah, but what do you care where you are, as long as there's a telephone.

JOHN. As it happens, Gwen wants this house. Whatever she wants is fine by me. Whatever makes me happy.

JED. I'm hip.

JOHN. Yeah, see, that's none of your business.

KEN. But, Jesus, John, the money you spend doing it. Come on, we're not blind. What are you buying, the whole record company now? How can you buy a—

JOHN. Oh, fuck, Talley. Stop being such a faggot. Look around you, wake up, for God's sake. You can buy anything!

SALLY. Not for a hundred and a quarter you can't.

JOHN. Okay, that was the wrong thing to say. Are you telling me you can't sell for that price.

KEN. I didn't say that.

JOHN. You can't sell to me for that price or you can't sell to anybody for that price? I'm not deaf to these insinuations and innuendoes that have been floating around. *(Pause.)*

KEN. *(Level.)* I was very angry when you took off for Europe without telling me, but that's long past.

JOHN. Don't dump that on me.

KEN. The three of us plan for six months to go to Europe to beat the draft, then Gwen drags you off a week ahead of schedule and you don't tell me, what the hell would you call it?

JOHN. No, I won't take that. You can't lay your goddamned fecklessness on me—I'm not responsible for anything that happened to you in—

KEN. Okay, forget it. Everyone loves you, everyone forgets everything. Nobody's dumping anything on you.

JOHN. What the hell would you call it? No. I told Gwen you changed your mind. I wanted me and my wife out of the whole steamy situation with both of you.

KEN. *(Shocked.)* You told her I changed my mind?

JOHN. Yeah. And we had a good cry and left in two days and how long did you stay in Oakland before you actually got called up? One month? Two months?

JUNE. Closer to three.

JOHN. So don't blame me. I thought you'd fag out. I thought you'd evade—

go to Canada. I didn't think you'd join the damn Army. Why did you go, anyway? Did it have something to do with Gwen and me?

KEN. No.

JOHN. Now I hope everyone heard that.

JED. That's enough.

JUNE. It was just easier to let them take you.

KEN. I have never known why I went, and the question has crossed my—

JUNE. You sat on your butt and let them take you because it was easier than making a commitment; you let them make your commitment for you.

JOHN. Hey, baby, I'll tell you something. The first thing you learn in business is to talk about one deal at a time. Kenneth says he wants to sell the place. Now, I'll give you a hundred thirty, that's as high as I go.

SALLY. A hundred thirty-five.

JOHN. You bidding against me or are you trying to up the price.

SALLY. I'm bidding against you.

JOHN. A hundred forty.

SALLY. A hundred forty-five.

JOHN. A hundred fifty.

SALLY. A hundred fifty-five.

KEN. Aunt Sally, what the hell are you doing?

SALLY. Jed and I scattered Matt all over the rose garden early this morning. It didn't take ten minutes. You can sell the place to me, Kenny, if you've got to sell it; and I'll give it to Jed. If you can't stay here, Jed can. And you're not selling the Talley place for a hundred fifty thousand. I'm prepared to go to two hundred twenty-six thousand. You're a rich man, Kenny.

KEN. Jed.

JED. You go on to Greece; I've got work to do here.

KEN. Well, you're welcome to it. A hundred seventy-five, that's the price, John?

JOHN. Leave me out of this.

KEN. Sally? Take it or leave it.

SALLY. I'll take it.

KEN. You've got it. John. I'm sorry you've been outbid.

JOHN. I don't need this hassle. I came here to see June. I didn't come down here looking to buy the Talley place. That was your idea.

JUNE. Why? See me why?

JOHN. What? Oh, Jesus. Could we walk down away from here a minute?

JUNE. I don't think so.

JOHN. I just want to talk.

JUNE. Here I am.

JOHN. Then could Shirley go inside for a while?

SHIRLEY. Certainly not.

JUNE. I don't think you want to go into that right now.

JOHN. I don't have to enumerate the advantages for the kid.

JUNE. Advantages? What the fuck are—

JOHN. Gwen and I both love her. I don't want to seem cavalier—

KEN. Of course not.

JOHN. Just look at the situation. What she is and what we could offer her. Not permanently, just half the year. Just a few months a year—

JUNE. You're out of your mind. You have the balls. You have the balls—

JOHN. Come on, I don't think you want Shirley to—

SALLY. I knew goddamned well he didn't want the house. No, young man.

JUNE. *(Overlapping.)* I don't give a shit who hears it. Out. You better leave now, and you better never—never mention Shirley again.

KEN. *(Standing.)* You better watch what you say, buddy; you're leaving yourself open for one hell of a non-support suit—

JOHN. I have said nothing. I claim no responsibility.

JUNE. Some things you cannot buy, baby! Now leave.

JOHN. But if I wanted to take it to court, I could get her— Don't think I couldn't.

JUNE. You try it!

JOHN. All right, forget it; can it. You just by God remember you had the chance.

SHIRLEY. I will live in St. Louis with my mother.

JOHN. Fine, baby, it serves you right.

KEN. You're leaving now—

JOHN. You damn right we are.

GWEN. *(Bursting into the porch, with Weston.)* Holy shit, they want me! They want me! We're in! Oh, sweet Jesus! Columbia bought our tape! They're releasing the fucker in two weeks! Holy shit, they flipped out! The man is talking like retainers of five thousand a month for the first six months, then renegotiate. The man is talking like we're fuckin' stars.

WESTON. *(Overlapping.)* No shit, he's like sellin' it to us. We didn't have to say shit.

GWEN. Two weeks! Two weeks! He's going to have the fucking record on the air. On the motherfuckin' air waves.

WESTON. He wants it orchestrated, though, he wants strings. Whoever heard of strings in a—

GWEN. Damn straight. Violins, fuckin' cellos, the works. Lay it on me. Voice of pain! Shitfire.

KEN. *(Overlapping.)* Gwen, no, no, Gwen, you can't do it. We can't let John do this to you.

GWEN. Honey, this is a piece of cake, and me and Wes are hungry.

WESTON. She's good.

KEN. It doesn't matter if she's any good. It's all a sham. It's just something John has cooked up to keep you away from your business so he can—

JOHN. Hold it, now; enough. That's not true.

KEN. I wouldn't be a friend to you if I didn't tell you—it's a dream. It's not real.

JOHN. Shut up right now… Baby, that's wonderful.

KEN. Gwen has a responsibility to something more important—

JOHN. That's it. Come on, we're getting out of here—move it—*(Pushes him aside. Ken goes down flat on his back.)* Oh, Jesus God, I forgot. I'm sorry, baby, I'm sorry. I forgot completely.

JED. *(Goes to Ken.)* Go on. Don't touch him. Leave. Move. *(He grabs the garden shears, threatening.)*

KEN. I'm not hurt! I'm not hurt! It's okay, Jed.

JOHN. I swear to God, I barely touched you!

JED. You take care of Gwen, I'll get him up!

KEN. I'm okay. Stop. *(A pause.)*

JOHN. Listen. I'm your friend. If you know it or not…*(Exits into house upstairs.)*

GWEN. *(To Ken.)* Boy, baby; with friends like you, huh?

KEN. Gwen, forgive me. It's none of our…

GWEN. John's doing nothing I don't know about. You think I'm blind? I gotta have John. And if he needs to wheel and deal behind my back, then he's welcome to it. With you flat on your back like a fuckin' turtle maybe you'll listen. You think you don't need Jed, you don't need to be useful—you'll sell the damn roof over your head to get out of facing yourself. You're on the edge of nowhere, baby, and you listen to me 'cause I *been* nowhere. Now are you gonna get to work or are you gonna lose it all? Huh?

KEN. I haven't worked out a syllabus, I haven't—

GWEN. You damn straight, we're all gonna have a busy summer. Fuckin' Columbia records. Come on, Wes, we gotta pack. Move your ass. Shirley, we're gonna listen to my tape. *(Exit, into house, upstairs.)*

WESTON. John's gonna freak. This cat is a different cat from the one John set up for us. Columbia outbid the outfit John bought. She's really good, only John don't know yet.

JOHN. *(Offstage.)* Wes, move your tail.

WESTON. I got to go pack. *(Runs to the door. Stops. Politely.)* It was very nice meeting you. *(Exits into house, upstairs.)*

KEN. *(As Jed starts to pick him up.)* Hold it a second. *(Ken pulls Jed down to him. A very long pause; Ken is nearly crying. Jed sits beside him, holding him.)* Jesus. That scares me. *(Fighting tears.)* Falling backwards is the one thing the guy always—*(Trying to joke.)* Jesus. I may never dance *Swan Lake* again. *(A pause. Jed rises and helps Ken to stand.)*

JUNE. *(To Jed.)* You're quicker than you look.

SALLY. I've never been so scared in my life. And I'm sixty-four years old.

JUNE. I thought you were sixty-one.

SALLY. I've lied about that since I was twenty.

KEN. It's impossible. I haven't looked at my notes; I don't even know what textbooks are available anymore.

JED. *(Gets tape deck; gives it to Ken.)* Yeah, Gwen said you got a lot of work to do.

KEN. You know you're all going to pay for this. *(To Sally.)* How are you feeling?

SALLY. Much better.

JUNE. Oh, sure. Where's that damned doctor?

KEN. Should we drive her back down to the office?

SALLY. No, no. And you don't have time. You have to talk to the Young kid.

KEN. Oh, God, I'll have to call the Youngs and tell them I can't see Johnny this afternoon.

JUNE. No, you go on…I'll take care of Sally.

SALLY. Could you understand what the boy was talking about?

KEN. Oh, sure. It just takes listening to a couple times. You won't like it at all. He's into science and the future.

JUNE. Well, why not.

KEN. But he doesn't have much faith in Sally's spacemen. He's very positive and negative and decidedly eccentric…teleportation, space travel, *(Turns on cassette player.)* and this is the way it ends—*(He reads from his yellow pad at the same time.)* "After they had explored all the suns in the universe, and all the planets of all the suns, they realized that there was no other life in the universe, and that they were alone. And they were very happy, because then they knew it was up to them to become all the things they had imagined they would find." *(Turns off the cassette player. Weston comes to the stairs, sits down, tuning his guitar.)*

WESTON. Gwen? You're going to play our tape?

SALLY. You know, if I sold that mausoleum in California, I could dump an awful lot of money into this place. I was just thinking out loud.

KEN. I frankly don't think you should be moved from here.

SALLY. I'm much too ill to travel…

JED. Oh, that's out of the question.

WESTON. *(Through window.)* Hey, Sally, I want you to hear this. Shirley!

SALLY. I'm coming!

GWEN. June!

JUNE. God love her. *(Yelling.)* Coming.

WESTON. Kenny!

KEN. We hear you. *(June goes in. Gwen joins Weston; he plays the introduction to his song. Sally gets up.)* Are you okay?

SALLY. Well, I can walk.

KEN. You're beatin' me. *(Sally goes in to listen to them. Shirley and Jed and Ken sit on the porch. Shirley is crying quietly.)* What's wrong, doll?

SHIRLEY. I don't care. The important thing is to find your vocation and work like hell at it. I don't think heredity has anything to do with anything.

KEN. Certainly not.

SHIRLEY. You do realize, though, the terrible burden.

KEN. How's that?

SHIRLEY. I am the last of the Talleys. And the whole family has just come to nothing at all so far. Fortunately, it's on my shoulders. *(She gets up with the weight of the burden on her shoulders. Gwen and Weston begin to sing.)* I won't fail us. *(She goes into the house. Ken and Jed listen a moment.)*

KEN. We had to put in all those damn lilies. If they don't bloom, it's your ass. And you and Weston have got to get cinders this afternoon for the penstemon.

JED. Oh, God.

KEN. Well, maybe he'll write us a song. *(He gets up. Sighs. Picks up the portable recorder.)* I've got to talk to Johnny Young about the future. *(They look at each other a moment. The singers continue. Jed looks out over the garden, still seated. Ken begins to work his way toward the door. The music continues as the light fades.)*

END OF PLAY

Talley's Folly

For Harold Clurman

Judd Hirsch and Trish Hawkins
in the Broadway production of *Talley's Folly*.

Photograph ©1980 by Gerry Goodstein.

INTRODUCTION

Helen Stenborg, who was playing Sally Talley, came to me during the rehearsals of *Fifth of July* and asked what Matt had been like; what he looked like and sounded like. Sally spends so much of the play reminiscing about him, Helen wanted a specific image to call up as she talks about their life together. I said, Can't you use Barney? Her husband is the wonderful actor Barnard Hughes. No, she said, Barney wasn't like that at all. I told her when I was writing the play I had imagined Matt to be something like Judd Hirsch, one of the outstanding members of our company with whom she had worked for over a year in *The Hot L Baltimore*. Judd in one of his jollier moods. She said Judd would work excellently.

That was the genesis of *Talley's Folly*. Imagining Matt and Sally on a date—this big, sexy, clumsy Jew coming from St. Louis down to Lebanon, Missouri, where nobody had ever seen a Jew before—was very exciting. I knew immediately that I wanted this to be unlike anything I had written. It would be much lighter, with a gloriously happy ending. But I also knew that nobody would trust me. I had written so many bloodbaths, that the audience would be sitting there saying, "He's gonna kill her. He's gonna finally get mad and strangle her." So at the opening of the play I had to reassure the audience that this really was going to end up a valentine. Hence, Matt's first speech: "This is a waltz, remember."

Naturally Matt would be Judd Hirsch. What a huge and varied instrument he has—or I should write *he is*. What an interesting and difficult challenge it would be to write a character for an actor who has that facility. And, since I had only seen him in comedy, there would also be the challenge to him (and to me) to reflect the depth and history of the European Jew. The logical actress for young Sally was Trish Hawkins. Judd and Trish were even dating, it seemed perfect.

The basic story, the outline, was almost written before I started. We knew from *Fifth of July* that Matt and Sally had a hot love life but no children. Why? We knew Sally had once been engaged to Harley Campbell and had not married him. What had happened? We knew Sally had been a nurse's aide during the war, that Matt and Sally had vacationed down here, that he enjoyed the countryside enormously in the midst of people who couldn't stand him. We knew they had seen a flying saucer and had no idea what it was, that they made love for the first time in a boathouse on the Talley property. No matter that there isn't a river that close to Lebanon. We also knew Matt loved swimming naked. That's something I wouldn't use in this one. To keep myself in the period, and the play in the period, I wanted to write it as if it had been written then. If this was going to be a love story, I wanted it to be like one of those romantic films of the 1930s and early 40s, gentle and bright. It should pass the Brene Office or whatever censorship apparatus they had back then. It's wonderful to work on a play with so many of the questions and shared events already laid out for you. It must be akin to what writers go through when they follow an outline—something I've rarely been able to do.

The largest challenge, I thought, would be the period itself. It should be circa 1944. I hadn't before written anything in any moment but the present. It helped that I remembered Lebanon at that time: Boys (we called them) coming home from the war, soldiers coming down from Fort Leonard Wood to skate at the roll arena, to meet girls and take them to the roadhouse outside town. My mother had been divorced for two years by then. She and her girlfriends sometimes dated soldiers. I have a feeling they were rather proper dates. Sometimes they even took me along: When the carnival was in town; one afternoon to whatever was the name of that big rock castle outside Lebanon. My mother had also been a nurse's aide and at this time was working at a clothing factory, making army fatigues. She was exactly Sally's age and she proved to be an invaluable resource, a great research tool. Why make something difficult for yourself? I pestered her with questions almost every day, so often she threatened to have her phone removed. She also said she should have shared writing credit but that was going too far, this was, after all, just research—and only a small amount considering all the research I did. Fortunately I enjoy it, and did a lot more than I needed. I knew the price of scrap iron on the day the play takes place, I was certain I was going to need that; couldn't work it in. A lot I used, a lot just helped to put me back in that time frame. I think the nostalgia I felt, remembering those times, helped soften the play, gave it the scent of honeysuckle and sound of a distant band playing across that imagined river. (I really did think there was a river very close to Lebanon. I remembered swimming there. What I didn't remember was the twenty minute car ride getting there.)

The writing went rather quickly. The first draft was finished in about three months; as I said, so much of it I knew already from *Fifth of July*. I kept thinking that Sally's brother or father or Harley Campbell, her old beau, would show up down there at the boathouse, hunting maybe, and stumble onto the lovers. But the play steadfastly remained just the two of them.

It was Circle Rep's practice to read a new play every Friday afternoon. Judd wasn't available for the reading, John Hogan read the part, quite creditably, and I don't think he was ever convinced he was wrong for it. Now comes the interesting part, at least to me, because it pertains to so much in the theater: To collaboration, to the nature of plays, to storytelling and plotting, to dramaturgy. Don't read this if you haven't read the play, as I'm going to give away the whole shebang. The two characters obviously love each other but both are terribly guarded; they have given up on the idea of marriage because of a secret they happen to share. In the first draft Matt came to Lebanon already knowing that Sally couldn't have children. Aunt Lottie had told him. Since, because of his hellish childhood, he refused to have children, he knew they were a perfect match. So the action of the play was Matt forcing Sally to admit she was barren. It played wonderfully. Everyone loved the reading. (I'm speaking relatively, you understand. This was a group that loved everything anyone else in the group did, offering supportive and helpful criticism, but only when asked.)

Everyone loved it, that is, except Marshall W. Mason, who was to direct. After many glowing comments and applause, Marshall and I retired to his office. He had (ominously) said nothing during the discussion period. I thought the play was perfect, so I had quite a chip on my shoulder. He said something like, "So the story, essentially, is Matt comes down to Lebanon and browbeats this girl into a hysterical admission that she's barren." I said yes and he said, "What's fun about that?" He pointed out that with Matt knowing she couldn't bear children he didn't even have to tell her he refused to bring children into the world. Except for being turned down, he had nothing more at stake. He didn't even have to browbeat her, he could just say, Lottie told me. It wasn't even dramatic. His actions were brutal with little cost to himself. However, if he did *not* know her situation, then he would first have to tell Sally he refused to have children and ask if she would have him with that condition. He had to *risk* something. Marshall must have been very convincing because the chip fell off my shoulder and very soon I was taking notes. I rewrote the middle third of the play. It was much more dramatic. I took it to Marshall, who had just opened a show and was exhausted. He said, "Let's read it. I'll read Matt, you read Sally." I don't think there was any design, any agenda, in that, he just wanted to do the better part. He read it quite well and said he thought I had adjusted it beautifully. I had had a completely different experience, and one I recommend to all writers as dense as I. I had sat there as Sally, watching Matt jump through hoops, and all I said was, "Oh, Matt" and "Come on, now, Matt." I didn't like my part. And I especially didn't like it when Matt finally told me he wanted to marry me but he didn't want kids. The writer had not provided me with the obvious response: "Who told you I couldn't have children?" I sat there livid because he had made me feel terrible about his lousy childhood and I thought it had all been a ploy. And all I did in the script was cave in. Back to the typewriter. Sally's part grew by a third. It is still not as flamboyant as Matt's but I think she now holds her own. She is much stronger and much more her own woman. We finally had the play.

But but but but. We had something else. We had a plot. If Matt knows she can't have children and it takes the whole play for him to convince Sally it's OK that she can't have children—it's a story. If he doesn't know, and if he presents his resolution, and then finds out that she can't have children any- way—it's a plot. What happens is a very strange phenomenon. When Sally finally screams out, in desperation, "I can't have children. I can't bear chil- dren!" there is an almost audible *click* as the last piece of the plot locks into place. It is an enormously satisfying moment. We feel the perfection of it. But it is also terribly disappointing. We feel like we have been manipulated. This has all been a carefully worked out artifice. It's very much like, "Can you say— coincidence?" Now, some people will probably feel none of these things, and some will only feel the weight and drama of the moment. But for some, in a part of their mind, they'll feel cheated. That's what a plot this starkly pre- sented does. It underlines the artifice. We feel elated and slightly disap- pointed at the same time. Marshall and I saw it immediately. Wasn't that odd. We decided to live with it.

Rehearsals went by so quickly and so smoothly that it seemed just a moment—and we were in previews. We were completely unprepared for the play's reception. Since this is essentially a sweet play, a romantic comedy, Marshall had worked very hard to underline the difficult lives each of these characters had experienced up to this night. Also it was a short play, ninety- six minutes without intermission. Most of our plays were considerably over two hours. It was unlike anything we had done. Granted the actors were wonderful, still there was a tension in the air. When I started writing the play Trish and Judd were going together. By the time we began rehearsals they were no longer going together. Somehow even that worked in the play's favor. But it was *so sweet!* I remember telling friends as they left the theater, during previews, not to worry: We had imperceptibly sprayed them with insulin as they left the theater so they wouldn't suffer any ill effects from all that sugar. They all said they loved it, but you never believe what your friends say unless the reviews are bad. Then you say, well, my friends *loved* it. After the dress rehearsal Marshall and I saw no one—we just rushed to the dressing room as Marshall had hundreds of notes. (When something is going well Marshall has a lot of notes. If he has only one or two you're in trouble). The first intimation that we were on to something came when I went downstairs to get a glass of water. The designers and their assistants were sitting in a circle on the floor of the lobby, drinking wine. I had to step over them. Jennifer grabbed my foot. I stopped and looked at them. She said wistfully, "Oh, Lanford, we've been sitting here saying, 'Oh, let it happen to me!'" For a moment I had no idea what she was talking about. Then I said something like, "Oh, good," and went about my business. But audiences were ready for a love story. Attention spans were growing shorter (a play at the Lucille Lortell Theater, down the street, was only sixty-five minutes long) and audiences were thankful for a ninety-six minute evening. And they wanted something like that to happen to them.

Opening night I stopped Harold Clurman in the lobby. I stammered and said, I'd like very much to—Oh, well—Talk to me after the play. He said he couldn't stay for the party, I'd have to catch him coming out. I was in the lobby after the show. He said, "OK, what's so important." I said I would like to dedicate this play to him if that was all right. He stammered again, saying this was not at all like his story, his life. I said of course I knew that, but I thought his teachings had contributed to the spirit of the play. He said, "Sure, why not, and rushed off. About five minutes later he was back in the lobby saying he was terribly sorry to have been so rushed, but he would be honored to have me dedicate the play to him. His review was as glowing as the others, and the first indication that he had even liked the damn play. Harold can be very gruff in person and very kind in print. The play was scheduled to be published almost immediately. Harold kept writing me notes, saying, Where the hell is my book? It was delayed, but I finally got it to him along with an embarrassing effusion of thanks for his generous spirit. Months later, when the Pulitzer was announced, I received a number of telegrams. The one I treasured most was from Harold. It said simply. "I see from the papers this morning that we're to be congratulated."

ORIGINAL PRODUCTION

Talley's Folly was first presented by the Circle Repertory Company, in New York City, on May 3, 1979. The cast, in order of appearance, was as follows:

MATT FRIEDMAN . . . . Judd Hirsch
SALLY TALLEY . . . . Trish Hawkins

Director . . . . Marshall W. Mason
Setting . . . . John Lee Beatty
Costumes . . . . Jennifer Von Mayrhauser
Lighting . . . . Dennis Parichy
Sound . . . . Chuck London
Production Stage Manager . . . . Fred Reinglas

THE SCENE

An old boathouse on the Talley place, a farm near Lebanon, Missouri

TIME

July 4, 1944, early evening

Talley's Folly is to be played without intermission.

Talley's Folly

A Victorian boathouse constructed of louvers, lattice in decorative panels, and a good deal of Gothic Revival gingerbread. The riverside is open to the audience. The interior and exterior walls have faded to a pale gray. The boathouse is covered by a heavy canopy of maple and surrounded by almost waist-high weeds and the slender, perfectly vertical limbs of a weeping willow. Lighting and sound should be very romantic; the sunset at the opening, later the moonlight, slant through gaps in the ceiling and walls reflecting the river in lambent ripples across the inside of the room.

The boathouse contains two boats, one turned upside down, buckets, boxes, no conventional seating. Overhead is a latticework attic in which are stored creels, bamboo poles, nets, seines, minnow buckets, traps, floats, etc., all long past use.

At opening: All this is seen in a blank white work light: the artificiality of the theatrical set quite apparent. The houselights are up.

MATT. *(Enters in front of the stage. Matt Friedman is forty-two, dark, and rather large. Warm and unhurried, he has a definite talent for mimicry. In his voice there is still a trace of a German-Jewish accent, of which he is probably unaware. He speaks to the audience.)* They tell me that we have ninety-seven minutes here tonight—without intermission. So if that means anything to anybody; if you think you'll need a drink of water or anything…

You know, a year ago I drove Sally home from a dance; and while we were standing on the porch up at the house, we looked down to the river and saw this silver flying thing rise straight up and zip off. We came running down to the river, we thought the Japanese had landed some amazing new flying machine, but all we found was the boathouse here, and—uh, that was enough.

I'll just point out some of the facilities till everybody gets settled in. If everything goes well for me tonight, this should be a waltz, one-two-three, one-two-three; a no-holds-barred romantic story, and since I'm not a romantic type, I'm going to need the whole valentine here to help me: the woods, the willows, the vines, the moonlight, the band—there's a band that plays tonight, over in the park. The trees, the berries, the breeze, the sounds: water and crickets, frogs, dogs, the light, the bees, working all night.

Did you know that? Bees work—worker bees—work around the clock. Never stop. Collecting nectar, or pollen, whatever a bee collects. Of course their life expectancy is twenty days. Or, in a bee's case, twenty days and twenty nights. Or possibly "expectancy" is wrong in the case of a bee. Who knows what a bee expects. But whatever time there is in a life is a lifetime, and I imagine after twenty days and twenty nights a bee is more or less ready to tuck in.

(In a craggy, Western, "Old-Timer" voice.) "I been flyin' now, young sprout, nigh-on to nineteen days an' nineteen nights."

(Imitating a young bee.) "Really, Grandpa Worker Bee?"

(Old-Timer.) "Yep. An' I'm 'bout ready to tuck it in."

(Slight pause. Reflectively.) Work. Work is very much to the point. *(Showing the set.)* We have everything to help me here. There's a rotating gismo in the footlights (do you believe footlights) because we need the moon out there on the water. The water runs right through here, so you're all out in the river—sorry about that. They promise me moonlight by the baleful, all through the shutters. We could do it on a couple of folding chairs, but it isn't bare, it isn't bombed out, it's rundown, and the difference is all the difference. And valentines need frou-frou.

We have a genuine Victorian folly here. A boathouse. Constructed of louvers, and lattice and geegaws. I feel like a real-estate salesman. Of course there's something about the term "real estate" that strikes me as wrong. Estate maybe, but real is arguable. But to start you off on the right foot…Everybody ready? This is a waltz, remember, one-two-three, one-two-three.

There was a time—or, all right, I think that has to be: Once upon a time—there was a hope throughout the land. From the chaos of the Great Depression, people found strength in union, believing their time had come. But even as this hope was perceived, once again a dark power rose up from the chaos in another land. Once again this country pitched its resources and industry into battle. Now, after almost three years of war, it has become apparent that the battle is turning. Once again we are told that "peace and prosperity" are in the air. But in the midst of battle, that "hope" the people had known has been changed into the enemy. Peace, and—more to the point—prosperity, is our ally now. Once again, we are told the country has been saved by war.

Now, you would think that in this remote wood, on this remote and unimportant, but sometimes capricious, river—that world events would not touch this hidden place. But such is not the case. There is a house on the hill up there, and there is a family that is not at peace but in grave danger of prosperity. And there is a girl in the house on the hill up there who is a terrible embarrassment to her family because she remembers that old hope, and questions this new fortune, and questioning eyes are hard to come by nowadays. It's hard to use your peripheral vision when you're being led by the nose.

Now I know what you're thinking. You're saying if I'd known it was going to be like this, I wouldn't have come. Or if I'd known it was going to be like this, I would have listened. But don't worry, we're going to do this first part all over again for the latecomers. I want to give you and me both every opportunity. So. Okeydokey. *(Checks pocket watch.)* Oh, boy, this has gotta be fast. So: *(Deep breath, then all in a run.)* They tell me that we have ninety-seven minutes here tonight without intermission so if that means anything to anybody if you think you'll need a drink of water or anything I'll just point out some of the facilities till everybody gets settled in if everything goes well for me tonight this should be a waltz one-two-three, one-two-three a no-holds-barred romantic story and since I'm not a romantic type I'm going to need the whole shmeer here to help me the woods the willows the vines the moonlight the band there's a band that plays tonight over in the park the trees the berries the breeze the sounds water and crickets frogs dogs the light the bees…*(Pauses. With a slight hill accent.)* Frogs, dogs…*(To stage manager in sound booth.)* Could we have a dog? I'd like a dog. *(He listens a second. Nothing. Then a furious, yapping, tiny terrier is heard.)* Fellas! Fellas! A dog! *(Beat. Then a low, distant woof-woof-woof that continues until Sally's entrance. Matt listens a beat, pleased.)*

Oh, yeah. Old man Barnette kicked out Blackie and called in the kids, and about now the entire family is sitting down to supper. Even Blackie, out by the smokehouse. But a car pulled off the road about a mile downstream, and someone got out. And at this hour it begins to be difficult to see, the chickens have started to go to bed, and noises carry up the river as though there was someone there in the barnyard. And Blackie wants to let everybody know the Barnette farm is well guarded. *(Beat. Then back to run-on narration.)*

Working all night did you know that bees work worker bees work around the clock never stop collecting nectar or pollen whatever a bee collects of course their life expectancy is twenty days or in a bee's case twenty days and twenty nights or possibly expectancy is wrong in the case of a bee who knows what a bee expects but whatever time there is in a life is a lifetime and I imagine after twenty days and...

SALLY. *(Off, yelling.)* Matt? *(Matt is silent. He almost holds his breath.)* Matt? *(The houselights begin to dim. The sunset and reflection from the river begin to appear; we hear the sound of the river and birds.)* Matt?

MATT. *(Softly, to the audience.)* This is a waltz, remember. One-two-three, one-two-three...

SALLY. *(Off.)* Are you in that boathouse? I'm not going to come down there if you're not there 'cause that place gives me the creeps after dark. Are you down there?

MATT. No.

SALLY. *(Coming closer.)* I swear, Matt Friedman, what in the devil do you think you're doing down here? *(Coming through the tall weeds and willow.)* Oh, my—everything is soaking wet here. Buddy said he chased you off with a shotgun. I thought, good, we're maybe rid of you. I saw your car parked up there, I could not believe my eyes! *(She enters.)* Not even you! And there you sit. Wiping your glasses. *(Sally Talley is thirty-one. Light, thin, quite attractive, but in no way glamorous or glamorized. Straightforward, rather tired, and just now quite angry. In this state she has a pronounced Ozark accent, but when she concentrates on what she is saying, the accent becomes much less pronounced.)*

MATT. The better to see you with, my dear.

SALLY. Don't even begin with me, Matt, I'm in no mood.

MATT. Were you hiding behind the window curtains when I was out in the yard talking to your brother? You like to hide from me so much.

SALLY. I got home five minutes ago. You know what time I get off work. Rachel and Ida dropped me out front, we could hear Buddy cussin' all the way out to the road.

MATT. You talk to your Aunt Charlotte? How did you know I'd be here?

SALLY. I was inside that house exactly thirty seconds. I walked in the door,

Momma and Buddy lit in on me like I was ten years old, screaming about the Communist traitor infidel I'd let in the house. Buddy said he run you off with a shotgun.

MATT. He had a large two-barreled weapon, yes, with apertures about like so.

SALLY. If they knew you were still on the place, they'd have Cliffy on you.

MATT. You want the sheriff, all you have to do is keep yelling. Your sister-in-law called him. He's probably at your house right now.

SALLY. *(Near whisper.)* Whatever possessed you to come down here and get into a fight with my brother? You know I can't stand livin' there as it is.

MATT. Sally, one of us had better go for a walk and cool off. Both of us can't be angry.

SALLY. What better happen is you better march right back up there to your car and head back to St. Louis.

MATT. No, see, the way they build those things now they require gasoline to really get them running good. Especially Plymouths.

SALLY. Matt Friedman, you did not run out of gas.

MATT. You want to go try it? See if you can get it to catch?

SALLY. Oh, if that isn't just…typical.

MATT. That's what saves it, I think. I was just thinking that that was typical.

SALLY. That car is gonna kill me. I mean, I'm a strong person, but that car is gonna do it. Not one time has that car gone from one place to another place without breaking down.

MATT. Sally, you don't deprecate a man's car. A man's car reflects his pride in himself and his status in society. Castigate my car, you castigate me.

SALLY. Well, good. And you may be full of hot air on most things, but you are right about that. That—that—hay bailer!—is a good reflection of you.

MATT. Boy, you get angry, you really are a mountain daughter, aren't you? Where's the still? I was looking for the still you said was down here.

SALLY. Matt, I'm exhausted. I've been up since five. I was at the hospital at six-thirty. I don't want to argue. The still was right there. They busted it up—broke it up.

MATT. Your dad get raided by Cliffy?

SALLY. Cliffy wasn't sheriff then, McConklin was sheriff. Him and Dad were half-partners in the still. They broke it up to sell for scrap after the repeal. Matt—

MATT. They were runnin' liquor, were they?

SALLY. Is the only thing keeping you here a gallon of gas for your car? 'Cause we have a can in the pump house.

MATT. Better wait till it gets a little darker if you're gonna start stealing Buddy's gas.

SALLY. You've alienated Buddy. You've almost paralyzed Olive.

MATT. *(Snapping his fingers.)* Olive! Olive! I could not think of your sister-in-law's darn name! I'm thinking pickled herring, I'm thinking caviar, I'm thinking boiled egg. I knew she was on a relish tray.

SALLY. Why are you always barging in places?

MATT. No, ma'am. I wrote you how many times I'd be down today.

SALLY. You barge into a person's home, you barge into where they work!

MATT. I telephoned your house here. I had a nice Missouri telephone chat with your Aunt Charlotte.

SALLY. Aunt Lottie would invite the devil into the parlor for hot cocoa.

MATT. Actually, I came here to talk to you father. That's the way I've been told these things are done in the South.

SALLY. You're not in the South. You're in the Midwest.

MATT. Sally, I've been all over the country, and there is New York City, isolated neighborhoods in Boston, and believe me, the rest is all the South.

SALLY. Would you please just tell me what happened up there so I'll know how to handle them?

MATT. Sally, I know I told you we'd have the whole weekend, and I've been looking forward to it just as much as you have, but there was—

SALLY. You are the most conceited, blind, deaf—

MATT. —just no way out of it. I have to go back tonight. We have a hearing on the iceman and his horse, there was no way—

SALLY. On what?

MATT. You know, I wrote you, the iceman, with a horse and wagon. We had him consecrated as a church and that worked for two years, till they caught on, but—

SALLY. I don't have any idea what you are talking about.

MATT. *(Going on.)*—churches don't pay taxes. We had him ordained. They didn't like it. So we set up a trust fund in the name of Daisy; now they want a hearing on that, because horses can't hold trusts. It was just sprung on us. I have to be back in St. Louis tomorrow.

SALLY. Would you just tell me what happened up there?

MATT. It was crazy to come down here, only I promised you, but we have to work fast here tonight.

SALLY. What was Buddy so mad about?

MATT. Did you hear me? I've only got tonight; I have to get back.

SALLY. Would you please just—

MATT. Sally, it is unimportant, but if it makes you happy! I came down here as I said I would; I parked my car, went to the front door, and knocked. Your sister-in-law—from the relish tray? You said?

SALLY. Olive.

MATT. Olive! I cannot remember the woman's—Olive! Olive! Olive came to the door, with very big eyes, shaking all over. I said, "Oh, hello, I'm Matt Friedman. I thought I'd come over this beautiful evening and have a chat with Mr. Talley." So she stood there doing her imitation of a fish, and—

SALLY. She did what?

MATT. She couldn't speak, I think. She was paralyzed. She goes—*(Imitates a fish.)*

SALLY. It isn't necessary to characterize every—

MATT. Sally, I'm trying to tell this in a way that I don't get angry again.

SALLY. Okay!

MATT. Finally, she swims off, after having said all of not one word, and Buddy came—does your entire family have such absurd names?

SALLY. His real name is Kenny. We call him Buddy.

MATT. Kenny? Is his real name? This is better, for a grown man, Kenny? Kenny Talley, Lottie Talley, Timmy Talley, Sally Talley? Your brother also does not know how to converse. Your brother talks in rhetorical questions: "You're Sally's Jewish friend, ain't ya? What do you think you want here? Did you ever hear that trespassing was against the law?"

SALLY. Oh, they're all such hypocrites and fools.

MATT. There was nothing hypocritical about it, believe me.

SALLY. You deserve it, coming down here. I told you Dad said you weren't invited back.

MATT. So Buddy said, "If you want to see your friend Sally, you can go to Springfield, where she works," and I said I'd wait there in the yard—and he went in and got a two-barreled hunting gun.

SALLY. And Olive called the sheriff.

MATT. I am omitting the yelling and the screaming and the deprecating.

SALLY. Who was yelling?

MATT. Well, there was your Aunt Charlotte yelling: "This man came to see me." And your mother yelling: "You are not to see my daughter." And Olive yelling, "Get back in the house" at everybody, at Charlotte, at Buddy, at the dog that was barking, at your bother's business friend—who was out in the yard to protect Buddy; he mostly said, "You tell 'em, Buddy, you tell 'em, Buddy." *(Pause.)*

SALLY. *(Moves away, turns to him.)* I'm not even gonna apologize, you had it coming to you.

MATT. Of course, your mother and Olive stayed up there on the screened-in porch, protected from the mosquitoes and Communists and infidels.

SALLY. *(Turning away.)* I have absolutely got to get out of that place. Rachel and Ida and I have been looking for an apartment in town for months.

MATT. *(Watches her. Lightly.)* Actually you don't get mosquitoes here, do you? Rich people always know where to build their houses. With the house on the hill, in the breeze, the river always moving, mosquitoes don't nest around here. The breeze blows them off. Do they nest? Mosquitoes? Do mosquitoes nest? Does everything that lays eggs nest? Do fish nest? That's a funny idea.

SALLY. Don't try to make me feel good, Matt, it isn't going to work. Fish spawn.

MATT. What do mosquitoes do?

SALLY. I don't know what mosquitoes do. They breed.

MATT. You know, I'll bet you're right. *(Beat.)* See, I thought you'd be glad to see me. That's my problem. I got no sounding board. I sit up there in St. Louis in this dusty office sneezing away, I get to daydreaming. I start thinking: *(Ozark accent.)* Well, now, listen here, Matthew, what ort to happen is you ort to head on down into them hills an—

SALLY. Please don't do that. Don't make fun of the way we talk. Oh! Everything you do! You're enough to make a—

MATT. *(Beat.)* Preacher cuss. *(Beat.)* Sailor blush.

SALLY. I don't make fun of your accent, I don't see why—

MATT. *(With an unconscious but pronounced accent.)* I have no accent. I worked very hard and have completely lost any trace of accent.

SALLY. Very well.

MATT. And daydreaming away up there, I said to myself: *(Bogart.)* This—un—Sally dame. She—uh—looks to me like a good deal, Matt. She—uh—showed you a good time. The least you could do is reciprocate.

SALLY. That's supposed to be someone, I guess. That isn't you.

MATT. What do you mean, "someone"? You don't know Humphrey Bogart?

SALLY. We don't go to the pictures.

MATT. How did you know he was a movie actor. He might be the Secretary of the Interior; he—

SALLY. My grandmother knows Humphrey Bogart and she's never been to a—

MATT. You don't castigate a guy's imitations, Sal.

SALLY. The Secretary of the Interior has been Harold Ickes since Sitting Bull.

MATT. You don't go to the movies?

SALLY. Pictures are an excuse to sit alone in the dark.

MATT. To sit together in the dark.

SALLY. Not necessarily.

MATT. But you go alone.

SALLY. Not always.

MATT. *(With sexual overtones.)* Oh, ho…now, that's—interesting.

SALLY. Sometimes with some of the other nurse's aides from work.

MATT. *(After a pause.)* That's a big business, isn't it? Caring for the wounded. It's a nice place for the boys to forget about the hard realities of making a buck when they get out.

SALLY. The boys we take care of have seen their share of hard realities.

MATT. It's a very sunny building. The boys all have a very sunny attitude. The doctors are very sunny, the nurses are very sunny, the nurse's aides are sunny. You expect the whole place to go up with spontaneous combustion.

SALLY. We try to be pleasant, yes. What would you have us do? Say, "Oh my gosh, you look horrible, I don't think you're going to make it through the night"? "Good Lord, you poor man, both hands missing and all you know is auto mechanics; you're never going to find a job you're happy with."

MATT. No, I wouldn't have you do—

SALLY. *(Almost angry.)* We don't have to fake anything. When you work with them every day you can see progress. Some of them will recover completely.

MATT. I'm not criticizing, I admire it.

SALLY. I was there last February when you barged in, I wasn't home!

MATT. Oh, yes, yes, that was funny. One girl said you had a cold that day, and another girl said you had gone to Kansas City to help requisition more beds. She was very imaginative, but under sympathetic questioning she was not a good fibber.

SALLY. So you drove all that way down to Springfield and all that way back for nothing.

MATT. It wasn't a wasted afternoon. I had the honor to be shown by a Negro private from California twenty-five different ways I can lose the game of checkers. Also, I had time to puzzle. Why would Sally tell every person with whom she works that if this hairy Jewish accountant comes down like a crazy man to see her…everybody tell him she's not here and Sally will hide in a closet.

SALLY. I was working in the kitchen that morning, where visitors are not allowed. It was not necessary to hide.

MATT. With little nurses coming into the kitchen every ten minutes to say: "Well, I don't know, Sally, he's still up there. Looks like he intends to stay all day." Puzzles don't waste my time, Sally. I'm very good at puzzles. I have great powers of ratiocination. I'm a regular Sherlock. He was a terrible anti-Semite. He was a rather shallow, ignorant man. Did you know that?

SALLY. I'm sorry, I wasn't listening. I was trying to figure out what "ratiocination" means.

MATT. Oh, forgive me. I don't have a speaking vocabulary. I have a reading vocabulary. I don't talk that much.

SALLY. I haven't noticed the problem.

MATT. Last year, weren't you always saying how quiet I was? Matt, why don't you say something—weren't you always asking me questions?

SALLY. *(Moving toward the door.)* I retract everything I said last summer.

MATT. *(Moving to cut her off with rather surprising agility.)* But unlike Sherlock Holmes, I'm not quick. I'm steady and I stay at something, but I'm thick. *First,* it took a long time for me to know something as thick as me. And *then,* going back over the mystery of Sally in the closet, I decided what was called for was an on-the-spot investigation.

SALLY. Matt, I'm—

MATT. *(Taking a notepad from his pocket.)* So I have a few questions I'd like to put to you.

SALLY. There is no mystery.

MATT. Mystery isn't bad, Sally. Mystery is the spice of life.

SALLY. Variety is the spice of life.

MATT. Well, variety has always been a mystery to me. Give me one choice and I can take it or leave it. Give me two and I can't decide. Give me three, I don't want any of it. Now—

SALLY. I cannot understand why you can't get the message. You sound like a functioning human being; but you've got a wire crossed or something.

MATT. A screw loose.

SALLY. You are one total, living loose screw. That much is certain. You've been away a solid year. The one time you come to the hospital to hunt me down I refuse to see you—

MATT. No, no, you didn't refuse, you hid in the kitchen.

SALLY. And you sat up there in that dayroom the entire blessed afternoon.

MATT. I was not made to feel unwelcome.

SALLY. *Not made to feel unwelcome?* You do not have the perception God gave lettuce. I did not answer but one letter and in that one short note I tried to say in no uncertain terms that I didn't want you to write to me. You have sent me an almost *daily* chronicle of your life in your office. The most mundane details of your accounting life. Why did you come back here?

MATT. It was a very pleasant way to begin the morning: writing, Dear Sal. Cleared out my head, like reading the newspaper, only not so depressing. I could tell you about the intrigue in the office; mull over the problems I anticipated. And knowing you—you sort of spoke along with me. Your carefully balanced and rational judgment was a great boon to my disposition. Improved the weather. And the weather in St. Louis needs all the improvement it can get. I'll bet I made you laugh.

SALLY. No, you did not.

MATT. No?

SALLY. Not once.

MATT. That's a blow.

SALLY. I knew you were trying to, but I didn't find anything particularly funny.

MATT. Not trying. I just thought you might. You didn't get lonely. It wasn't like being away from me this whole year, was it?

SALLY. Not at all.

MATT. Didn't you come to look forward to the mail in the morning?

SALLY. I dreaded each new day.

MATT. Now see, if I believed that, I'd leave.

SALLY. I did gain a fondness for the calm respectability of Sunday.

MATT. Holidays must have been nice.

SALLY. Holidays were a benediction.

MATT. Did you make the recipe I sent you? I couldn't make it because I don't have a timer. Baking in an oven, I forget what I'm doing and I go off and leave. I come back, the apartment is terrible. I cook well—

SALLY. —I don't cook. Why don't you just go on up the road to the Barnettes? It isn't that far. They'll give you enough gas to get into town.

MATT. *(Pocketing the notebook.)* You have no sense of nostalgia, Sal. You have no romance.

SALLY. No, I do not. Not right now. I can't remember feeling less romantic.

MATT. Alone. Together again in the sunset—well, sundown—twilight.

(Pause, looks around and out over the river.) This country. I mean, this countryside. Is so beautiful. Do you think about that when you live in it all the time? Surrounded by all this lovely scenery? Or do you take it for granted?

SALLY. We know it's beautiful. Why wouldn't we appreciate it? There has to be some compensation in the place. It isn't particularly fertile; it's rocky; it's got poor drainage; it's all hills.

MATT. How can it have poor drainage if it's all hills?

SALLY. Hills have nothing to do with drainage. Water has to soak into the ground, not run off. The weather is too dry in the summer, the crops just curl up in the field. The spring is nothing but a cycle of floods. The winters are too cold, and damp, and…

MATT. But it's beautiful. *(He has been rubbing his hands on a side of the upturned boat. His finger has just jabbed a hole in the side.) Gottenyu!* Look at that. That goes right through. Not what I'd call seaworthy. Riverworthy. When was the last time anybody was down here? Aside from you and me coming down here last summer?

SALLY. I wouldn't know.

MATT. Ought maybe to fix the place up.

SALLY. Nobody has any use of it any more. You couldn't get materials now if you wanted to.

MATT. Fancy place to let rot away. Nobody even knows who spent all that much time building some crazy place like this. It isn't really grand, it's just silly. Is it not silly? Must have broken a lot of jigsaw blades.

SALLY. Uncle Whistler.

MATT. What?

SALLY. Everett Talley. Built the boathouse in 1870. Built follies all over town. He wanted to build a gazebo up by the house, but Grandpa said it was a frivolity, so he built a boathouse.

MATT. And made it look like a gazebo.

SALLY. Well, that's what he wanted to do in the first place. He did the bandstand in the park across the river. The town didn't want it, but he'd seen it in a picture somewhere so he went over and built it. They tried to stop him, he went right on; said they could tear it down after he had finished. Painted it maroon and pink and gold. Said, "Now, tear it down." Eventually they used it for high school band concerts.

MATT. Sounds like a frustrated guy.

SALLY. Not at all! Why does everything have to be cynical? He was not in the least frustrated. He was a happily married man with seven kids. He made toys. Tap-dancing babies and whirligigs. He got pleasure out of making things for people. He did exactly what he wanted to do. He was the healthiest member of the family. Everybody in town knew him. They all called him Whistler.

MATT. Because he was the artist in the family?

SALLY. Because he sang and whistled. He used to go stomping through the woods singing *"Una furtiva lagrima"* at the top of his lungs; nobody outside the Talleys knew what he was singing, so they all said he was crazy, but he certainly wasn't frustrated.

MATT. *(He has found an ice skate.)* What is that? An ice skate? Somebody had big feet. Do you skate?

SALLY. No.

MATT. Me too. Did you use to roller skate on the sidewalk?

SALLY. There isn't a sidewalk closer than a mile and a half, in town.

MATT. Me too. All the other kids had skates. Fly past me, knock me down. I was only five. Some memories linger.

SALLY. In St. Louis?

MATT. *(Beat. He does not answer her.)* In the winter they skated on the lake. Frozen solid. I tried another boy's skates once. Nearly broke my neck. Well, that's what I should have expected. I am not what you would call a beautifully coordinated individual.

SALLY. Oh, don't put those on!

MATT. That roller rink in Lebanon where the soldiers all hang out. That's the principal recreation here, it seems.

SALLY. People come up from Springfield.

MATT. Fellas and their dates?

SALLY. Girls looking for soldiers.

MATT. Looks like everybody is having a good time. All that drinking and skating, I'd get sick.

SALLY. They do.

MATT. You go?

SALLY. I went once, Matt, I didn't like it. *(He has put the skates on his feet.)* Don't stand up in those, you'll go right through the floor.

MATT. No, no, it's all a matter of balance. *(Stands, nearly falls over, grabs the wall.)*

SALLY. Don't do that— Oh, for crying out loud.

MATT. Unfortunately, I have almost no sense of balance at all. *(He is holding on.)* What do you do? You have to push off to start. Then you glide.

SALLY. You don't have to push off, but I suppose you could.

MATT. Eventually, you come to a standstill. How do you keep going?

SALLY. You take steps. Step, push. And you glide on that foot. Your weight on that one foot.

MATT. How do you get your weight off one foot and onto another?

SALLY. The other foot has to come up.

MATT. How can the other foot come up?

SALLY. Lift it! *(She goes to him, pulls one foot.)* Oh, for godsake, lift it!

MATT. *(Unsteady, still holding on to the wall.)* Oh… One foot.

SALLY. Now, you're gliding on that one foot. Before you start to slow down, you lean your weight over onto the other.

MATT. Oh, sure. What's to catch me if I shift my weight off of this foot?

SALLY. The other foot. you've got two, stupid.

MATT. Sally, I'm awkward, I'm not stupid.

SALLY. Put the *other foot* down! *(He does.)*

MATT. *(On both feet again.)* That's much easier.

SALLY. Now, lift the other foot.

MATT. I know, I know. And glide on that. *(He has taken hold of her and let go of the wall.)* Why don't the skaters get tangled up?

SALLY. Because they're synchronized.

MATT. I'm not going to worry about what you do, okay? You'll confuse me. *(Singing "Over the Waves," waltz-temp, low at first, gaining confidence.)* La-la-la-la-la-la-bop-bop-bop—

SALLY. *(For one moment they appear to be skating.)* Come on, not so loud.

MATT. La-la-la-la-la-la-la-la-bop-bop-boom-bop-bop—

SALLY. Come on, Matt, stop. They'll hear you across the river.

MATT. I'm having an old-fashioned skate with my girl.

SALLY. I'm not your girl, Matt. Come on. Let go, you're ridiculous.

MATT. Don't let go. Don't let go! We're coming to the end of the pond.

SALLY. *(Has disentangled herself. He is flailing his arms with nothing to hold on to.)* I'm going to go get gasoline for your car.

MATT. *(As if heading for the edge of the pond.)* I'm going too fast! I don't know how to turn. Sally! I'm gonna crash! Help! The trees are looming up in front of me. They're coming right at me. Fir trees and big old maple trees. Oak trees! They're black against the snow. Firelight flickering on them from the campfire. They're frozen hard as stone and deadly. It's the end of a brilliant career! Here they come. I can't slow down! Here they come! AAAAAAAAaaaaaaaaaa! *(Falls down.)* Oh, oh…I'm serious— Where are you going! Sally?

SALLY. *(She has stood with her arms crossed, watching him. Now she turns to leave.)* I'm going for your gas.

MATT. Sally? Hey, I can't run after you in these.

SALLY. Good. I'm good and sick of you running after me, Matt. *(She is gone.)*

MATT. Come on. *(He tries to run after her.)* Where do you think you are going—*(As his leg crashes through the floor, he grabs at the overhead lattice. It gives way and falls on him, dumping the reels, creels, baskets, nets, etc., over him.)* Oh, my God! Sally? Help. Sally? *(He fights his way clear of the mess to see her standing in the doorway again.)* I fell through the floor.

SALLY. *(Somewhat concerned.)* Where are you hurt? What did you hurt?

MATT. Sally. Come on—uh…*(Fends her off a moment.)* I appreciate your concern, but—just let me think a second. *(Pause.)* Uh, no, in all honesty, I think I'm not injured at all. Except maybe my head. That stuff came down on me. *(Laughs.)* Look at you standing there with your arms crossed. *(Tries to rise.)* Uh. There's one problem. I don't know how I'm supposed to get out of this. My leg's through the floor. Give me a lift.

SALLY. Oh, good Lord. *(Tries to help.)* They must have heard you up to the house; across the river.

MATT. I was having fun. It's very good exercise, skating.

SALLY. *(Giving up.)* I can't. You're too big. And you're not helping.

MATT. I'm helping, I'm helping.

SALLY. You'll have to get out by yourself. What a baby.

MATT. It's not so bad here. *(Looking around.)* It's not an uncomfortable position. My vanity is a little confused, but outside of that.

SALLY. You're not going to be so comfortable when you get your foot snake-bit.

MATT. Oh, my God. *(He manages to scramble out of the hole.)* You know all the right things to say. *(Looking his leg over.)* I think I'm not injured. No, I'm not even skinned. The wood is too rotten to scrape me even.

SALLY. You could have scratched yourself on a rusty nail and gotten blood poisoning.

MATT. No, I had a tetanus shot before I came down. That's what you have to get when you go fishing. I read about it. In case you prick you finger with a fish hook. Most painful thing I ever paid to have done to myself. *(Sits, takes off the skates.)* Were you serious about the snakes?

SALLY. Copperheads, water moccasins, cottonmouths. I mean, they won't prey on you. But I imagine if you stuck your foot right in their nest, they wouldn't like it.

MATT. Snake's nest? *(He gets up, pushes something over the hole.)* Had you told me about the snakes last year when we came down here, there would never have been an affair between Sally and Matt. *(Sits again to put his shoes on.)*

SALLY. There was no affair.

MATT. Of course there was an affair. How many times in seven days did I see you?

SALLY. I don't know.

MATT. Seven.

SALLY. Seven.

MATT. Seven. I got hoarse screaming over the music of that dance band. I could hardly speak all week long.

SALLY. The kids nowadays like it so loud they don't have to think.

MATT. I don't blame them.

SALLY. Neither do I.

MATT. You didn't mind me talking to you. Out on the porch of the Shriners' mosque.

SALLY. I didn't mind talking to you; I didn't mind you driving me home; I didn't even mind changing the tire.

MATT. I thought we made a very good team. Most girls would have stayed in the car. You at least held the flashlight.

SALLY. *Held the flashlight?*

MATT. Well, and told me how to change the tire.

SALLY. And lit matches so you could see, when the flashlight batteries burned out. I could have done it much faster myself. What I minded was the very next evening walking two miles when the carburetor failed.

MATT. I told you to wait in the car. I told you not to come.

SALLY. What is someone going to say, with me sitting alone in the car on a road where lovers park, where I have never been before in my life. Even during school.

MATT. I tried to hitchhike us a ride; you hid in the bushes every time a car came by. I'm looking around for you, the drivers all think I'm drunk and pull over into the other lane. You almost caused three head-on collisions that night.

SALLY. Aside from that night, the other times I saw you were a lot of fun. Except maybe the night you came to dinner.

MATT. I am not responsible for your family. That evening was your idea.

SALLY. Everyone is always saying what a crazy old-maid Emma Goldman I'm becoming, I wanted to show them how conservative and ignorant I really am.

MATT. You are not conservative, you are not ignorant, and Emma Goldman, believe me, was no old maid.

SALLY. You know what I mean. Between being what they consider out-and-out anti-American and being over forty years old, and having a beard, you made a grand hit with Mom and Dad, let me tell you.

MATT. I could tell.

SALLY. You left the house, Dad said, "That man is more dangerous than Roosevelt himself."

MATT. What they were hoping was that I would be a proper Christian suitor and take crazy Sally off their hands.

SALLY. *(She gets up to go.)* No, at least they've stopped hoping that. That's something.

MATT. Where are you going? When we're getting on so well.

SALLY. We are not getting on so well.

MATT. *(Manages to get between Sally and the door, blocking her way.)* Sally, listen. You're scared and I'm scared, but we both have to realize that we're going to deal with this before either of us leaves.

SALLY. There's nothing to deal with, Matt.

MATT. No, there's quite a lot. We can't have it both ways. You can chase me away or you can put on a pretty dress. But you can't put on a pretty dress to come down here and chase me away. *(Beat.)* You remember I've seen you come home from work in your uniform.

SALLY. I changed out of my uniform at work tonight.

MATT. Because you thought I'd meet you in Springfield, outside the hospital.

SALLY. I didn't know you'd be down here; I thought I'd come down here to listen to the band.

MATT. You were coming to the boathouse because this is where we came last year.

SALLY. This is my place. I come down here every day.

MATT. Okay, fine, I'll believe that. You go to the boathouse to forget your family. Maybe you have a cigarette to unwind, knowing you can't smoke up at the house; maybe you take a nip from a whiskey bottle you keep here somewhere.

SALLY. I won't stay up there forever. I'm as eager to leave as they are eager to get rid of me.

MATT. Maybe get an apartment in Springfield. Share with Rachel and Ida, so the three of you don't have to drive to work every morning.

SALLY. They're nice girls.

MATT. They're very nice. Maybe get a pet dog. A dachshund, maybe, name him Matt. Smoke all you want to in your own apartment. Go out to the movies on Saturday night. Maybe go sometimes to the USO dances? Not get too involved with any of the boys, not Sally.

SALLY. Is that bad?

MATT. No, ma'am, it is not. You do real work at the hospital. All the boys said they liked you best. All those other nurses, though, with their eyes they were saying: "Don't go away, Matt, Sally is gonna come around."

SALLY. They enjoyed the game.

MATT. Yes, me too. But they weren't telling me to go away.

SALLY. Well, then I'm telling you to go away; nothing will come from it, Matt—

MATT. See, they could tell that I was in love with you, and they were telling me you might be in love with me, and wouldn't that be a catastrophe.

SALLY. *(Beat.)* I don't think I even know what that means; I don't know if you know what that—

MATT. Aside from that, though, you're afraid you might love me.

SALLY. I don't think *that* is even a desirable state to be in—

MATT. Agreed, a hundred percent; all you have to say is, No, I am not.

SALLY. Why don't you just leave and make us all happier.

MATT. I don't know that leaving would make you happy. It wouldn't make me happier. It would be easier. See, I can take no for an answer; I can't take evasion, I can't take I'm scared, I can't take hiding in the kitchen.

SALLY. Just put it out of your mind, Matt. It's impossible.

MATT. So the future is pug dogs and apartments and USO get-togethers and drinking with the girls.

SALLY. It sounds wonderful.

MATT. Sally has decided she is an eccentric old maid, and she is going to be one.

SALLY. I'm looking forward to it.

MATT. *(He sighs. Pause. Gets out a notebook.)* Well, see, I'll show you how far Sherlock got. My first solution to the Sally-in-the-closet puzzle—

SALLY. Kitchen.

MATT. Sally hiding in the kitchen—was, she don't want nothing to do with this Jew-type. *(Mild Jewish accent.)* It no matter that she never saw one before, she has heard great much about dem. Days alvays beink shased from place to place, must be somethink wrong. Anyvay, *shiksas* are gullible breeds and belief everythink they hear.

SALLY. Oh, you don't think that at all. I'm a liberal Midwestern college graduate. You were very exotic to me. I reread the Old Testament.

MATT. Well, I hate to disillusion you, but I didn't reread the New Testament.

(Tearing off the page of the notebook; throwing it away.) So it is not that. Everything must be in a list for me or I get confused. Then I said maybe the reason Sally is so scared is it's this *(German accent.)* Yerman she can't abide. All the boys are off fighting these Yerman types, there's one right in the middle of us.

SALLY. There are old families of German descent here.

MATT. Ha-ha. You know nothing about dis Friedman. Might be anybody. Dis enemy maybe infiltrate de home front, ja?

SALLY. Don't. That's creepy.

MATT. You should only know. So! She does not think of Matt as a German. *(Tears off another page, looks at the next.)* Then Matt says: *(Carefully.)* This Sally puzzle. She's how old? *(Sally freezes.)* Stop looking at yourself, Matt. It is not just Matt she is not liking. She is *well over* how old? All her friends and all her relatives were married by what age? And with all the prospering young men down here, some—

SALLY. All the prospering young men are off to war, Matt.

MATT. I think we are getting somewhere. Well, then all the handsome and pathetic and brave soldiers at the hospital she sees every day.

SALLY. They're kids. They're ten years younger than me; more, most of them.

MATT. This has got to be the most particular girl that ever was. Whoever heard of such a situation? Where is her bright-red hair net? Where're the rolled garters on her legs to drive men out of their mind. Why isn't she exposing half her bosom with a plunging neckline like every other female? Where is the come-hither? The invitation? *(Moves to Sally.)* Here is an unmarried, attractive, not fanatically religious young lady who actually thinks of herself as a human being rather than a featherbed. And you say there is no mystery? Also, I talked to the patients at the hospital, remember? Some are not so young. And they all say, "Are you Sally's beau? Every time we say something sweet to Sally, try to get fresh, she says, 'Come on, now, I got a beau.'"

SALLY. *(A long pause. She is trying to speak and can't. After two attempts she says shakily.)* There's time…enough…for

MATT. *(Pause. Quietly.)* It's just a friendly conversation, Sally. No reason to be upset.

SALLY. Oh, come…on. My life is no concern to you. If we get through the war, there's time to think about the future.

MATT. Nobody thinks like that any more. Live for today.

SALLY. Everything is upside down.

MATT. *(Turns her to face him.)* No, no. We're not waiting for when Johnny comes marching home this time.

SALLY. I can't hear a word you're saying. You have a thing of blood on your face.

MATT. *(Alarmed. A spot of blood from a scratch has appeared over one eye.)* Blood? Where? How did I get?

SALLY. You said that junk fell on you. Don't touch it. Don't—just put both your hands down. *(She takes a handkerchief from her purse, and a bottle from a hiding place. Lights a lantern, and hands it to him.)* Hold this.

MATT. *(Looking at bottle, as she dabs handkerchief.)* What is that?

SALLY. Never you mind.

MATT. What is that? *(She dabs at his forehead.)* Ai! That stings. What are you putting on…?

SALLY. Gin. You're not hurt; don't faint. Sit down.

MATT. I'm inoculated; it won't give me lockjaw.

SALLY. I'm sorry to hear it.

MATT. I had a tetanus shot. Ouch.

SALLY. I know. Because you read in a book how to be a fisherman.

MATT. *(As she chases him.)* Some skills have to be acquired, you know. Man is not born with a knowledge of the river or nobody would ever drown. Ouch! This is a professional nurse's bedside manner? Also, I read. In my business I had to learn to ready very fast because they change the tax laws every week.

SALLY. *(A last dab at him.)* One more.

MATT. So now I read like a madman, and I retain nothing at all. But I read like lightning.

SALLY. I read very slowly and practically memorize every word.

MATT. Jack Sprat. Am I okay?

SALLY. You'll live. *(She takes a nip from the bottle and passes it to him. He takes a drink, reacts, hands the bottle back.)*

MATT. You have Sen-Sen for your breath? *(She opens her purse.)* No, no. *(He takes a cigarette, offers her one. She sighs, takes it. He gets a lighter from his pocket. It doesn't work. She opens her purse, produces a lighter, and lights his and hers. Looking around.)* Poor Whistler. He should see what is happening to his boathouse. He'd sing *"Una furtiva Lagrima."*

SALLY. I used to think that he made the place for me. I was little when he died, but I thought he knew I'd come along, so he built it just the way it is—falling down—the way people used to build Roman ruins for their gardens. That way nobody else would come here and discover the magic of the place except me.

MATT. It was falling down? Even then?

SALLY. Well, it wasn't that long ago. I played in it when I was eight or ten, I'm twenty-seven now, so—

MATT. No, you're counting wrong.

SALLY. I'm what?

MATT. You're thirty-one.

SALLY. I am certainly not thirty-one. Who do—

MATT. Oh, my goodness. She does have a vanity as well as a temper. You are thirty-one because you were fired from teaching Sunday school on your twenty-eighth birthday and that's three years ago.

SALLY. What?

MATT. I've become great friends with your Aunt Charlotte. There's a counterspy in your very home. You're infiltrated. I didn't tell you. You're ambushed. I've come up on you from behind.

SALLY. When did you talk to Aunt Charlotte?

MATT. Last year. For a second today. And every few weeks during the winter. On the telephone. *(He laughs.)* I had never heard of anyone being fired from Sunday school before.

SALLY. I quit, we didn't get along.

MATT. I like it better the way she told me. The preacher told you you were supposed to be teaching from the Methodist reader, not from Thorstein Veblen.

SALLY. They were having problems with union organizers at the garment factory.

MATT. Some of the kids' mothers work there.

SALLY. They asked me what was happening.

MATT. I like that. So you read to them from…?

SALLY. *The Theory of the Leisure Class.*

MATT. How much of the garment factory does your family own?

SALLY. Almost twenty-five percent. And more than that of the bank. Dad and the minister and the newspaper editor suggested we all concentrate on the text: "And he who does not work, neither shall he eat."

MATT. And scare the pants off the sluggards.

SALLY. Make the unreligious infidels buckle down.

MATT. Be good Christian workers.

SALLY. I also read from St. Augustine.

MATT. "Profit is a sin."

SALLY. "Businessmen will never enter the Kingdom."

MATT. He was also a terrible anti-Semite.

SALLY. Worse, he was Catholic.

MATT. Sally, you know that unmarried daughters are supposed to help the menfolk keep the social status quo.

SALLY. Organize food baskets for the poor.

MATT. Keep their mouths shut.

SALLY. There was a time when Dad had great hopes for me.

MATT. No wonder they are so eager to get you out of their house.

SALLY. You're older than I am.

MATT. Oh, more than you know. I'm forty-two.

SALLY. That's about what I imagined.

MATT. Sally, you don't say that. Whatever you think.

SALLY. Under the draft by the skin of your teeth.

MATT. Yes.

SALLY. You could have volunteered.

MATT. Yes.

SALLY. You've been married?

MATT. No, ma'am.

SALLY. Why?

MATT. Never asked anybody. Nobody ever asked me.

SALLY. You should have heard the other nurse's aides, after you left. They thought you were the bee's knees.

MATT. They still say that down here?

SALLY. They still say cat's pajamas. Only something is wrong. Something is goofy, isn't it? A single man, forty-two years old. It doesn't make sense that a good man hasn't made a fool of himself at least once by your age.

MATT. Well, puzzles. Why does the chicken cross the road? A man I know says some riddle to me every day. I say, "Don't tell me, don't tell me." Later in the day I say, "Okay, I give up." Puzzles and jokes.

SALLY. They couldn't quite put you together so they decided you weren't quite right. Maybe you had a wife and six kids in Germany.

MATT. You like jokes? Ben Franklin was standing at the kitchen window one morning flying his kite out the window. And his missus, Mrs. Franklin, comes in, looks out at the kite, and says to Ben, "You need more tail." (Sally reacts.) And Ben says to her: "That's what I told you this morning. And you told me to go fly a kite."

SALLY. I heard that before I was twelve.

MATT. I hadn't heard that before. Mrs. Blumenfeld in the office told us that yesterday morning.

SALLY. English wasn't your first language. What was?

MATT. Questions and answers. What is the shortest month? May is the shortest month, there are only three letters in May.

SALLY. German? Yiddish?

MATT. What was Matthew's first language? It doesn't come out funny. What does it matter; he can't talk to the old man at the cafeteria in Lithuanian any more. Not the way he would like to. Some. Pieces: "The weather is hot today." "Yes, the weather is hot. I read the Germans marched into Russia." "Yes, what happened to the German-Russian friendship, ho, ho, ho?" I yell to him like he was deaf.

SALLY. Where were you born?

MATT. I don't know.

SALLY. Where was the sidewalk they skated on?

MATT. *(Almost abrupt.)* I lived in many cities. *(Sighs, maybe sits, or walks around.)* Oh, dear. We are a lot alike, you know? To be so different. We are two such private people. A guy the other day—I eat at this cafeteria, I talk to a lot of nutty guys—

SALLY. I don't want to hear another story, I—

MATT. No, no, no, this is not like that. I came down here to tell you this. This guy told me we were eggs.

SALLY. Who? You and me?

MATT. All people. He said people are eggs. Said we had to be careful not to bang up against each other too hard. Crack our shells, never be any use again. Said we were eggs. Individuals. We had to keep separate, private. He was very protective of his shell. He said nobody ever knows what the other guy is thinking. We all got about ten tracks going at once, nobody ever knows what's going down any given track at any given moment. So we never can really communicate. As I'm talking to you on track number three, over on track five I might be thinking about...*(Puts his hand on her back.)* Oh, any number of things. *(Really asking.)* And when I think you're listening to me, what are you really thinking?

SALLY. *(Removes his hand.)* And you think he's right or you think he's wrong?

MATT. Well, that's two ways of looking at it. I told him he was paranoid. Ought not to worry too much about being understood. Ought to work at it. We...*(Puts his hand on her knee.)* Got our work cut out for us, don't we? I told him...

SALLY. *(Gently pushes his hand away, and crosses her legs.)* What?

MATT. *(Up and pacing.)* Well, it's all right there in his analogy, ain't it? What good is an egg? Gotta be hatched or boiled or beat up into something like a lot of other eggs. Then you're cookin'. I told him he ought not to be too afraid of gettin' his yolk broke.

SALLY. Where were you born?

MATT. He didn't appreciate it either.

SALLY. Why are you being such a private person? Such an egg?

MATT. *(His back to us, staring out.)* Where was Matt born? Uh, Rostock maybe or Dansk or Kaunas, but probably Kaunas, which became the capital of...

SALLY. Lithuania.

MATT. What *was* Lithuania. *(Turning.)* So! There! Omelet!

SALLY. When did you come to America?

MATT. This is one you haven't heard: This is a city joke. The Kaiser's architect had a little outhouse he wanted plastered and painted, so he asked for bids from three contractors: a Polish man, an Italian, and a Jew.

SALLY. Matt—

MATT. So first the Pole says, "Well, that job will cost you three thousand marks." Kaiser's architect says, "How do you figure that?" The Pole says, "One thousand for the plasterer, one thousand for the painter, and one thousand for me." So the Italian says, "That will be six thousand marks." Kaiser's architect says, "How is that six thousand marks?" The Italian says, "Two thousand for the plasterer, two thousand for the painter, two thousand for me." So he goes to the Jewish contractor and he says, "That job will be nine thousand marks." Nine thousand marks! How can you figure that? So the Jew says, "Three thousand for you, three thousand for me, and three thousand for the Pole."

SALLY. You said you were German, why were you born in Lithuania?

MATT. Probably Lithuania.

SALLY. Did you come here with your family? *(Pause.)* To this country? *(Pause.)* Or don't you know that either.

MATT. I know, I know. *(Pause. Finally decides.)* Very well, Miss Sally Talley. There was a Prussian and a Uke (Ukrainian, yes?) A Prussian and a Uke and a Lat and a Probable Lit, who all traveled over Europe.

SALLY. Matt, you're maddening—I don't know if this is a story or a—

MATT. I will tell this, Sally, in the only way I can tell it. The Prussian had been a soldier, but then he realized that, being Jewish, he could not advance in the Kaiser's army, so then he became an engineer.

SALLY. There's no such thing as a Prussian Jew.

MATT. *(Rather Prussian.)* Prussian is the way the Prussian thought of himself, and Prussian he was. *(She sighs, perhaps says, "Very well.")* So he became a Wandering…Engineer. The Kaiser sent the Prussian and the Uke and the Lat and the Probable Lit to study engineering wonders: many months in the Swiss mountains to watch the building of a funicular, yes?

SALLY. Yes.

MATT. And in the evening the Prussian liked to sit stiffly and talk with other stiff Prussian Jews sitting around the cafés of the capitals of Europe. But unfortunately, one of the people with whom the Prussian spoke was—

SALLY. Matt, you're confusing me and I don't know if this is a joke or this is—

MATT. This is the joke about how the Probable Lit came to America that you said you wanted to hear. So one of the people with whom he spoke was an inventor named—who remembers—such is fame—who had discovered how to get nitrogen out of air. Like magic. So one day the Prussian and the Uke and the Lat and the Probable Lit lit out for Naples but were detained in Nice, where there is a large police force, because people try to board boats there to cross borders, Europe being mostly made up of borders that people get upset when you try to cross. Europe is the child's game of May I. You know May I? "Captain, may I cross into Yugoslavia?" "Yes, you may take three scissor steps." "Okay, I take three scissor steps." "Oh, oh, go back to Czechoslovakia. You forgot to say, 'May I.'"

SALLY. Who is the Uke and who is the Lat? You're the Lit and the Prussian is your father? Who is the Uke?

MATT. This is all on the up-and-up, Sally, the Prussian was married to the Uke. She said she was Sephardic, but that wasn't true.

SALLY. *(Knows somehow that he is talking about something important.)* Okay. I want to understand this, Matt. Who was the Lat?

MATT. The Lat was their daughter, who had been born in Latvia two years before the Probable Lit had been born probably in Lithuania.

SALLY. I didn't know you have a sister.

MATT. *(Looking across the river. Low.)* It turned out to be of little consequence, people in Europe being very wasteful of people.

SALLY. *(Beat.)* And your family was detained in Nice?

MATT. Yes, by the Nice police. Which was very unlucky, as the French are very much the natural enemy of the Prussians, and the French very much wanted to know from the Prussian engineer…What? *(Beat.)* Something he had overheard in a café.

SALLY. *(Long pause. Troubled answer.)* How to get nitrogen from the air.

MATT. Like magic!

SALLY. Why?

MATT. Everyone was happily looking forward to the Great War.

SALLY. This was when?

MATT. This was 1911, the Lit was nine. And this nitrogen is not used in the fields as fertilizer. This nitrogen is used in the manufacture of gunpowder. So one should be very careful what your friends tell you in cafés. *(This is difficult to say, and there is a bitterness underlying it which he does not show.)* So the French torture the Prussian—

SALLY. Oh, no—

MATT. Who, being Prussian and Jewish, says nothing, and the French decide to torture the Lat daughter to make the Prussian speak.

SALLY. Matt, you don't have to say anything, I know—

MATT. The consequences being that the Lat fell into a coma from which she did not recover and the French were convinced that they had the wrong Prussian, Uke, Lat, and Lit, and let the whole lot of them go. So they went to the authorities in Germany, leaving the little Lit with his uncle in Lübeck. The irony turned out to be that the German government reasoned that this gregarious Prussian engineer knew something vital to the interest of the Kaiser—

SALLY. Oh, no—

MATT. Well, as he did. So the Prussian and the Uke tried to slip across the border into Denmark. But, we understand, they forgot to say, "May I?"

SALLY. They wouldn't kill their own people just because they knew something they might or might not tell—

MATT. —Well, they didn't consider them their own, of course. And people were not killed in Germany. They were indefinitely detained.

SALLY. I never heard that there were persecutions in the First World War.

MATT. I thought you said you reread the Old Testament.

SALLY. How did he get to America? The Lit?

MATT. Who said the little Lit came to America?

SALLY. How did he get to America?

MATT. Norway to Caracas to America on a banana boat.

SALLY. By himself? Or with refugees?

MATT. Refugees, smefugees. With the uncle from Lübeck and his wife and four kids.

SALLY. Little kids?

MATT. What does it matter what size kids? No. Grown people. Not little kids. *(Beat.)* There is always something thrilling about the broad canvas of a European story, isn't there? *(Pause.)* But I am afraid that the Probable Lit had seen too much. No allegiances would claim him any more, no causes.

SALLY. So the Lit didn't volunteer for the army.

MATT. Oh, war. What did he know except war; life was war, war was life. Against the French he would almost have gone this time. No. *(Looking at her.)* The resolve was never to be responsible for bringing into such a world another living soul. He would not bring into this world another child to be killed for a political purpose. This boy knew blank about sitting alone in a room in a city without a woman to talk to. *(Pause.)* So the little Lit was a little crazy, and I'm afraid as he grew older he got a little crazier, but he has witnessed nothing to cause him to alter his conviction. *(Watching her closely.)* And what woman would be interested in such a grown Probable Lit with such a resolve? *(Pause. She doesn't answer.)* Anyway, he doesn't think about it. The day is over in a second. I spend my life adding figures. It breaks my head.

SALLY. *(Very level.)* He does. The Lit.

MATT. Does what?

SALLY. You said "I." You mean the Lit. The Lit spends his life adding figures.

MATT. Yes, well, I do too. We are much alike. We work together.

SALLY. You've both gone to a lot of work for nothing.

MATT. What work? What do you mean?

SALLY. Or do you naturally invent stories about your sister and father and mother being killed by Germans?

MATT. One by the French; two by the Germans.

SALLY. You've been talking to Aunt Lottie? Who else have you talked to? People in town? Have you looked in the Lebanon newspaper? The old files? I don't know how detectives work.

MATT. This is bad. Why are you speaking like this?

SALLY. Why did you tell me that story?

MATT. To make you see why I had not spoken last year.

SALLY. That's what you came down here to tell me?

MATT. Yes.

SALLY. Well, now you've told me. Now I know. Now you can leave.

MATT. *(Worried.)* I have said something I don't know that I have said.

SALLY. *(She hurries to leave.)* It was a calculated risk; you just miscalculated.

(Hides the gin, grabs her jacket and purse.) You're not good at manipula-
tion. I've been worked over by experts. *(Blows out the lantern.)* They're
good down here. *(The boathouse is flooded in moonlight.)*

MATT. Sally, you have mistaken something—

SALLY. —Get gone now. Leave before I hit you with something. You can
walk to the Barnettes', they'll give you some gas for a couple of coupons.

MATT. Now who is making the disturbance?

SALLY. *(Angry; quite loud.)* Get off this property or get out of my way so I
can go back to the house, or I'll disturb you for real.

MATT. We are going to settle this before anyone goes anywhere.

SALLY. I won't be made a fool just because I fell in love again, Matt, and I
won't be pushed around again.

MATT. You're not getting away from me.

SALLY. Get out of here!

MATT. Do you realize what you said? Did you hear yourself?

SALLY. *(Yelling toward the door.)* Buddy! Cliffy! Here he is. Matt Friedman is
down here! *(Her last words are muffled by Matt's hand as he grabs her and
holds her fast. She tries to speak over his lines.)*

MATT. *(Grabbing her.)* Vilde chaya! You are a crazy woman! We could both
be shot with that gun. People do not scream and yell and kick. *(She stops
struggling.)* People are blessed with the beautiful gift of reason and com-
munication. *(He starts to release her.)*

SALLY. Cliffy!

MATT. *(Grabbing her again.)* How can such a thing happen? When they
passed out logic everybody in the Ozarks went on a marshmallow roast.
You are rational now? *(He releases her. She moves away, Matt stands where
he can block her exit.)* Life is going to be interesting with you. You're hurt?

SALLY. No.

MATT. My hand is bleeding. Where did you hide the alcohol? *(He goes to the
gin bottle, keeping an eye on her.)* I called my uncle and my aunt. Seventy
years old. They say, Matt, don't get mixed up with the *goyim*. They have
my cousins call me; old neighbors I haven't heard from in years. I say I
must live my own life. I come down here protected from tetanus; I am
getting rabies from an *alte moid.*

SALLY. *(Level.)* Why did you tell me about your family, and about you?

MATT. *(Pouring the gin on his hand.)* Because you asked me. Why have you
not married? Where were you born? How did you get to this stupid
country? Because I am a crazy person. Your nurse friends all say something is wacky with Matt that he has never made a fool of himself over

some woman; I said, Matt, go down, tell Sally who you are. Once in your life *risk* something. At least you will know that you did what you could. What do you think she is going to do, bite you?

SALLY. *(Pause.)* Charlotte told you nothing. She may be silly. She may like you.

MATT. One does not necessarily follow the other.

SALLY. But she doesn't gossip about me. She didn't tell you anything.

MATT. So you tell me. No, Charlotte told me nothing except that there was something to tell. I said, Charlotte, Sherlock thinks that there is some dark mystery down here and Charlotte said, Mr. Holmes, Sally will have to tell you that herself.

SALLY. There is nothing to tell.

MATT. You were screaming up to the house for the sheriff because there is— Oh, my—*(Listens.)* They could all be coming down here now.

SALLY. They're all listening to the radio.

MATT. Saved by Miss Fanny Brice. We stick together. Oh, my gosh! I do not know how to begin! I am walking into an unfriendly church in my underdrawers, here.

SALLY. What are you talking about?

MATT. You don't have that dream? I congratulate you. That is a terrible dream. I mean, I am at such a disadvantage here. *(With an energy born from frustration.)* None of my skills is appropriate to the situation I find myself in. And I have amazing skills. I could be an attraction in a sideshow. Give me a list of three, six, up to fifteen numbers, five digits each, I'll tell you the sum immediately. In my head, Mr. Adding Machine. Everybody gapes. How does he do that? He's got it all written down. I know the multiplication table up to seventy-five times seventy-five. Truly. It's something I know. What is sixty-seven times sixty-eight? Four thousand five hundred fifty-six. I have amazing skills. Only I feel like Houdini in the iron box under the ice at the bottom of the river. I forgot where I put the key to the handcuffs. Such a frustrating dream.

SALLY. One of the boys at the hospital is an artist. He's developed a facility for when a dream starts to go bad. It starts to get scary. He, in the dream, changes it all into a drawing, wads it up, and throws it away.

MATT. Freud wouldn't like it.

SALLY. Oh, drive him crazy.

MATT. I am foolish to insinuate myself down here and try to feel like one of the hillbillies. Who ever heard of this Friedman? I don't blame you. I won't be Matt Friedman any more. I'll join the throng. Call myself…August Hedgepeth. Sip moonshine over the back of my elbow.

Wheat straw in the gap in my teeth. I'm not cleaning my glasses, I'm fishing for crapies. Bass.

SALLY. Sun perch.

MATT. Oh, heck yes. Only I'm not. I can't even take off my shoes without feeling absurd.

SALLY. People don't walk around with their shoes off here, sipping moonshine. It isn't really the Hatfields and the McCoys. The ones who go barefoot only do it because they can't afford shoes, Matt…I…

MATT. Matt? Who's that? I don't even hear you. My name is August. Call me August.

SALLY. I couldn't possibly.

MATT. That's my name as of this minute.

SALLY. Matt, you—

MATT. Who? Huh? Wha?

SALLY. *(A pause. Finally.)* August…

MATT. I don't like it. What is that fragrance? What are you wearing?

SALLY. It isn't me.

MATT. Smell.

SALLY. Honeysuckle.

MATT. That's honeysuckle? No wonder they make songs about it. It blooms at night?

SALLY. No, that's something else. It blooms during the day, the night, whenever.

MATT. It's wonderful.

SALLY. You've never had to grub it out of a hedgerow.

MATT. You know that folk song? *(Sings.)* "Lindy, did you smell that honeysuckle vine last night? Honey, it was smellin' so sweet in de moonlight."

SALLY. No. I mean sure, but I don't know it.

MATT. We heard the Lebanon band play it last summer. Isn't that a Missouri folk song?

SALLY. No. I don't know. I don't know Missouri folk songs.

MATT. *(Sings.)* "Oh, God, I'd lay me down and die, if I could be as sweet as that to you." *(Directly to her, low and trying to sing well.)* "Oooooo-oooooo. My little Lindy Lou…"

SALLY. Don't sing to me, it's ridiculous. And my name is not Lindy Lou. It's Sally Talley. *(They both smile.)*

MATT. I know, I came down to talk to you about that.

SALLY. Well, I'm not going to change my—*(Dead stop. Count fifteen.)*

MATT. Why is your chin trembling? You okay? Sally?

SALLY. You didn't say that. Don't say that.

MATT. It's what I want to say.

SALLY. Well, don't. Well, don't talk to me about your socialism, talk about your work or something, like you did in your letters.

MATT. I don't talk Socialism, I don't talk Communism, I talk common sense. I don't think much of isms. In no time at all you start defending isms like they were something tangible. What are you afraid of? Why—

SALLY. *(Cutting him off.)* And that's what made Buddy so angry? And Olive? Talking common sense?

MATT. No, your brother is a baiter. You want to change the subject? Fine.

SALLY. A what?

MATT. *(Almost angry.)* A baiter! A baiter. He baits people. Buddy thinks that if all the factory workers went on strike for better wages, as they are trying to do in his factory, it would bring the country to its knees. He is a very poetic speaker.

SALLY. Well, it would bring Buddy to his knees, and that's a position with which he is very unfamiliar, believe me.

MATT. What are you afraid of?

SALLY. People are working now at least.

MATT. Economics, you want to talk? I say to you: This is my life. This is what I want. Say no or say yes, and you say: Talk about economics?

SALLY. Will there really be strikes after the war is over?

MATT. *(Glares at her.)* You are playing games, yes?

SALLY. I don't know what—

MATT. You are a peach. After the war they'll strike, yes. People say. Shaking in their boots. Sure. They'll strike. Everybody from the soda jerks to the grease monkeys. It gives them the illusion that the system is working.

SALLY. *(Also worried. Trying one more diversion.)* People are afraid to admit it, but I think they're worried about what's going to happen when the boys come back.

MATT. *(Increasingly angry.)* Down here they're afraid to admit it? I'm glad to hear it. It shows humility. Humility is good for the soul. In St. Louis they tremble in their beds at night. Headlines in the papers. One businessman said the war had to last another two years or the nation would never recover.

SALLY. They're afraid that there will be another Depression.

MATT. They who?

SALLY. They. They. Who do we ever mean when we say they?

MATT. Man I know says, "They-sayers are all liars."

SALLY. They see it happening all over again: the Depression, unemployment, with the factories shut down, higher taxes.

MATT. No.

SALLY. What do you mean, no?

MATT. No. It won't happen.

SALLY. You can't know that.

MATT. There is a lot I do not know. On people I am utterly ignorant. On girls I am more than ignorant. On money I am an expert only. On taxes I am an authority. Businesses ask *me* about taxes. People who cry depression are blind and frightened.

SALLY. Why should it be different this time?

MATT. You are worried? About what is going to be?

SALLY. Yes. It was no fun. Hobos coming up to the back door four and five at a time. Every day. Asking for work and having to accept handouts.

MATT. It's different. It won't be like that again. Roosevelt himself will be the one passing out lollipops.

SALLY. I don't know why you're acting like this. All I—

MATT. How much money do you have?

SALLY. What?

MATT. *(Furious.)* You're an average person in a less-than-average job. You've been working only two and a half, three years. How much money do you have saved? You have nothing to spend it on, you put it in a savings account, you buy bonds to save capitalism, excuse me, democracy—er—a—freedom of speech, were you not terrified to express yourself—how much have you saved?

SALLY. What's wrong? I'm not going to let you talk to—

MATT. Forget it. How much?

SALLY. *(Beat.)* I do know how much money I've saved. That's what bothers me. Money makes me greedy and guilty at the same time.

MATT. So how much?

SALLY. Half my check every week for three years. I make thirty dollars a week.

MATT. Twenty-three hundred forty dollars!

SALLY. A little less. Twenty-two hundred.

MATT. Multiply that times one hundred twenty million people.

SALLY. You're the mathematician, what does it come to.

MATT. A lot of money. That nobody had before the war. Burning a hole in everybody's pockets. How many people have bought war bonds? Eighty-five million people! How much money is in saving banks? One hundred thirty billion dollars! Everybody is going to be spending and building and working. The sideshow is over! End of financial exhibition. I'll go. Why did I come? You aren't going to be honest with me.

SALLY. Honest about what?

MATT. About you, about me, about Sally and Matt. You think I intend to sit here and talk finance? What will happen after the war. Why should there be an after-the-war?

SALLY. I was being perfectly honest with you.

MATT. Perfectly honest and perfectly evasive. Perfectly mysterious and perfectly frightened out of your wits. *(Bogart.)* "You know somethin', baby? You dames are all alike. Ya yella. Ya all got a yella streak a mile wide right down the middle of ya back."

SALLY. Is that supposed to be Cagney?

MATT. *(Crushed.)* No; oh my goodness! Cagney! That's still Bogart. You have no sense of flattery.

SALLY. And we're all yella. You know that many women, you can make a generalization like that?

MATT. Oh, good grief. Now what are you going to be? Jealous and possessive about something you don't even want? No. I know no women. What I told you I have never before spoken for the same reason that you speak nothing to anybody, because we are terrified that if once we allow ourselves to be cracked—I think people really do think that they're eggs. They're afraid they are the—who is the eggman, all the king's horses and—

SALLY. Humpty Dumpty.

MATT. We all have a Humpty Dumpty complex. So now I take a big chance. I come down here to tell you I am in love for the only time in my life with a girl who sees the world exactly as I see it. I say to you, I am sorry, Sally, I will not have children, but if there is a life for the two of us, will you have me or not? You scream and yell bloody murder, you kick, you—ah, breathe fast, what do you call it, breathing fast in and out, in and out—?

SALLY. Hyperventilate.

MATT. You hyperventilate and say, Matthew, talk about finance. *(Sighs.)* Oh, boy, oh, boy.

SALLY. *(A long pause.)* You can come with me to the road. I'll get you some gas. I'll go into the yard by myself.

MATT. The car isn't out of gas.

SALLY. *(Beat.)* What is it out of?

MATT. Hope! The car is out of hope. The car is in fine running condition.

I turn the key, it goes; I turn if off, it stops. I turned it off. I didn't say it was out of gas, I said it needs gas to run. You assumed it was out of gas. *(Pause.)* I wasn't talking to Buddy about isms up at the house, I was telling him about you and me down here in the boathouse last summer.

SALLY. Oh, my God! Oh!

MATT. Hey, come on, you'll drown out Fibber McGee.

SALLY. You didn't!

MATT. They'll arrest us both. Shhhh! They'll hear you swear right across the river at the park. You want to hear the band play in Whistler's band shell? So the night shouldn't be a waste?

SALLY. You didn't.

MATT. They ought to start any time. We can watch the fireworks.

SALLY. They won't have fireworks; you can hear the band from here. Matt, you have no idea how prejudiced Buddy and Olive are! Really!

MATT. You kidding me? I don't imagine your father will let you sleep under his roof after Buddy tells them. Your aunt thought it was very likely you'd be kicked out of the house. We think maybe they'll shave your head.

SALLY. Aunt Lottie put you up to this?

MATT. She said you were anxious to get out of the house, but you didn't have much courage. She is a very bold strategist.

SALLY. You told her about last summer?

MATT. No, she told me. You told Rachel, Rachel told her cousin Rose, Rose told your Aunt Charlotte.

SALLY. I'll brain them, every one.

MATT. You been listening to anything I've said?

SALLY. What? Oh, Matt, I told you, put it out of your head.

MATT. You're hard. You're tough.

SALLY. Well, I can't think about it now.

MATT. Maybe you better.

SALLY. There is no place to go or I'd be out of there, Matt.

SALLY. There's a hospital in St. Louis. Saint Ann's. St. Louis's St. Ann's. Where you could work. They're crying for help.

SALLY. Too long a drive.

MATT. Well, it happens my apartment is conveniently located four blocks away.

SALLY. You have room for three nurse's aides?

MATT. I rescind the offer. You like St. Louis? The Browns, you never know.

The Cardinals are okay. We can go to the game, watch the Cooper brothers.

SALLY. Matt, you can see I don't want you to talk like that.

MATT. I hear you say that. I think I see something different. You aren't afraid of me. This minute, are you afraid of me right now?

SALLY. I've never been afraid of you.

MATT. Put everything I've said behind. I didn't sing "Lindy Lou" and ask Sally to marry me. Sally didn't say, Don't sing. We are friends talking together, looking at the river and the upside-down black trees with the shaky moon in the water. *(Suddenly noticing.)* Hey! There's no color. In moonlight. What a gyp. Very little color. Look at you.

SALLY. *(Looks at him.)* Some.

MATT. You might as well have blue eyes. Amazing the things you get so used to that you don't know them any more. Okay. So I ask you. Why did your aunt say, "There is something you don't know, Matt, and something only Sally can tell you"?

SALLY. It was a long time ago.

MATT. You're thirty-one years old. How long—

SALLY. It was another life, really.

MATT. So what happened in this other life?

SALLY. Say I was disappointed in love. It was a long time ago. I was another person.

MATT. No, I don't believe in disappointed in love.

SALLY. It was more of a financial arrangement than anything.

MATT. Oh, well. Disappointed in a financial arrangement, I understand.

SALLY. I was engaged to Harley Campbell, his dad owned—

MATT. I don't believe it.

SALLY. You don't even know who he is.

MATT. I met him up at the house. He was the one that was saying, "You tell 'em, Buddy. You tell 'em, Buddy."

SALLY. Well, he used to be very good-looking.

MATT. I don't believe that either.

SALLY. *(Not rhapsodic; detached, but this is an unpleasant memory.)* He was a guard on the basketball team; I was a cheerleader. We grew up together. We were the two richest families in town. We were golden children. Dad owned a quarter of the garment factory; Harley's dad owned a third. These two great families were to be united in one happy factory. We used to walk through the plant holding hands, waving at all the girls; they loved us. When the workers asked for a showdown to discuss demands, Dad brought us right into the meeting, onto the platform. Everybody applauded.

MATT. The youth, the beauty...

SALLY. The money. Here they are, folks. The future of the country. Do you love them or do you love them? Now back to work. They still don't have a union.

MATT. So how did it happen that Sally was disappointed in love?

SALLY. It all became academic. The Depression happened. Maybe we didn't look so golden. The factory almost closed.

MATT. I know the Depression came. So how did it happen that Sally was disappointed in love?

SALLY. *(With some difficulty.)* I was sick for a long time. I got TB and missed school. I didn't graduate until a year after Harley did. It was a good excuse to drift apart. *(Easier.)* Then he went to Princeton, became engaged to a girl from New Jersey, his father killed himself.

MATT. Because he was engaged to a girl from New Jersey?

SALLY. Because by then it was 1931. He was in debt. He thought he would lose the factory. He didn't know how to live poor.

MATT. So?

SALLY. Harley quit school, Buddy and Harley and Dad worked at the factory, trying to save it. They're doing fine now.

MATT. I know. A government contract for army uniforms. So?

SALLY. Harley's wife left him eight years ago; he remarried a girl from Rogersville.

MATT. *(Looks at her a moment.)* So that's the truth, the whole truth, and nothing but the truth, so help you, Hannah.

SALLY. Yes.

MATT. You're real cute. *(Pause.)* Might as well get the gas, don't you think?

SALLY. You're not out of gas.

MATT. Yes, maybe I am. Maybe I lied.

SALLY. Well, if that's what it takes.

MATT. You know what I'm thinking? Over on track number nine? That Sally may not be who I thought she was, after all.

SALLY. Maybe not.

MATT. May not be. Maybe not. What kind of an answer to a mystery is that? What happened to change this Golden Girl into an embarrassment to the family? Into a radical old maid who is fired from teaching Sunday school? Why would this nice Harley leave you after all this time while you were sick with such a romantic disease? See, I'm a logical person. I have to have it all laid out like in a list, and that isn't logical.

SALLY. His family didn't want him to marry me, obviously.

MATT. They thought you weren't good enough for him?

SALLY. Come on. (*As she starts to move past him to the door, he reaches out and takes her wrist. The band, rather distant, plays a fanfare.*)

MATT. What?

SALLY. Yes. Don't do that.

MATT. Mr. Campbell was in debt and worried about being overextended, but the rich partner's daughter gets TB and the wedding is off?

SALLY. I don't know.

MATT. There's your music. Wasn't Harley the richest boy in town, you said?

SALLY. Yes.

MATT. And Sally was the richest girl in the countryside. This was the match of the decade. Bells were going to ring for such a match.

SALLY. Well, they didn't.

MATT. When the Depression comes, rich families must pool their resources.

SALLY. They didn't see it that way.

MATT. The Campbells are a large Missouri family, are they? Fifteen little Campbells?

SALLY. No.

MATT. Only Harley and his brother?

SALLY. Harley and his sister.

MATT. Harley was the only son of a very prominent Laclede County family.

SALLY. Yes.

MATT. So why didn't they want their only son to marry the beautiful, popular, cheerleader Talley girl whom he had been going steady with for three years?

SALLY. They didn't like me.

MATT. All those years he dated you over their protest?

SALLY. Not on your life.

MATT. No, because Harley did not do things against his parents' wishes.

SALLY. No.

MATT. But in fact you didn't graduate with Harley. You were delayed a full year.

SALLY. That's beginning to hurt, Matt.

MATT. You're pulling, I'm not pulling. (*Releases her, but stands in her path.*) Why weren't you good enough for Harley?

SALLY. I got sick.

MATT. You got TB and went to Arizona, where you lived for the rest of your life.

SALLY. No.

MATT. You gave this contagious disease to their only son and he went away to Arizona and was never heard from again.

SALLY. The TB was not serious. There were complicating circumstances that caused me to be out of school.

MATT. There were complications. Sally was pockmarked and ugly and nobody wanted anything to do with her.

SALLY. You might say that.

MATT. This only son was repulsed by the sight of you.

SALLY. No, Matt. I was in the hospital for a month. I had a fever.

MATT. This Harley has a morbid fear of hospitals. I'm getting a fever is who's getting a fever.

SALLY. They didn't want it.

MATT. But your dad insisted.

SALLY. He didn't want it either.

MATT. You were pale and white and would not look good in a wedding dress.

SALLY. Matt.

MATT. You were a tramp and a vamp and would have ruined the reputation of this prominent family. Is what the story is?

SALLY. He was the heir. He had to carry on the family name!

MATT. And you were irresponsible; you had uncontrollable kleptomania and could not be trusted around the family money.

SALLY. I was sick! I had a fever.

MATT. You were delirious and drunken and no family would allow such a woman to marry their only son.

SALLY. *(She tries to run past him.)* I was sick for a year.

MATT. *(Holds her again.)* You were not sick. You went away. Why did you go away?

SALLY. I was at the house.

MATT. *(Driving.)* Why were you in the house for a year?

SALLY. I had a fever.

MATT. No. Because you had disgraced yourself.

SALLY. I had a pelvic infection.

MATT. Is that would you told people?

SALLY. They didn't know what was wrong with me.

MATT. Why were you hiding in the house?

SALLY. They couldn't get the fever down!

MATT. Why were you hiding?

SALLY. *(Hitting him.)* They couldn't break the fever! By the time they did, it didn't matter.

MATT. What were you hiding—

SALLY. Because it had eaten out my insides! I couldn't bear children. I can't have children! Let go of me. *(She breaks away, crying, falls against something, and sits.)*

MATT. What do you mean?

SALLY. I couldn't have children.

MATT. Sally, I'm here, you're okay. It's okay.

SALLY. Go away. Go away.

MATT. *(Sitting beside her.)* I didn't know. I thought you had had a child.

SALLY. I have had no child. There was no scandal. I was no longer of value to the merger.

MATT. It's okay. It's okay.

SALLY. Oh, stop. That's what I tell the boys. It's okay. Only they're dying of blood poisoning. Don't comfort me. I'm fine. Blast you. Let go.

MATT. I thought you had had a child by someone else. You're so crazy.

SALLY. I only wish I had.

MATT. This was a result of the TB?

SALLY. *(She looks at him for a long moment. Then finally, no longer crying.)* The infection descended into the fallopian tubes; it's not uncommon with women at all. And so there couldn't be an heir to the garment empire. *(Almost laughing.)* It was all such a great dance. Everyone came to the hospital. Everyone said it made no difference. By the time Harley graduated, the Campbells weren't speaking to the Talleys. By then Dad was looking at me like I was a broken swing. It was a very interesting perspective.

MATT. Did you think that your aunt had told me you couldn't have children and I was making up the story of my life just to tease you?

SALLY. Possibly.

MATT. *(To the sky.)* Eggs! Eggs! Eggs! Eggs! We're so terrified. But we still hope. You take a beautiful dress to work— Did you tell the nurses I was coming to see you?

SALLY. No!

MATT. And look at me. For five years I have been wearing the same tie to work. It is a matter of principle with me not to wear a different tie. I buy a new tie to come and see Sally. You see how corruption of principle begins.

SALLY. I had nothing to do with that.

MATT. Is that a new dress, by the way? I don't know that dress.

SALLY. Yes. It's no big deal.

MATT. It is an enormous deal! It is the new New Deal! It is a Big Deal!

SALLY. You didn't even say you liked it.

MATT. I like it, I love the dress. *(Pause.)* I was sitting up in St. Louis all this winter in a terrible quandary. It is not that I have been happy or not happy, but that I have not thought that I *could* be happy. *(Beat.)* But this winter I was terribly unhappy and I *knew* I was unhappy. I had fallen for a girl and could not give her the life she would surely expect, with a family, many children. *(Pause. Taking her hand.)* You know what has happened? Some mischievous angel has looked down and saw us living two hundred miles apart and said, "You know what would be a kick in the head? Let's send Matt on a vacation to Lebanon."

SALLY. You believe in angels?

MATT. I do now, most definitely. Her name might be Lottie Talley, maybe. *(Pause.)* We missed your marching band.

SALLY. They'll play all evening.

MATT. *(Pause.)* So. We'll go up to the city tonight. Leave the car here—

SALLY. Oh, Matt, it's absurd to be talking like that; we're practically middle-aged.

MATT. So. We'll go up to the city tonight. Leave the car in town, take the midnight bus.

SALLY. *(Pause.)* I'll be up in a week or so.

MATT. *(Pause.)* I'll stay here at the hotel in Lebanon and wait.

SALLY. You have to work tomorrow.

MATT. So what?

SALLY. *(Pause.)* We'll go tonight. *(They kiss. The distant band strikes up a soft but lightly swinging rendition of "Lindy Lou." They laugh.)*

MATT. "Lindy Lou." *(Pause. They are sitting holding hands, perfectly relaxed. Matt looks around.)* You live in such a beautiful country. Such a beautiful countryside. Will you miss it?

SALLY. Yes.

MATT. Me too. Once a year we'll come back down, so we don't forget.

SALLY. All right.

MATT. *(Looks at her for a long while, then his gaze drifts to the audience.)* And so, all's well that ends…*(Takes out his watch, shows time to Sally, then to audience.)*…right on the button. Good night. *(They embrace.)* *(The music continues as the light fades.)*

END OF PLAY

TALLEY & SON

For Bruce McCarty

Laura Highes, Helen Stenborg, Edward Seamon, Lindsey Richardson, Jimmey Ray Weeks, and Elizabeth Sturges in the Circle Repertory Company production of *Talley & Son*. Photograph ©1985 by Gerry Goodstein.

INTRODUCTION

While I was writing *Talley's Folly* it was fun imagining what was happening up at the house during all this time. I knew I would write it because I wanted to see the other people in the family that everyone (even in *Fifth of July*) had been talking about.

Also I had been trying to think of a part, a play, *some way* to take advantage of the talent of Liz Sturges. She was so exciting and we seemed to have so little work for her. I had been trying for years to come up with something for her to do; which is not the way I work—I have to know the character first, then fit the actor to it. The first image for her play was: In a house where smoking was strictly forbidden, especially in the formal parlor and nobody, certainly not the ladies, swore, Liz would walk through the house, lighting a cigarette, saying, "Oh, kiss my ass!" This had to be the Talley's front parlor—and this had to be Aunt Lottie.

I wanted, again, to write a play of the period—a play in the style of the 1940s. Only instead of a romantic comedy, this would be one of those pot-boilers, the sort of influenced-by-Ibsen plays Lillian Hellman was writing at the time. I'm not terribly good at plotting potboilers, so it isn't surprising that the first one (like the first waffle) wouldn't quite work.

I wrote *A Tale Told* immediately after *Talley's Folly*. It should have been *A Tale That is Told*, everyone kept confusing it with Shakespeare's A tale told by an idiot, etc. (Idiot? Fool?). The only clue I had as to the existence of Timmy Talley was in a long list of Talley names that Matt reels off satirically. Who the hell was Timmy Talley? We knew that Lottie was Sally and Matt's ally and was rather frisky. We knew about Olive and the rest of the family. I decided Buddy would be on leave from Italy and Timmy would be killed in the Pacific, just as Mr. Talley's first son had been killed in the First World War. He's the son of Talley & Son Garment Factory, not Eldon.

It was my intention for a time to continue the Talley Saga to include most of the wars the family had seen, all written in the style of the period. It would be fun to either camp or even do straight one of those turn of the century plays like *A Face on the Bar Room Floor*—and we would end with the beginning—the house being build just after the Civil War, not by slaves, but by freed slaves. That play would be a musical, a hard-assed Minstrel Show. It is very unlikely now that I'll do that, but it was fun planning it, and it gave me countless details for this play.

I liked *A Tale Told* well enough, and the production was gorgeous. It gave me a chance to meet the marvelous actor Fritz Weaver who came down the hall for the first rehearsal saying, I'm four decades too young for this part, and twenty minutes later, at the first reading, was completely Calvin Talley.

But Timmy drove me mad. He said nothing in the first act, then wouldn't shut up in the second. I thought his monologue on how he had been killed was as good a piece of writing as I had accomplished. On stage, in the playing, I'm sorry—we're in the middle of a melodrama here and I want to know what's going to happen next and this guy is stopping the show. In other words, Get the hook. It was an interesting play that was generally indifferently received, except for the production, and I knew I could do better. There are still things in the earlier play that I hated to see go, and I would have loved to bring Matt back and see him tangle again with the Talley family, but, no. Sally and Matt are soon on their way. Leave it alone.

I did know that I wanted to connect this play with *Fifth of July*. June would be crying upstairs, Kenneth would be conceived during the play—off stage. And then there was the Young family.

The Youngs actually existed, and they scared me to death. On my way from my grandmother's house to Shirley's, aged five to about seven, I had to pass the Young's. Most of the houses were respectable, if not architectural wonders, but the Young place was a shambles of huts and lean-tos in the middle of a three-foot-high weed patch. The grandmother really did stir a steaming cauldron in the back yard, making soap, and the kids were the terror of the neighborhood. There seemed to be an endless supply of them. They came running out to push me around every time I passed the house. Once when Shirley had just had her smallpox vaccination (Shirley is based on my best friend when I was about seven) she and I walked from her house to my grandmother's. Two of the young girls ran out to accost us. One of the girls egging the other on, kept saying, "Hit her on her vaccination!" There was a mulberry tree in their yard and all the kids' faces were stained purple during the season. They also did gather blackberries and sell glasses of jelly and buckets of berries at a sidewalk stand, but I never went near it. I was certain it would all be poisoned. I never knew for sure (I was seven) but it was rumored that one of the girls in the family was a complete slut. I did know that the older brother of one of my moneyed playmates dated her secretly while he was engaged to a girl from one of Lebanon's better families. He and Avalaine's usual trysting place was a clearing in the middle of the woods. We seven-year-olds crept up on them once but they were making so much noise, they frightened us away. I recognize all that puffing and groaning and screaming now but at that age we couldn't imagine what horrible murder was taking place. It wasn't too difficult to conjecture an earlier liaison of the two families that would become another excellent connection to *Fifth of July*, and finally tie the two enterprising families together by blood. Even more fun because only the audience would know.

Calvin Talley is based on Shirley's granduncle. We seldom saw him but when we did we teased him something awful. That was when he was out of it. When he was cogent, God help you if you got in his way. And once, when he was pretending, it was I who got banged across the nose with a, "There! Gotcha!" It took forever to stop the bleeding and both my eyes were black for weeks. Viola is based loosely on my mother (Violetta) who, after she left the garment factory and was remarried, cleaned house and the motel that belonged to the Talleys—or the family that I've named the Talleys. They are only a rough model, financially at least, of the clan. I knew them only from sitting in the hallway sometimes when mother was cleaning, and hearing them rushing about their huge house. I've met them in a dozen disguises in a dozen rich neighborhoods since.

You grab characters from everywhere, filling out the family: Buddy is based on the uncle of a friend who came home from the war a different person. I had known him as a great buddy to all the kids in the neighborhood. His name was Kenneth but they called him Buddy. He came back from the war early, from a relatively light assignment, his nerves completely shot.

This is the logical end to the Talley saga. These wounded and angry and wounding people—caught on the night America started locking her doors. And on the night Sally made her getaway with Matt.

ORIGINAL PRODUCTION

Talley & Son was produced by Circle Repertory Company, in Saratoga Springs, New York, at the Little Theater, Saratoga Performing Arts Center, on July 8, 1985. The play opened in New York City at Circle Repertory Company's theater on November 22, 1985. It was directed by Marshall W. Mason; the set design was by John Lee Beatty; the costume design was by Laura Crow; the lighting design was by Dennis Parichy; the sound design was by Chuck London Media/Stewart Werner and the production stage manager was Jody Boese. The cast was as follows:

Viola Platt . . . . Lisa Emery
Olive . . . . Laura Hughes
Netta. . . . . Helen Stenborg
Lottie. . . . . Joyce Reehling Christopher
Eldon . . . . Farley Granger
Buddy. . . . . Lindsey Richardson
Emmet Young . . . . Steve Decker
Harley Campbell . . . . Richard Backus
Mr. Talley. . . . . Edward Seamon
Avalaine Platt. . . . . Julie Bargeron
Timmy . . . . Robert MacNaughton
Sally . . . . Trish Hawkins

"Thou has set our iniquities before thee, our
secret sins in the light of Thy countenance.
For all our days are passed away in Thy wrath;
we spend our years as a tale that is told."

Psalm 90

CHARACTERS

CALVIN STUART TALLEY, eighty.

LOTTIE TALLEY, his daughter, forty-five.

ELDON TALLEY, Talley's son, fifty-two.

NETTA TALLEY, Eldon's wife, the same age.

KENNETH (BUDDY) TALLEY, Eldon's son, twenty-nine. In the uniform
     of an Army Staff Sergeant.

OLIVE TALLEY, Buddy's wife, twenty-eight.

TIMMY TALLEY, Eldon's son, twenty. In Marine fatigues.

SALLY TALLEY, Eldon's daughter, thirty-one.

EMMET YOUNG, a handyman.

VIOLA PLATT, the washerwoman, thirty-five, looking older.

HARLEY CAMPBELL, Eldon's business partner, thirty-one.

SCENE

The front parlor of the Talley place; a farm near Lebanon, Missouri

TIME

Independence Day, 1944, at sunset

Talley & Son

ACT ONE

The formal parlor of the Talley place, a large and elegant farmhouse constructed in 1865, just outside Lebanon, Missouri.

On the upstage wall is a fireplace flanked by double sliding doors that open to a wide, imposing hallway, showing on one side the front door and at the other the entrance to the kitchen and dining room.

At stage left, large double French doors open to a porch that surrounds the house; at stage right, matching doors of solid mahogany open to the office.

In one of the windows is a two-star flag indicating that the family has two sons in the war.

The room has been furnished luxuriously at (perhaps) the turn of the century. It is comfortable, if a little stiff, but verging on threadbare. The floor shines, the room is spotlessly clean.

Timmy Talley stands near the fireplace. He speaks to the audience.

TIMMY. America won the Second World War today. It'll be August next year before anybody knows it, but we took Saipan, and from Saipan we'll take its little cousin island, Tinian, and from Tinian a B-29 can finally take off for Japan and get back again, and then the war's over. I'm a little early here. This is the Fourth of July; I'm due here on the sixth for Granddad's funeral. I got my pass in my pocket. And while I'm here we're gonna have this big powwow about the family business. See, Harley Campbell and Dad own this garment factory, Talley and Son. Now some big company's wantin' to buy us out. Dad wrote me I'd better get my butt back here quick before Harley sold off everything but my stamp collection. *(Eldon comes in.)* Hey, Dad, that was one hell of a fire-and-brimstone letter. Hey, could you look at me for a change? What you don't know—I got a letter from you and one from Harley and one from Mom. Dad? *(Eldon goes into the office. Timmy looks back to the audience.)* Last thing I knew I was bumping along on a stretcher, some guy's hand over my eyes. I was yelling, "I gotta see Dad, man, get me up. Everything going all right, I'm home for the sixth." I think everything didn't go all right. *(Sally runs down the stairs, followed by Lottie.)*

LOTTIE. Sally. Sally. I thought you locked yourself in your room.

SALLY. Oh, I am so mad, I really am.

TIMMY. That's my sister.

LOTTIE. Sally, Buddy and Olive don't have the sense…

SALLY. Oh, I am very angry with both of them, and Mother, too.

LOTTIE. Mr. Friedman was as polite and gentlemanly as anyone could ask.

SALLY. Most of all I am angry with Matt Friedman.

LOTTIE. It wasn't Matt—

SALLY. How dare he get himself into a fight with my brother.

LOTTIE. Matt wasn't fighting; he was going to sit on the porch and wait for you. Buddy chased him off with a shotgun.

SALLY. Oh, Lord.

LOTTIE. I hit Buddy with a broom, and I'm glad.

SALLY. Why did Matt come down here in the first place? He knows how we feel about him. Oh!

LOTTIE. He said he wanted to talk to your father.

SALLY. Aunt Lottie, I wish you would get all that romantic twaddle out of your mind.

LOTTIE. Well—

SALLY. If there was a place to move to, I'd move there tonight.

LOTTIE. I know, darling.

OLIVE. *(Coming down the stairs.)* Sally, I just got June to sleep. You're going to wake her right up.

SALLY. Well, I wouldn't want to do that.

LOTTIE. Where are you going, Sally,

SALLY. Out. Out. I'm going out.

LOTTIE. Sally, stay here and talk to me.

SALLY. I am very angry with this entire household. *(She slams out the door.)*

LOTTIE. *(At the door.)* Sally!

TIMMY. *(To audience.)* I think my sister's very angry with this entire household.

LOTTIE. *(Calling.)* Sally, come back up here.

OLIVE. Aunt Lottie, you might have some consideration. You're going to wake June right up.

LOTTIE. I'm not speaking to you, Olive. *(She storms off outside. Olive goes back upstairs leaving Timmy alone in the parlor.)*

TIMMY. Boy, this family. This house. This room. This is where we always liked to come and play 'cause we weren't allowed to. We'd lay around on the rug playing Monopoly, but Sally'd always lose interest and I'd just lose—Buddy'd beat up on Sally and Sally's old boyfriend Harley'd beat up on Buddy and all three of them would beat up on me 'cause I was the youngest. About the only thing we did together was save up our dimes and sneak off down to the Lyric Theater to see a picture show, 'cause we weren't allowed to do that either. If the family ever went to the movies, they could watch us win the war next week on the Movietone Newsreel. They could see me die.

VIOLA. *(Off, calling loudly.)* Mr. Eldon? Anybody at home? Mrs. Talley?

OLIVE. *(Upstairs, whispering, overlapping.)* Viola, hush up. Oh, my goodness.

VIOLA. *(Continuing.)* Mr. Eldon?

TIMMY. Is anybody going to get the door?

VIOLA. Anybody to home here? Miss Charlotte?

OLIVE. *(Continuing.)* Oh, good Lord, would somebody shut that woman up. *(Netta appears from the back hall.)* Mother, I just got June to sleep. She's gonna wake her right up.

TIMMY. That's Mom.

NETTA. Why didn't you come around to the back, Viola?

VIOLA. I thought you'd all be gone off to the celebration; I couldn't raise nobody.

OLIVE. Oh, good Lord, Viola, shush. I swear, yelling through the house to wake the dead.

NETTA. Olive's just trying to get the girl to sleep, Viola.

VIOLA. I was wondering if your husband was at home, Mrs. Talley.

NETTA. I don't know if Eldon's here or not. What is it? I'll tell him.

VIOLA. No, no, don't bother, ain't important.

LOTTIE. *(Coming in from outside.)* Damn her hide.

NETTA. *(To Lottie.)* I hope you are thoroughly ashamed of yourself after the spectacle you made here this afternoon.

LOTTIE. I'm not talking to you, Netta. *(She settles at a table where she will work crossword puzzles and play solitaire.)*

NETTA. Lottie, now that we got rid of that Jew, I'd like Buddy to have one nice evening with the family. Nora and I are trying to cook supper for ten people, with Olive running in and out, in and out, in and out, and that's enough for me to put up with, thank you. Viola, I'll get the laundry; I've not even got it sorted yet.

VIOLA. I can do that.

NETTA. No, we don't want any more people parading through the house. It's all upside down. *(She exits.)*

TIMMY. Mom's having a hard time out there. My big brother, Buddy, is home, too. He's on special leave, and Mom and the cook, Nora, are making him a welcome-home-soldier supper. The kitchen looks like a cyclone went through it.

VIOLA. Miss Talley, I got to talk to your brother, it's kinda important.

LOTTIE. I can't tell you where he is.

VIOLA. Well, I'll come back after I get the laundry to soak, 'cause I better talk to him.

LOTTIE. Can't it wait till tomorrow? You look done in.

VIOLA. No, no, it better not wait.

OLIVE. *(Entering.)* Well, I thought you'd slipped a cog and was talking to yourself. It's a miracle June went back to sleep with all that commotion. Does this room smell? I've had the windows opened all day; I think it still smells. I guess you heard my Buddy came home on leave last night—

VIOLA. I saw him, yes.

OLIVE. And Timmy gets home from the Pacific day after tomorrow, so we're all together for one day at least.

TIMMY. I guess I'm gonna miss the party.

OLIVE. We're all trying to have everything so perfect. I can't quit thinking they're sending Buddy right back to Italy Thursday morning. I swear my prayer is that the war ends this night and he doesn't have to go back at all.

VIOLA. He's been over to Italy?

OLIVE. You knew that. He was at the wheel of General Mark Clark's car last month when they drove the Krauts out of Rome. We wired him how his granddad was failing; General Clark wrote an order for Buddy to come home, right on the spot. Then, too, he'd got his arm hurt awful bad— *(Lottie snorts.)*—so he couldn't drive. Lottie, he doesn't let on, but I can tell he's in terrible pain.

LOTTIE. He's General Clark's driver and he gets himself wounded during a victory celebration, falling down the Spanish steps.

OLIVE. They were under fire all winter, thank you. They sustained terrible casualties, Lottie. They only liberated Rome.

NETTA. *(Entering with laundry.)* Viola, come around to the back next time.

OLIVE. Mother, you ought to let me carry that.

NETTA. I'm sorry, Olive, don't call me Mother. It just makes me jump.

OLIVE. I'm sorry. I know.

NETTA. I can't visit—Nora and I are turning the goose. *(Exits to kitchen.)*

OLIVE. I'm sorry. Did you folks put up any of that blackberry jam this year? That's the first thing Buddy asked for.

VIOLA. That's all gone.

OLIVE. Blackberry season's hardly over. I don't imagine you've had—

VIOLA. We sold all that.

OLIVE. Don't step there, honey, with those rubber soles. I'll be down on my hands and knees again all night.

VIOLA. You tell Mr. Eldon it's important that I talk to him.

OLIVE. *(Overlapping some as Viola exits.)* Don't yell in the hall; you'll wake— Don't go out that front door—you'll *(Door slams.)* I have never seen such a lack of the most basic social graces in my life. These cushions need recovering, don't they?

LOTTIE. Not tonight.

OLIVE. Aunt Lottie, there is no call for you to be catty.

LOTTIE. While you're bragging about Buddy and Timmy getting special leave, Mrs. Platt's brother Vaughan was killed in Cherbourg last week.

TIMMY. Vaughan was?

OLIVE. I don't think I know him.

TIMMY. Worked at the garage.

LOTTIE. He was that good-looking guy who used to pump gas for you.

OLIVE. Oh…Well, I'm sorry to hear that, but Viola Platt should be able to rejoice in another's fortune even in the midst of her own sorrow. I know the whole family is ignorant and distrustful, but I will not believe they're unfeeling. *(Sotto voce.)* And her daughter, Avalaine Platt, has been seen with these eyes out with our handyman, Emmet Young, and I would not repeat the condition they were in. *(The office door opens, Eldon enters.)* Oh, good Lord. I thought I'd seen a ghost.

ELDON. Thought it was about time we found out what Dad's been counting up in there all these years. Turns out we're a lot more comfortable than we thought we were, Sis. You ought to go out and buy a hat.

LOTTIE. No, it wouldn't set right on me, brother dear—you can buy the hat.

ELDON. I just might.

LOTTIE. Get a new pair of britches, too. You're getting too big for those.

OLIVE. I'm not saying I couldn't use a few new things.

ELDON. Would you look how radiant she is. One night with Buddy home and I never saw anyone looking…so well rested.

OLIVE. Dad!

ELDON. She's put on a frock, maybe even a brush of makeup?

OLIVE. No, I—Well, if I *had,* I guess I have good reason.

ELDON. You've got the parlor shining, too.

OLIVE. Mother and I thought we'd air it out. But it does seem so callous.

LOTTIE. Olive's getting the parlor ready for Papa's funeral—that ought to be quite a celebration.

OLIVE. Lottie, it's not like that at all.

ELDON. No, we just count our blessings and go on with what has to be done.

OLIVE. *(At office door.)* What's Mr. Talley been hiding in here?

ELDON. Hey!

OLIVE. Well, it's no business of mine. Dad, I'm fixing you and buddy a little surprise for supper, so I'd better get crackin'. *(Exits.)*

ELDON. I wish Olive wouldn't call me Dad.

LOTTIE. Did you see Sally on the road?

ELDON. Sally was the last thing I was looking for.

LOTTIE. The Talleys are up to their usual standard of hospitality this afternoon.

ELDON. How's that?

BUDDY. *(Coming down from upstairs.)* Olive, where did you say you put my house shoes?

OLIVE. *(Off.)* What, what?

NETTA. *(Off.)* What, what?

ELDON. Well, there's another country heard from.

TIMMY. Hey, Buddy.

BUDDY. *(Looking into the room.)* Hey, Dad, where you been? We had our fireworks early this Fourth.

NETTA. *(Entering.)* Eldon Talley, you have an absolute talent for leaving the house if you're going to be needed.

ELDON. What did I do this time?

BUDDY. He missed the fun, didn't he, Mom?

NETTA. I'll fun you.

BUDDY. You know that Jew you said Sally dragged home to supper last year? He came down from St. Louis for a visit.

ELDON. The hell you say.

NETTA. If he'd stayed ten minutes more, Sally would have driven up with him standing right there on the porch.

BUDDY. I took out that old shotgun; he started shaking like a hound shittin' razor blades.

NETTA. *(Loving it.)* I won't have that army-barracks talk in here.

BUDDY. You oughta seen him hightail it—

NETTA. Your sister was a lot of help, too.

BUDDY. Aunt Lottie, you still ticked at me?

LOTTIE. You want to talk to me, Buddy, you talk about something else.

BUDDY. I think Aunt Lottie's kinda sweet on him.

NETTA. Yelling Sally wanted to see him. That's just Sally being willful. She doesn't want to see that man.

LOTTIE. She came home from work at the hospital and everybody lit on her like she—

NETTA. I am still her mother, I hope. And I know as well as I'm standing here that she brought that—man home last year out of spite. I can't understand a word he says; I swear I think he's a Communist.

ELDON. Well, he's something.

NETTA. He *is,* he's a lunatic. I told Olive to call the sheriff, nobody could find you.

ELDON. I told you I was in town. Took advantage of the holiday to see what's going on down at Dad's bank.

BUDDY. That's all right, me and Harley gave him a fine reception.

ELDON. Yeah? And how come Harley to be here? Soon as I'm not?

BUDDY. How's that?

ELDON. I'll bet Harley didn't happen to mention how great it is that Delaware Industries wants to buy the factory either.

TIMMY. Delaware Industries! That's the company I was telling you about.

BUDDY. No, he said we ought to talk. Sounds interesting.

ELDON. Anyone'd think so to hear Harley tell it.

BUDDY. Interesting, interesting, that's all I said.

ELDON. Well, you and Harley can be interested all to hell and back, some people in the family aren't going to be that all fired excited about selling out.

BUDDY. What's that supposed to mean?

NETTA. No business talk, now. You know how you two are.

ELDON. Your Harley's having pipe dreams about being on the board of some big corporation, sitting on his can smoking a cigar.

BUDDY. Heck, it's pretty hard to argue with getting paid for doing nothing.

ELDON. Oh, we'd get paid. The devil spends half his day just sitting down writing out checks.

BUDDY. You're so proud of Talley and Son—

ELDON. Damn right I am.

BUDDY. Well, you ought to be happy somebody's noticing it.

NETTA. Eldon, don't talk now—

OLIVE. *(Entering.)* Well, good morning sunshine in the middle of the afternoon. Did Viola wake you up, yelling for Dad?

BUDDY. I woke up because I was smelling Nora's Christmas goose. I could almost see the snowflakes flying.

OLIVE. You said you wanted to have Christmas on the Fourth of July. Did you have a good nap?

BUDDY. I slept like the dead once I finally got the chance.

OLIVE. *(Thrilled.)* Oh, don't say that! Oh! You! Oh! *(Playful to instant serious.)* Mother, do you think Granddaddy is strong enough to come to supper tonight?

LOTTIE. He'll be right at the head of the table.

ELDON. He was up this morning. Even managed to dress himself.

NETTA. We haven't seen him that strong in over a year.

BUDDY. Did you find those house shoes?

NETTA. I looked, Buddy, I think they might be gone.

BUDDY. They can't be gone, I've been dreaming about those shoes all through Italy.

OLIVE. Well, if we can't find them, we can surely buy you a new pair.

BUDDY. I don't want a new pair. I want my damn house shoes.

OLIVE. Well, they've taught you a few new words.

BUDDY. I told you to send them to Rome.

NETTA. We haven't got any of your mail from Rome yet.

OLIVE. I'm going to write to your company commander about all that censoring, too. They hardly touch Timmy's letters, they cut yours all to pieces.

BUDDY. Whata you hear from the fair-haired kid?

ELDON. Oh, we hit the jackpot yesterday.

NETTA. I got fifteen, Eldon got ten.

LOTTIE. I even got one.

NETTA. Lottie even got one.

ELDON. We really hit the jackpot.

BUDDY. I can't wait to see him, tell him to send his sister-in-law a grass skirt.

OLIVE. A sarong.

ELDON. I'll tell you. The Pacific sounds real disappointing in that department.

TIMMY. I didn't see one native female under sixty-five.

BUDDY. We don't always tell it all.

OLIVE. I didn't hear that.

BUDDY. Classified information.

OLIVE. Are you going to put on your shoes or are you going barefoot?

BUDDY. I was hoping to be able to put on my damn house shoes.

NETTA. Just don't be getting so free with that talk.

LOTTIE. Oh, shit.

NETTA. Lottie, really!

LOTTIE. Everybody knows Olive burned those shoes last April.

OLIVE. Lottie Talley, when I do—I could even say, more than my share—I can't remember during spring cleaning if I might have accidentally thrown out—

NETTA. *(Overlapping above.)* Olive had no way of knowing Buddy'd be asking for those slippers.

BUDDY. *(Overlapping.)* It's O.K., it doesn't matter. Good Lord.

OLIVE. If they're so important, then they're still around. Now, there's coffee on the stove.

NETTA. There's going to be no shortage of coffee for you.

OLIVE. And there's sugar.

ELDON. They've saved up their stamps for a month.

NETTA. Eldon, we've done nothing of the kind.

ELDON. We've killed the fatted calf.

NETTA. We've killed the fatted goose and I'm not joking; I've never seen so much grease in my life.

BUDDY. Coffee sounds good. I heard the Italians made such great coffee. Wooee! I had to spit it out on the ground. Tasted like they'd burned it.

ELDON. You won't spit this out. *(Buddy and Olive exit.)*

NETTA. Buddy, don't get in Nora's way out there. *(Sotto voce.)* She's about out of patience with Olive. Are those your dad's records?

ELDON. I'll say one thing, he's made it fun figuring out what he's been up to in there. Everything's in code and symbols and God knows what.

NETTA. He always did keep things pretty close to his chest.

ELDON. I love it, it's not like figuring someone's books, it's like doing a puzzle. I swear, if Dad went into town to buy a bottle of Coca-Cola, he'd write in the ledger: "One B CC, five cents."

NETTA. You'll have to ask him what some of—

ELDON. And spoil the fun? Not on your life.

NETTA. We don't know how much time—

ELDON. Besides, every time I ask him about anything, he goes senile on me. That's his new trick. Do you remember a Carl Saper? *(Netta shakes her head.)* Lottie?

LOTTIE. Let me in there, I'll burn the office and its contents.

ELDON. You ever heard of him?

LOTTIE. Just be sure you keep that door locked.

NETTA. Well, not to keep you out.

LOTTIE. That's right, you ask Olive what that means, she's probably got it all worked out.

NETTA. I'm sure nothing as piddlin' as a Yale padlock ever kept that one out of—well, nobody wants to hear mother-in-law talk. But yesterday she—

OLIVE. *(Entering.)* Mother!

NETTA. *(Jumps a foot.)* Oh, Olive! Scare me out of ten years' growth.

OLIVE. Did Granddaddy come through here?

ELDON. No, ma'am, we've been allowed to get something done without his supervision this afternoon.

OLIVE. I went in to see if he wanted to come to supper tonight; he isn't there. He isn't strong enough to go upstairs, is he?

NETTA. I looked in after dinner and he was dressed and sitting up. Told me to get out, so I got.

LOTTIE. He's come back to life out of contrariness.

OLIVE. Granddaddy?

NETTA. Lottie. *(Going off, calling.)* Mr. Talley?

BUDDY. *(Entering.)* He's not around to the side.

NETTA. *(Off.)* Well, this is absurd. Mr. Talley?

OLIVE. Dad, did you park the Packard in the drive when you came back from town.

ELDON. I took the pickup.

OLIVE. Well, where'd you leave the Packard?

ELDON. Same place I always—

OLIVE. 'Cause unless someone's moved it, I can't see it out there.

ELDON. It's right in front of the pickup.

OLIVE. Well, I'm sorry, but it isn't.

ELDON. Well now, blue eyes; don't fly off crazy. Emmet's probably washing it around behind the barn.

OLIVE. Emmet Young is sitting on his duff, like he always is, whittling a stick.

ELDON. *(Yelling out the window.)* Emmet! Emmet, come in here.

OLIVE. Someday somebody's gonna hold a stick-whittling contest; I'm gonna enter Emmet Young and make my fortune.

NETTA. *(Enters.)* Oh, good Lord, he couldn't have got up and taken that car off.

ELDON. He doesn't even know how to drive it; he doesn't know the shift.

NETTA. Maybe he's out to the barn to look at the horses.

ELDON. There's no insurance on the car with him drivin' it either.

BUDDY. There's not been a horse on the place since I was a kid.

NETTA. Tell him that, and tell him they don't skate down on the mill pond anymore.

ELDON. He remembers what he wants to. *(Emmet enters.)* Emmet, have you seen Dad since dinner time?

EMMET. Not since this morning. I been down to the pump house.

ELDON. You hear the car drive off? You see it?

EMMET. I had the auxiliary pump goin', I wouldn'ta heard nothin'.

ELDON. Well, look around and see if you can see the Packard. Damn it all. *(Emmet leaves.)*

NETTA. I better call Cliffy. Good Lord.

BUDDY. Don't bother the sheriff. I'll take the pickup and go along the road. We'll catch him.

OLIVE. Dad can do that. Or Emmet can go. *(Chasing after him.)* Buddy, we have to go up and look in on June. Well, then I'm coming along.

BUDDY. You're helping Nora cook supper, I thought. *(He exits.)*

OLIVE. Buddy Talley, I swear. You just got home, honey. You're only on leave for seventy-two hours. Honey! *(Storms back to the kitchen.)*

NETTA. She's going right back to that kitchen. Nora's going to flat quit on us. *(Everyone has left except Eldon and Lottie.)*

ELDON. I knew Dad was half senile, but I—*(Pause. He notices that Lottie is standing frozen, doubled over in pain.)* Are you in pain? *(Pause.)* I wish you'd let the others know you're sick. *(Pause.)* I wouldn't think it would be so painful. *(Pause.)* Is there…*(She shakes her head, catches her breath.)* Is it passing?

LOTTIE. *(Nods.)* Oh damn.

ELDON. Better?

LOTTIE. *(Blissfully, breathlessly.)* Oh! Gone! Gone completely. Blessed relief. Oh, wonderful. Oh, I'm walking on air. Nothing left of it at all.

ELDON. I wouldn't think it'd hurt so much.

LOTTIE. Oh, who knows anything about it. Oh my, I feel lovely. Oh, wonderful! It certainly is taking its time, isn't it?

ELDON. Enough of that.

LOTTIE. It's only pain, after all.

ELDON. When do you go back to see the doctors?

LOTTIE. I think they've lost interest. All the girls have kicked the bucket
except five of us. One of those is about to go, poor thing. The other four
of us are holding out on them. The doctors'd like to close the books,
publish their reports. We're not going to let them. We're in a race to
the...*(Laughing.)* Well, I was going to say to the bitter end. That's the
damned truth. *(Phone rings.)* That's for me.

NETTA. *(In the hall.)* I got it, Lottie.

LOTTIE. I'll get it. You know better than that. *(Standing in the hall, within
sight. Netta is out of sight.)*

NETTA. Hello.

LOTTIE. Who is it? Is that for me?

NETTA. Would you just sit down, Lottie, everything isn't for you. It's Cliffy.

LOTTIE. What's the sheriff doing calling here? Let me talk to him.

ELDON. Is Dad all right?

NETTA. Well, is he all right? We've been worried sick.

LOTTIE. I don't want you tying up the telephone here tonight.

NETTA. He's all right. They're bringing him back. Harley is. *(On the phone.)*
What say?

ELDON. You're quick enough when the phone rings.

LOTTIE. If that's my one pleasure, I don't want it denied me.

ELDON. Who's the secret admirer.

LOTTIE. I have my enjoyments.

ELDON. Lottie, with all those long-distance calls all winter, I hope you
haven't been talking to that Friedman character, trying to plead Sally's case.

NETTA. *(On the phone.)* We appreciate it.

LOTTIE. Eldon Talley, I don't know what you're talking about.

NETTA. Good-bye now. *(Coming into the parlor.)* He's all right.

ELDON. What happened?

NETTA. I don't know, Eldon. Cliffy says they're driving him back. *(Exits.)*

LOTTIE. With Olive sprucing up the parlor for his funeral, the least Dad
could do is oblige everybody by dying.

ELDON. I don't want to hear that, Lottie. We just count our blessings and
go on with what has to be done.

LOTTIE. What are you so feisty about tonight?

ELDON. Nothing at all. Maybe I'm excited about Timmy coming home, having Buddy here. Work agrees with me. I guess I'm not the martyr you are.

LOTTIE. Me? Shit. If that clock company hadn't gone out of business, I'd have sued them for every dime they had. Made a bundle. When did ol' Marie Curie kick the bucket? Ten years ago, bless her, or I'd sue her, too. 'Course ol' Marie didn't tell us to point the brushes with our tongues.

ELDON. Oh, come on.

LOTTIE. Give you the willies? Every one of us did it. Had a little pot of radium paint to paint the clock dials with. Point the brush on our tongues, dip it in the little pot of radium paint, paint a number, point the brush on our little tongues.

ELDON. Come on, now, just shut up about it.

LOTTIE. What did we know about radium poisoning? The foreman told us not to. Thought it was unsanitary. Gave us little sponges for the purpose. Only one girl used it that I know of. Didn't like the taste. Hell, I couldn't tell it had any. 'Course, she went too—poor baby. Cancer of the bone.

ELDON. Oh, God.

LOTTIE. Well, Eldon, that's the rewards of a delicate palate. *(Olive runs to front door and out. Timmy follows her.)*

NETTA. *(Entering.)* They're pulling up out front. Harley brought him back.

ELDON. Where the devil had he got to?

NETTA. He did, he took the Packard. Harley's driving him back in it. *(She exits again.)*

BUDDY. *(Entering.)* Harley's got him. Looks like he's OK; they're bringing him in. You never saw anything like it.

NETTA. *(Off.)* Come on, back up, here we go.

OLIVE. *(Off.)* Upsy-daisy!

HARLEY. *(Off.)* I tell you, he is a cuss!

TALLEY. *(Off.)* Wooo! Oh boy.

HARLEY. Wooo, I bet! You shoulda seen it. I was—*(Entering with Talley, Netta, and Olive)*—just driving by; I saw the car had run into a ditch up at the hill. I thought—

ELDON. Is he all right?

HARLEY. —What the hell's going on—excuse me, Netta. Oh, he's fine. Old man Talley's got more guts than an army mule. Ain't ya?

TALLEY. Who? Who?

HARLEY. He's been sayin' that all the way. I parked my car, got out, and there he was up on the hill—dressed for the dead of winter, standing in the middle of the graveyard. Caretaker—*(Netta and Olive say, "Oh my Lord," "Oh no.")*—said he'd been taking up one spot and looking around, then moving to another spot. Admiring his site, maybe.

BUDDY. Selecting his site, maybe.

NETTA. Oh, his place is all laid out.

ELDON. He's right by Momma.

TALLEY. Who? Say who?

NETTA. He's overexcited.

OLIVE. You don't want to stay here, Granddaddy. You want to go into your room?

TALLEY. Here, you! Blamed woman. Let me be. Who? Say who?

NETTA. What, Mr. Talley?

TALLEY. Who?

HARLEY. Sounds like a goddamned owl.

NETTA. Harley, don't be disrespectful. This is still Mr. Talley's house.

TALLEY. Blamed woman, get her off me.

ELDON. He's not hurt none.

OLIVE. I've never seen him so rambunctious.

HARLEY. Shoot no, try to hurt him.

TALLEY. Who?

ELDON. What kind of shape is the car in?

NETTA. He doesn't hear. Mr. Talley, you want to go? You want to go to your room?

HARLEY. It drives good. That's the miracle. I don't think he knows where the brake is on it.

OLIVE. Granddaddy? You want to go?

TALLEY. Blamed woman.

ELDON. He doesn't know how to drive it at all; he doesn't know the shift.

HARLEY. Run it into a ditch to stop it; might be scratched up. *(Eldon exits.)*

NETTA. The important thing is, he's not hurt.

HARLEY. Son-of-a-gun, you opened up the parlor. They're really putting on the dog for you.

TALLEY. Fine room.

HARLEY. Yes, sir, beautiful room.

TALLEY. Fine room. Chair. Chair.

NETTA. Help him to his chair, Buddy.

OLIVE. Here you go, Granddaddy.

TALLEY. Get me to sit down. What? Who?

NETTA. This morning he was sharp as a tack. He went into his office.

HARLEY. It's good to see old Buddy, isn't it? All dressed up like a soldier. I thought you'd be in civvies for one day at least.

OLIVE. You're always in the service, Harley. You know that.

HARLEY. I didn't know I was gonna be impressed or I'd have prepared myself.

OLIVE. Uncle Sam may need you at any time, night or day.

BUDDY. And he ain't the only one.

TALLEY. Who? Oh boy. *(Smiles, grunts.)* Oh boy. *(Smiles, grunts.)* Oh boy.

NETTA. What's that, Mr. Talley? Oh no. No, Papa, not here. Oh dear, Olive, help me get him into the bathroom—Oh, Mr. Talley. Oh no.

HARLEY. Wooooee! Oh boy, for sure.

BUDDY. Well, Momma said, "It's his house."

HARLEY. Netta, you said, "Do you want to go?" and he went.

OLIVE. Both of you, now.

NETTA. Don't you laugh.

HARLEY. Never in my life seen a man so pleased with himself.

NETTA. *(She and Olive have moved Talley to the door. They stop.)* Mr. Talley? No? Well, come on. Wait. Don't you laugh, you'll be like this someday. I think that was a false alarm. Do you want to go to the bathroom?

TALLEY. Chair.

NETTA. He's fine. He's been gassy is all. Don't you laugh.

ELDON. *(Entering.)* Whole side of the car is scratched from front to back.

NETTA. Don't you want to take off your coat?

OLIVE. Are you too warm?

TALLEY. Who?

NETTA. What does he think I'm saying?

OLIVE. Aren't you too warm?

HARLEY. I haven't seen a coat of that quality in twenty years.

NETTA. Oh, he was always a dresser.

OLIVE. Weren't you, Mr. Talley?

TALLEY. Hey, hey. Let me go! Blamed. Blamed. *(Olive has got Mr. Talley's overcoat off him.)*

BUDDY. Look at that suit material.

OLIVE. Well, it wouldn't hurt you to have one good suit. When you own the garment factory in town, you might as well dress like it.

HARLEY. Shoot—nothing like this ever came out of Lebanon. One hundred percent cashmere, made by hand in Boston. Him and Dad both thought they were hot stuff. Only good it did Dad was give him something fancy to be buried in.

NETTA. It isn't just show.

HARLEY. Wait till you see me tonight. I'm gonna put on the dog for you.

OLIVE. Everybody's gonna look their best tonight.

ELDON. That's the nicest bonus of having the boys back—the girls all show them a little leg.

OLIVE. Dad.

ELDON. You wouldn't know it to look at her tonight, but Olive is often as not in men's trousers when you're not here.

BUDDY. She's wearing what?

OLIVE. They're slacks and you're never gonna see me in them.

BUDDY. Good.

ELDON. That's one thing we're not gonna manufacture down at the plant.

HARLEY. No, sir.

BUDDY. Shorts and halters maybe.

ELDON. Now that's something we might consider.

OLIVE. Nobody in this town would wear those, I hope.

BUDDY. Oh, I could name a couple.

ELDON. I bet you could.

TALLEY. Who?

BUDDY. Olive, I thought you aired out the room, I swear it still has a smell.

(Harley whispers something to Eldon.)

NETTA. Now! You. That's the coal furnace; the room's been closed up since last winter.

ELDON. I remember when I was a boy, we heated with wood. The whole house when you came into it had that wonderful smell of wood smoke. I always—

TALLEY. No, sir.

ELDON. What say, Dad? I think he's calming down.

TALLEY. Said coal. This house was fired by a coal furnace. Bought and paid for it myself. School was coal, church was coal, City Hall was coal. Me and Elijah Scott bought a half interest in the delivery service. Talley place got a new furnace, everybody in town had to have one.

ELDON. Well then, what am I remembering?

TALLEY. You're remembering laying with one of your floozies out in her daddy's smokehouse.

LOTTIE. Yes, he's calmed down to normal.

HARLEY. I think.

TALLEY. You're thinking of some roadhouse speakeasy. Contracted for the school delivery, contracted for the Municipal Building... Me and my brother, Whistler, gave that river land for a park to the city. Gave it free and clear.

HARLEY. Yes, sir, and you've had the whole town by the gonads ever since.

TALLEY. Yes, sir. Knew it at the time. So did they. Sit down Mr. Campbell. I can't look up.

HARLEY. Yes, sir. That old boy used to scare the tar outta me.

BUDDY. I love him. General Clark put me on a plane to get me back for Granddad's funeral; I get here and look at him—ornery as an ox.

ELDON. We just count our blessings, Buddy, and go on with what has to be done.

HARLEY. Hey, I saw that Jew's dilapidated old Plymouth.

ELDON. The hell you say.

HARLEY. Parked down the way.

ELDON. If I thought he was still on the property, I'd go out hunting.

HARLEY. Looks like he'd run outta gas, pushed it off the road.

BUDDY. Don't get excited, Aunt Lottie, he's long gone now.

LOTTIE. I'm sure he is, thanks to you.

HARLEY. So that's Sally's new beau.

BUDDY. Yeah, isn't he a prize?

HARLEY. She sure can pick 'em.

LOTTIE. You two, I'm gonna get out that broom.

HARLEY. Listen, I got to go to the draft board yet; this stop wasn't on my schedule. I still haven't had a chance to go home and change my clothes, wash up.

NETTA. You look fine.

HARLEY. No, I said. A big dinner like you got planned, Mary Jo would have a conniption if we didn't dress up and turn out.

ELDON. I'm not used to these fancy late-supper parties.

NETTA. Not with the family, anyway.

BUDDY. That's right, Dad. I'm about starved.

HARLEY. *(Sotto voce.)* Occasion like this, might break out some of that old Prohibition stump water you used to run.

ELDON. Come on now, what the old man don't know won't hurt him. That was in my greener years.

HARLEY. I remember it had a pretty potent kick.

ELDON. Not at all, now, not at all. Sometimes we let that age ten or fifteen minutes.

OLIVE. The women didn't hear that.

HARLEY. So, you guys had a chance to talk about that Delaware Industries offer? You read those brochures I left you?

BUDDY. I looked at the pictures.

ELDON. He was just telling me how he didn't know anything about it.

BUDDY. Only what you wrote me, Dad, that's what I know. And what Mom was tellin' me out in the kitchen.

NETTA. Buddy, now. No factory talk, and none tonight, or the women will just leave you sitting at the table.

HARLEY. I think it's beautiful. 'Course I don't know the first thing about it, to hear Eldon.

BUDDY. I'm always willing to listen.

OLIVE. She's not joking now.

HARLEY. O.K., O.K. *(Lighting a cigarette, gives Buddy one.)*

OLIVE. Harley Campbell and Kenneth Talley! You two, if you want to smoke a cigarette, you step outside or into another room. Mother'll have your hide.

HARLEY. Son-of-a-gun, I clean forgot.

OLIVE. Oh, I'm sure. I'm not kidding now!

HARLEY. I know, I know. What a bossy woman. Come on. I don't know how you put up with her.

BUDDY. Oh, I need it. Keeps me in step. *(Olive chases them out the French doors.)*

OLIVE. You can't tell me Mary Jo allows you to smoke in the parlor, I don't care how modern you are. *(Lottie lights a cigarette, Olive exits.)*

NETTA. She's going right back to that kitchen. She's already put so much spice in that pie, the devil himself couldn't eat it.

ELDON. That was a pretty clever maneuver to get Buddy outside. What's he telling him out there?

NETTA. Eldon, I'd like it to be peaceful this evening. Nothing can be decided till Timmy gets home, anyway.

ELDON. I know that. Tell Buddy. Tell Harley.

NETTA. You can all talk on Thursday. I don't want you and Buddy in an argument. *(She exits.)*

ELDON. I know.

TALLEY. All gone. All gone. You. Sally. Answer up when you're spoke to.

ELDON. That's Lottie, Dad.

TALLEY. We all of us got to go, young lady. You scared of going?

LOTTIE. Well, I'm hoping not to see you there, Daddy, wherever it is. *(She looks to Eldon.)*

ELDON. I didn't say anything.

TALLEY. I ain't. Ain't anxious; ain't scared. I've lived a good, clean, Christian life.

LOTTIE. If there's a heaven, Daddy, you'll burn in hell.

ELDON. That's not called for.

TALLEY. Charlotte Talley, besides painting numbers on fifty-cent watches, what have you done? Run off to be independent, come hangdoggin' it back ten years later—

LOTTIE. Thirteen. And if there'd been another place to go—

ELDON. She got sick, Dad.

TALLEY. Stood right here on this carpet with her college certificate in her hand and called me a curmudgeon. Said she was going off to work among the poor people. Didn't like being rich. Ended up painting clock faces in a factory in Connecticut. That place closed down and where did she go? Speak up. Chicago. Working in some socialist outfit. Trying to teach something to the colored kids. Guess they couldn't stomach her either, 'cause the first thing you know, here she comes back again.

LOTTIE. I stayed in Chicago until I got too weak to work. And it's the only time I've been of any use to anybody.

TALLEY. And what you got to show for it?

LOTTIE. More than you could imagine.

TALLEY. Come hangdoggin' it back, looking for the curmudgeon to feed you. Fine family I raised; fine children, the two of you.

LOTTIE. I'm not going to have a conversation with you, Daddy; I choose the people I talk to.

TALLEY. Comes a time in a man's life he totals it all up; adds it all up. I go and the place goes to blazes.

ELDON. We'll just have to do the best we can. *(Low.)* If we ever get the chance.

LOTTIE. Amen. He's not afraid of going because he doesn't think he will.

ELDON. He may not, Lottie, he may not. He's never made a will... He's used a different lawyer for every transaction. Did you know he owns half the Bassett Farm?

LOTTIE. He's probably got something on Leslie Bassett, the poor bugger.

TALLEY. Place has gone to the devil.

ELDON. The Bassett farm? Did Leslie take out a mortgage from you?

TALLEY. Talley place, I say. Wouldn't invite a dog in here. All going to the devil without me.

ELDON. Dad, with the war on, everything is run down. *(Low, where Talley can't hear.)* And you are still very much with us.

TALLEY. Yes, I am, sir, and you'll learn to respect the fact. If Stuart had lived, you'da seen something.

LOTTIE. Oh boy.

ELDON. Just don't start that, Dad.

TALLEY. Day Stuart was born I changed that factory name to Talley & Son. It wasn't named for you, I can tell you.

ELDON. I know. And from the day Stuart died you never set foot in the place.

TALLEY. Look at you with that ledger. You go in that office, all those papers, you know what you'd do? You'd alphabetize them.

ELDON. Well, that's more than you've done. What does that signify? Can't even read it. Carl Saper, December 1913. *(Talley laughs.)* What's funny? Is he laughing or crying?

TALLEY. Well, sir. Old Carl Saper had thirty acres' wild land. Had eighty-five black-walnut trees on it. Wasn't worth nothin.'

LOTTIE. But you took it away from him anyway, didn't you, Daddy?

TALLEY. No, lady.

LOTTIE. From Carl and Ruth both.

TALLEY. No, sir. Loaned him a bundle, mortgaged the land. Nine thousand dollars, fifteen years. Dern fool tried to raise geese. Didn't know the first thing about it. Feathers everywhere. Said he couldn't pay that year. Couldn't pay the interest, couldn't pay the principal; said, "Don't take the land away, leave the land in my name and take the walnuts for payment. Black walnuts sellin' for forty cents a gunnysack, hulled." Well, sir, I went down there, looked the place over, said, "Next year you pay, this year what I can make off that thirty acres of bottom land is mine." Wrote it out, notarized by Norma Ann Comstock. Had the colored boys from Old Town pick up the walnuts, haul 'em to the exchange. Called a company in Minneapolis, Minnesota; they came here, cut down the walnut trees for fancy lumber to make veneer out of 'em. I made eleven thousand dollars off that no-count wild land in 19 and 13. Told old Saper, now you got good pasture land. I should charge you for clearing it. Fool tried to sue me. Hadn't read the paper. Read what you sign, I told him. Use your eyes. Know the worth of a thing. *(He laughs.)*

LOTTIE. *(Without looking up.)* Is he laughing or crying?

ELDON. Just when you think his mind is gone, it's back.

TALLEY. Dern fool sold at a loss not to sell to the Talleys. See what's happening and happen first.

LOTTIE and ELDON. *(With Talley.)*...happen first.

TALLEY. Eldon never looked up from his bookkeeping. Start keeping books, you end up keeping books.

ELDON. I don't keep books, sir. I have a girl who does that for me, and she has an assistant now.

TALLEY. Only thing you ever did on your own was run whiskey to St. Louis during Prohibition.

ELDON. You'll find I've done a little better lately. My factory is worth double what your bank is.

TALLEY. Thought I didn't know how you was enhancing the Talley name with your whores.

ELDON. I don't spend half the week at church shaking hands with all my neighbors and the other half at the bank foreclosing on their mortgages, no. My factory is putting out the best quality pair of army fatigues made anywhere, no thanks to you, and after the war Timmy and I intend—

TALLEY. Fine children. Get me up. Up.

ELDON. All right. Don't listen; you never did.

TALLEY. Won't have it. Fine children. Up. Up. Get me to my room, blamed. Blamed.

ELDON. *(Over.)* Here, don't go alone; wait and I'll help you.

VIOLA. *(Entering.)* Excuse me, Mr. Eldon. Everybody was around to the kitchen, so I came to the front.

TALLEY. If you had any gumption, you'd tell those Delaware boys to soak their heads. Got no gumption.

ELDON. I did, thank you, and it's no business of yours.

VIOLA. I knocked, I couldn't get nobody to hear. I didn't want to wake up the baby again.

LOTTIE. Come on into the room.

TALLEY. Who?

VIOLA. Mr. Eldon, could I have a minute of your time?

ELDON. *(Moving Talley to the door.)* I can't talk now.

VIOLA. This is important to you, Mr. Eldon.

TALLEY. Me and Elijah Scott got a furnace; everybody in town had to have one...

VIOLA. Eldon. *(Pause.)* If I could just—talk to you a minute.

ELDON. Not right now, Viola. This isn't a good time. Or place.

TALLEY. Who's here?

VIOLA. I gotta tell you something.

ELDON. Fine, come to the factory on Friday or next Monday, talk to Mrs. Willy. *(He and Talley leave.)*

VIOLA. Well…I guess I been put in my place. The Talley's was always good at that.

LOTTIE. Sit down, Viola, before you fall.

VIOLA. I walked from the house; one of the boys took the truck. Is that Mr. Eldon's boy out there with Mr. Campbell?

LOTTIE. Yes, that's Kenneth. Worked at Dad's bank before the war.

VIOLA. Shoot, when was I ever in your bank? He looks good in his uniform. The young'un's a sailor, ain't he?

LOTTIE. Timmy's in the Marines; out in the Pacific. He'll be back day after tomorrow.

VIOLA. I remember Timmy from the garment factory. All them sailors over fighting in their white uniforms. I wouldn't want to do their laundry.

LOTTIE. I don't imagine.

VIOLA. *(Sighs, sits.)* No, Miss Charlotte. I tell you, I'm plum might worn frazzled this evening. I didn't get no sleep. I was up with the twins.

LOTTIE. Twins? I don't remember you having twins.

VIOLA. Oh, Lord help me, that's all I'd need. Mrs. Niewonker's two. I'm taking care of them while she's at the hospital having another one. Avalaine didn't come home and I couldn't get my boys to help.

LOTTIE. That's not men's work, I know.

VIOLA. Hell, ain't nothin' men's work to hear them tell it. Avie's the worker. Just last month she and me washed down the whole Farley house. 'Course now she's run off.

LOTTIE. Avalaine run off? Where to?

VIOLA. Who with is more like it. Who knows. She just took off, off and took. Seventeen years old, looks twenty-five. She was hanging down to the roll arena and around the Blue Line.

LOTTIE. What the hell is the Blue Line?

VIOLA. Roadhouse. A mile outside of town.

LOTTIE. Well, if you're worried, you want me to call Cliffy for you?

VIOLA. Oh hell, Lottie. I told her to go. I said, you fly away on. Fly away on. There ain't nothin' here. Don't talk to me about opportunity. It's all the same. You're workin' for the Talleys or you're working for the Campbells or you're working for the Farleys. You fly away on and don't slow down to say I'm leavin'. *(Laughing.)* And I guess she didn't.

LOTTIE. I guess not.

VIOLA. Can't blame 'em for doin' what you told 'em to do.

HARLEY. *(Entering with Buddy.)* It's clearing up. I swear this morning it looked like it was gonna rain like pourin' piss out of a boot. Oh, Lord, excuse me, ladies, I didn't know you was in here.

VIOLA. *(Pause.)* Well, none of that work is gonna finish itself.

HARLEY. Viola, I thought the service for Vaughan was very well handled.

VIOLA. Thank you, Mr. Campbell. I appreciate it. And thank you for coming by personally with the telegram. Mom appreciated it.

NETTA. *(Entering.)* Viola, did you need something else?

VIOLA. No, nothin', thank you.

LOTTIE. I'll tell Eldon.

VIOLA. No, don't trouble him about me. I'll come by the office like he said. I shouldn've known not to come up to the house. All you have a nice evening, now.

LOTTIE. You, too, Mrs. Platt. *(Viola exits.)*

HARLEY. I was down at their place, you never seen people living in conditions like that; all the windows wide open to the outside; flies thick as freckles on a turkey's egg.

LOTTIE. You're a rich man, Harley. You ought to send them some screen wire if you're so concerned.

HARLEY. Old man Platt would have it sold and drunk up before nightfall. I was the one took the telegram to her mother, said her son was killed. None of 'em can read. I had to read it to them.

BUDDY. That ain't easy. Who was he?

LOTTIE. Viola's brother. Vaughan.

NETTA. Vaughan Robinson.

HARLEY. Older than you, worked at the garage. Used to pitch for the softball. Lord, I'll tell you, I'd rather be over there fighting than back here bringing the word.

BUDDY. It isn't anything you have to do.

HARLEY. No, I do. I figure if I'm on the draft board helping to send you all over there, then when the telegram comes. I'm the one who should bring it to the family. I don't know. I started doing it, now people expect it. I'd a whole lot rather be in the middle of it over there with you.

BUDDY. I'm not in the middle of it. From what I read in the paper, says France is the middle of it.

HARLEY. We were all watching Anzio this winter, I can tell you. That didn't sound any too good.

BUDDY. Yeah, got pretty cold. We hadn't expected that.

NETTA. We all thought it was going to be another Corregidor.

BUDDY. No, no, it rained, there was a lot of mud. Did you worry about me, Aunt Lottie?

LOTTIE. Yes. I still do.

BUDDY. Well, don't.

NETTA. There's no hope of getting anything out of Buddy. Timmy's letters are full of the jungle and what everything is like. All we get out of Buddy is, "Well, there's not much to write." *(Eldon enters.)*

BUDDY. It's darn boring most of the time. Harley ought to be glad he's here with something to do.

NETTA. The washerwoman was just here looking for you.

ELDON. From what we read, it sounded like the Krauts had you guys in some kind of pincer action about half the time—

BUDDY. No, no, 'course it's a heck of a lot different from what it looks like from home. Half those guys Harley's so hot to join over there are gonna be killed and the other half would go AWOL if they had the chance. *(Timmy enters.)* So how's business on the home front, Dad? Harley says we're still making a killing down there.

ELDON. I don't know if you could say that.

HARLEY. Hell, we don't even sleep anymore. We're both of us down there twelve hours a day.

BUDDY. You still personally inspecting every pair of fatigues that goes out of the place?

ELDON. I am, yes, rejecting one out of five 'cause we've taken on more than we can handle.

TIMMY. Hey, Dad, you know what?

NETTA. Come on now, you can talk about this after supper.

ELDON. We're not going to talk about anything, honey, till Timmy gets home.

HARLEY. Hell, Timmy'll make enough off this deal to start up a shop of his own if he loves it so much.

ELDON. Well, that factory's more Timmy's concern than any of ours. I've always figured Buddy'd want the bank and the factory'd go to Timmy. As far as I'm concerned, Sally gets nothing unless she changes her tune.

BUDDY. Shoot, the sooner Sally just waltzes on out of here, the happier everybody will be.

HARLEY. Especially with the sort she's been hanging around with lately. *(Lottie stomps out of the room.)*

ELDON. I think the Talleys got to have one in every generation.

NETTA. You know how she is about Sally. She's tried to influence that girl since the day she was born.

HARLEY. Well, I'd like to include Timmy and everybody, too, but it's the Fourth of July and we got till the tenth. That's cutting it a bit close for comfort.

BUDDY. Who the heck is Delaware Industries, anyway. I never heard of them.

HARLEY. You know all their products.

ELDON. It doesn't matter, I tell you, it's not gonna happen.

HARLEY. You know everything they make. I can't think of one right off the bat.

ELDON. Country Oven Bread.

HARLEY. Country Oven Bread.

ELDON. Baked in Pittsburgh.

NETTA. Tastes like it, too.

HARLEY. They started out as an insurance company.

ELDON. That tells you right there how far they can be trusted.

HARLEY. Used to be in Delaware, now they've moved to Baton Rouge.

ELDON. That's interesting, too. Delaware Industries, Baton Rouge, Louisiana. Man said they had a company that baked bread, had a company that made coils for a car, owned natural gas in Kansas and Oklahoma. I said to the man, "It used to be a fellow was in the business of making something. When someone asks me what business I'm in, I say, "As long as the war's on, Talley & Son is in the business of making army fatigues." What business do you say you're in?" And the man says, "Well, we're in the business of making money."

HARLEY. Nobody told me we didn't want to turn a profit down there.

ELDON. Harley, I love you like a son, but I'm not going to get into this argument with you.

BUDDY. I don't know what they want with us, anyway.

HARLEY. Well, see, they're starting reconversion plans for postwar production.

BUDDY. Whoa!

HARLEY. That may sound a little funny to a soldier.

BUDDY. No, heck, I see it, everybody's looking ahead; you'd be a fool not to.

ELDON. And, looking ahead, we put in an order, which was Timmy's idea by the way.

HARLEY. The timing maybe, who's to say whose idea it was?

TIMMY. Harley was dead set against it.

ELDON. Soon as the war is over, three thousand bolts of nylon will be coming to us every week.

BUDDY. I thought you couldn't get it.

HARLEY. The Du Ponts needed the money, if you can believe it, and we had it that day.

ELDON. If you can't buy the nylon, take over the company that has it, next best thing.

BUDDY. Heck, better.

HARLEY. Hell, yes; excuse me, Netta. We have them over a goddamn barrel.

BUDDY. Excuse him, Mom. Where did these jokers come from?

HARLEY. We've only been working for them for three years.

ELDON. As of last January, Harley's got us working their orders a hundred percent.

HARLEY. You think a jerkwater outfit like us could get a war contract?

ELDON. No, they got the executives, they got the lobby in Washington, they got the credit, they got the pull, and they got the contract! And they do not own a single darned sewing machine. Everything is subcontracted to a bunch of dummies like us.

HARLEY. But now they've got the government to build them a plant down in Louisiana so they can get the whole operation under one roof.

ELDON. Now if that's not slicker than snot on a doorknob, I don't know what is.

BUDDY. I'm sorry, Dad, I don't see your point.

HARLEY. He thinks they're going to take over his name and turn out crap.

ELDON. I do, yes; among other things, I do. And it may be old-fashioned to have pride in the product that has the name Talley & Son on it—

HARLEY. I can't make him understand they don't want his damned name either.

ELDON. I didn't build something up to have it torn down. And Timmy is expecting that factory to be there for him when he gets out, and it's gonna be there!

HARLEY. Eldon, I tell you I'm tired! I tell you when Dad shot himself, I went right from the graveyard to the factory without changing clothes and cut pants till after midnight, was back on the job at six the next morning—thirteen years ago, and I haven't let up yet. Didn't even have time to order a marker for Dad's grave. Now, it killed him, but it's not going to kill me. *(Pause.)*

ELDON. Maybe we all should take a month off after the war; start treating ourselves.

NETTA. There's a stone now.

ELDON. Honey.

HARLEY. What say?

NETTA. On your dad's grave.

HARLEY. Oh, I know. I went back five years later, somebody had put up a stone. Must have been Mom. Made for the both of them, her birth date already cut into it. She's all the time afraid someone might say they had to spend a nickel on her. Thinks we're still living in the Depression. I gotta go.

NETTA. She's a good—

TALLEY. *(Entering.)* Blame it, blame it.

OLIVE. *(Trailing him.)* Granddaddy, don't you want to lie down?

NETTA. What's he doing up?

OLIVE. He came through the kitchen. I thought he was trying to head back to the Packard.

BUDDY. Olive.

OLIVE. Well, is he all right?

TALLEY. Blamed woman. Stop houndin' me. Whole blamed family buzzing like a swarm of gnats in here.

HARLEY. Eldon, I didn't work any harder than you and Tim, but I'm about due for that vacation.

ELDON. You go with Delaware and you retire completely. They don't want any of us down there.

TALLEY. Buzz, buzz, buzz, buzz…

OLIVE. I thought they offered you and Harley and Buddy an executive job as—

ELDON. Boy, everybody in the family has to put in their two cents. They offered me and Harley and Timmy, and Buddy, I guess, if he wants it, a position on their board of directors or board of— What is it?

HARLEY. Advisory board.

ELDON. Which means our names in a list on their stationery. For what it's worth, Harley, that place has been my life. And it's going to be Timmy's life.

NETTA. Eldon.

ELDON. Well, honey, what else, except for my family, have I had?

NETTA. I wouldn't know.

BUDDY. They want to move the plant to Louisiana?

HARLEY. The machines sure, use the building here for a warehouse.

NETTA. What would happen to all the girls who work down there? Where would they go?

HARLEY. Oh, good Lord, Netta; they'd go to Louisiana. Hell, excuse me, damn it, they're—excuse me—riffraff anyway. Divorced women, unmarried mothers. The town would be better off without them.

NETTA. Now you're sounding like Mr. Talley.

HARLEY. Well, it's about time somebody did.

TALLEY. Never did care. Never did. No interest in that factory down there. Tell you why.

ELDON. Oh, Lord.

HARLEY. 'Cause you was having too much fun down at the bank.

TALLEY. Sir, when I'm talking.

HARLEY. Yes, sir.

TALLEY. Tell you why. Moral corruption. Never trusted those women. Broken homes and moral weakness. Just like others I could mention.

ELDON. But won't.

TALLEY. Sir, they're a bunch of no-goods making pants for another bunch of no-goods who are somewhere making shirts for the first no-goods. Scum of the earth.

ELDON. Right, Dad. You want to go to your room?

TALLEY. Harley, my boy, you'd do well, sir, to remember who the head of the Talley household is.

ELDON. You hear that? He's as lucid as a windowpane when he wants to be.

HARLEY. Boy, am I late for everything. Listen, I got to go to the draft-board people, I'm miles late.

BUDDY. They'll be closed by now.

HARLEY. Hell, the telegraph office doesn't close now till eleven.

NETTA. You be back here by eight and don't forget.

HARLEY. I'm gonna be busier than a cat with two tails till then, let me tell you.

BUDDY. I'll run you into town.

OLIVE. Buddy.

BUDDY. It'll only take five minutes to drop him at the Laclede Hotel and be back.

OLIVE. We have to check on June, remember?

BUDDY. The telegraph office still at the hotel building?

HARLEY. No, no, I'll borrow your pickup, if that's all right?

ELDON. Sure, take it.

BUDDY. No trouble.

OLIVE. Buddy!

BUDDY. June's all right. Oh. Maybe I'd better.

HARLEY. Yeah, you check up on little June and maybe talk about getting her a little brother.

ELDON. We'll thrash this out; you'll see the light. *(He walks Harley to the door.)*

BUDDY. Honey, you want to come upstairs and check up on June? Maybe check up on Kenny, Jr., while we're at it.

OLIVE. Oh! You!

ELDON. *(Returning.)* Buddy, we're expecting your support on this.

BUDDY. Yes, sir. I know, sir. *(He and Olive exit.)*

TALLEY. Old Whistler up there singing his songs.

NETTA. What's he talking about?

ELDON. The graveyard, I guess. Had an adventure, didn't you?

TALLEY. Yes, sir. Drove the Packard. Good driving car.

ELDON. Dad, do you think you can come into the office now. There's things we should go over.

TALLEY. Singing *"Una furtiva lagrima."*

ELDON. Boy, you hear what you want to, don't you?

NETTA. Don't get him upset.

ELDON. Sure.

NETTA. Eldon, this business deal isn't more important than keeping peace in the family.

ELDON. I know. *(Netta exits.)*

TIMMY. Dad?

ELDON. Dad?

TALLEY. Still going at it. Talkin' a blue streak.

TIMMY. Yes, sir, your brother Whistler was going a blue streak and you were answering him right back. Caretaker thought he had a madman on his hands, didn't he? *(To Eldon.)* What I want to tell you, sir—remember how you always said, "It makes a difference when you do something right?" Well, what I didn't know was everybody wasn't doing it the way we were. I didn't know we were anything special. But then—*(To audience.)* See, the Marines get real cocky about what they look like—if you're on ship, you dress sharp. And they try to fit you right on your first issue at least. But those fatigues leave the factory about as stiff as a cardboard, so the guys all try to break them down, soften them up; then they iron a crease in them. So, once about a dozen of the guys tied their new fatigues to a hook and dragged them along behind the ship for about a week. They came out of that salt water soft as a chamois cloth. Only most of them had shrunk about an inch. I told the guys my dad's factory must of made the ones that hadn't shrunk 'cause we always shrink the material before we cut it. Dad, you know what? They ironed them out, put them on, and in the pocket of every good pair they found a little wadded-up strip of paper that said "Inspected by E. Talley." I was real popular, for about a week. *(To Eldon.)* I knew you'd like to hear that. But, Dad, I spent my whole life lookin' for things that I knew you'd like. All the time I spent down at Talley & Son, since I was eleven, was just so you'd notice me.

ELDON. Dad?

TIMMY. He really is asleep this time, he isn't just playing possum. *(Eldon goes into the office. Timmy looks out the window.)* Oh boy! Here comes trouble. *(Avalaine Platt steps into the room through the French doors.)*

AVALAINE. Mr. Talley. Mr. Talley. Is Mr. Eldon in? *(Pause. She realizes he isn't going to speak. She walks to the front hall door, listens. There is a noise from the kitchen. Avalaine goes past Talley to the back door and listens. Timmy has gone.)*

TALLEY. Whistler won't shut up. *(Avalaine whirls around and looks at him.)* Dead and buried, still won't quit yammering. *(Avalaine looks around the room; Talley does not seem to know she is there. After a second she sits across the room from him, staring.)* Old Whistler up there whistling, telling his tales. Can't hear yourself think.

AVALAINE. There you sit, you petrified old stick. You don't have a brain left in you evil old head, do you? You'd think the devil would come and collect his own before you became an embarrassment. Emmet said you was crazy half the time. I didn't believe it. *(Pause.)* Who is it that's going to tell the mayor and the Town Hall how to run their business now? *(Pause.)* I used to think you went stalking through Old Town at midnight, stealing babies to eat for breakfast. *(She stands.)* You're just a dried-up old stick, ain't ya? *(She walks to him.)* Ain't ya? Just a dried-up old horse. *(She tickles him on the ear.)* Ain't ya? Huh? *(Talley sits still for a moment. Then with one swift move he slaps her across the mouth, knocking her flat to the floor.)*

TALLEY. There! Got ya! Ha!

AVALAINE. You son-of-a-bitch.

TALLEY. Get her out of here. *(She yells in pain. From several places throughout the house people call, "What's going on?" Eldon opens the door from the office.)*

ELDON. Jesus Christ!

NETTA. *(Off.)* What in the deuce is going on?

ELDON. *(Overlapping.)* Never mind, I'll take care of this. This isn't for you. *(Closes door.)* You better go on down the road to you mother, Avalaine, she's looking for you.

AVALAINE. You think you got her and everybody else under your thumb, don't ya? Nobody dare say nothin'.

OLIVE. *(Looking in.)* Dad, what's going on?

ELDON. Just close that door there and never mind. *(She does. Talley goes into the office.)* You just go on now, you can go across the fields. *(Avalaine holds her hand to her face. Her nose is bleeding.)*

AVALAINE. That son-of-a-bitch broke my nose.

ELDON. I'm not going to call the sheriff, because you're going to go home now.

AVALAINE. Well, I'll tell you, Mr. Eldon, I've stayed with my mother's family for seventeen years; I got to thinkin' it's time I moved up here to live with my daddy.

ELDON. It wouldn't do for you to say anything against the Talleys, Avalaine.

AVALAINE. You thought Ma wouldn't tell me about you and her.

ELDON. Whatever you've been told, there's nothing to tell. I'm surprised you'd believe lies like that. *(Olive and Netta open the doors.)*

NETTA. I said, what's going on?

ELDON. Just stay out of here. *(He closes the doors.)*

AVALAINE. As it happens, since Buddy Talley practically raped me last time he was home…

ELDON. I won't have you interfering with Buddy's life, and you're not going to interfere here with the Talleys.

AVALAINE. And since he come by the house to ask me to go into the woods with him last night, my ma thought it best to tell me as how Buddy Talley was my part-brother.

ELDON. That's not true, Avalaine, and I know you mother wouldn't say it.

AVALAINE. She thought she'd better let me know so's I don't conceive no two-headed bastards, both of us being your kids.

ELDON. I've heard all I'm listening to. You get out now.

AVALAINE. I tell you what, Papa. The Talleys are well treated in this town. I come up the hill to get my own. I figger you owe me my piece of all this.

ELDON. Avalaine Platt, the entire town knows you're a whore for sale to any buyer. Our own handyman, Emmet Young, has as much as told me—

AVALAINE. No more, no more, Papa, no more. I done what was necessary, but it ain't necessary no more, is it?

ELDON. You better go on down the hill, Avalaine. I'll talk to your mother. If you people are in trouble, maybe the Talleys can help. Now, you better just go back down the hill and I won't call Cliffy on you for breaking in the house.

AVALAINE. The window was wide open. *(Harley opens the double doors.)*

ELDON. Just stay out a minute—

HARLEY. Eldon—*(He can say no more. He carries a telegram, hardly sees Avalaine; stands frozen a few feet inside the door, unable to speak.)*

AVALAINE. You can call in the whole damn town as far as I'm concerned. I didn't steal nothing.

HARLEY. Eldon!

ELDON. Harley, we have a problem here, I'm trying to talk to someone right now.

HARLEY. Eldon, I'm sorry. *(A long pause.)*

ELDON. It's Timmy.

HARLEY. I'm sorry. *(Olive opens the door. Netta comes through bringing an ice bag. Olive and Buddy enter the room. Lottie comes from upstairs. Talley enters from the office.)*

OLIVE. Was she looking for her mother? What is that girl doing up here?

NETTA. I don't know what you're thinking, screaming at this child when she should have an ice pack on that face.

ELDON. Buddy, Olive. Not now.

NETTA. Eldon, I want to know why that girl isn't taken care of. She could have her nose broke.

OLIVE. Not now, Mother.

NETTA. What's the matter? Have I said something? Well, why are you looking at...What is it? Harley?

ELDON. It's all right, honey.

NETTA. Harley? *(Looking at Harley. He holds out the telegram.)* That isn't true. That isn't true. *(Pause.)* Harley...(She takes a few uncertain steps toward Harley and faints, falling to the floor.)*

CURTAIN

END OF ACT ONE

ACT TWO

Later that evening. Lottie, Timmy, and Eldon are in the dark living room. The only light comes from the hall.

NETTA. *(Off from upstairs.)* I don't know why you say I fainted. I didn't faint.

OLIVE. *(Off.)* It doesn't matter, Mother.

NETTA. *(Off.)* Olive, please don't call me that.

OLIVE. *(Off.)* I know, I'm sorry. Should you be up?

NETTA. *(Appearing in the hallway.)* I'm fine. I can't just lay there.

OLIVE. *(In hallway.)* You rested some. You had a little nap.

NETTA. I didn't go to sleep. I couldn't sleep now. How could I sleep? *(She exits to the kitchen. Buddy enters from the front door.)*

OLIVE. Buddy, did you get Nora home O.K.?

BUDDY. Yeah. *(Eldon comes from the dark living room into the doorway, a letter in his hand.)* What's that?

ELDON. Oh—I've been reading Timmy's—have you read this?

BUDDY. I didn't get a chance to see the ones that came yesterday.

ELDON. Listen—"Last night we spent on the deck of the transport bobbing up and down about a mile off two islands that are part of the Marianas. The big one is just another tangle of jungle and mangos, with all these razorback ridges running down it like the Arkansas backhills, only more so."

TIMMY. That's Saipan.

ELDON. "The little one is the first real farm island we've come across. It looks like a five-by-ten-mile Missouri."

TIMMY. That's Tinian. I took one look at Tinian and I thought I'd been witched. I thought I was home. I thought I'd woke up in the middle of the night and was looking out the back window of my room into Leslie Bassett's farm.

ELDON. "They just floated a flat chunk of Leclede County out to sea and tied it up in the Marianas."

OLIVE. Maybe you ought not to read that now, Dad.

ELDON. I was trying to get to this part. You remember what a baseball nut he was.

OLIVE. *(To Buddy.)* Come on, honey, you're just going to get yourself upset. *(She exits to kitchen.)*

BUDDY. In a sec'; I'm fine. What?

ELDON. *(Reading.)* "These islands are supposed to be a cakewalk. Ha. Ha. They said that about Tarawa. There's three big islands in the Marianas that are important to us and it looks like we'll be taking them on in order: short to second to first."

TIMMY. Saipan to Tinian to Guam.

ELDON. "Tinker to Evers to Chance…"

TIMMY. When we got the word we were going to the Marianas, some dog-face lieutenant said, "Marianas—shit, they sound like they were named after some Nip's Wop whore." We told him that the Spanish Jesuits named them for Queen Mariana, and the Jesuits were a tough band to tangle with. Boy, he was pissed beyond all proportion. It's amazing the pride some people take in their ignorance. 'Course he was already renaming them the Eleanors. We told him Mrs. Roosevelt wouldn't want 'em after we got through, but he was all sozzled on patriotism. Well, half patriotism, half this cache of Nip beer, which, considering the Nips made it, is a hell of a lot better than Sterno and lemon extract, let me tell you. *(Eldon goes out. He gives Buddy the letter.)*

BUDDY. *(Reading.)* "This shouldn't be bad, I'll let you know. We just got the call to hit the landing boats, so I'd better close. Tell Buddy, before he makes Rome, I'll be in Tokyo. Sorry about my handwriting, I'm writing this standing in line. Hurry up and wait."

TIMMY. *(With Buddy.)* Hurry up and wait.

OLIVE. *(Entering from the kitchen.)* Buddy, don't hang around here in the dark, honey.

BUDDY. I'm not.

OLIVE. Where's Dad?

BUDDY. He went outside. *(They move into the dark living room.)*

OLIVE. Buddy, I can't take it here. We have to get a place of our own, a place in town.

BUDDY. I know; we will.

OLIVE. I never had a mother and dad that I remember. I thought this would be my family, but you see what it's like.

BUDDY. I know. Soon as I'm back. Not now.

OLIVE. Honey, we can't even talk.

BUDDY. I know.

OLIVE. The prices are just going to keep climbing. We might as well do it now as some other time.

BUDDY. I know. When I come home.

OLIVE. Honey, I know it's terrible to talk about it now, but you never answer any questions I write you.

BUDDY. I get them so long after you write…

OLIVE. Would you agree to a place if I find one? We can't have a minute to ourselves here.

NETTA. *(Entering.)* Don't stand in the dark, you two.

BUDDY. Are you all right, Mom?

NETTA. I wish everyone would quit asking me that. I have never blacked out in my life. For some reason I thought there was a chair right behind me. I know there isn't a chair there, but I thought there was and I put my hand back to steady myself, and there wasn't a chair there and I went over. I certainly fell down, but I didn't faint. I've never fainted in my life. Come on back into the kitchen with me and Harley. Don't hang around in here by yourselves. Where's your father?

BUDDY. He went out front.

NETTA. He's taking this very hard. Oh, Lord. Olive, I know, but don't let Eldon see you crying. And don't say anything, or—I don't know. I don't know. *(She goes out the front door.)*

OLIVE. Said she didn't faint. Her eyes rolled back in her head and she went down like a sack of potatoes.

BUDDY. Olive, good Lord.

OLIVE. I'm sorry, it's just—*(Buddy starts for the kitchen.)* Buddy, honey?

BUDDY. Come on into the light. Harley's in the kitchen all by himself.

OLIVE. Mother'll come back—and Dad.

BUDDY. Come on into the light. *(He goes. After a moment Olive follows.)*

TIMMY. Nora, the cook, who used to be about my favorite person in the family, got so upset when they told her about me that she couldn't finish cooking supper. Buddy had to drive her home. They didn't have any vegetables at all. It's a good thing Olive made that pie.

ELDON. *(Coming from the front with Netta.)* I don't want anything said in front of Dad.

NETTA. I know.

ELDON. If we ever got him to understand what had happened, it'd probably kill him.

NETTA. I know.

ELDON. Those two grandsons mean more to him than almost anything. Aren't you eating?

NETTA. I don't want anything, no. I'm fine. Eldon, come into the parlor now. You want to listen to the radio while Olive and I clean up.

ELDON. I don't know that I do; I have to get some air, the house is stifling. *(He steps back outside. After a moment she returns to the kitchen.)*

TIMMY. Mom said Dad is taking this really hard, and he is. He went out to the barn and leaned up against the cattle stanchions and cried like I've never seen. 'Course when I was eight years old I went running out of the house, ran into that same room, leaned up against that same stanchion when my hamster died. And Dad came and found me there, so he maybe was remembering that, too.

NETTA. *(Entering with Harley, Buddy, and Olive.)* Just see if he doesn't want to come in with us.

BUDDY. The sky cleared up.

HARLEY. There's even going to be a moon.

BUDDY. It's hot, but it's a beautiful night.

NETTA. I know, but he shouldn't be out there alone, brooding. *(Harley and Buddy go out.)* I don't know what to do for him.

OLIVE. I know.

NETTA. I just don't think he should be alone out there; he's not resilient like we are.

OLIVE. I know.

NETTA. He's got no bounce. I don't know what to say. I can't think of a thing to do for him.

OLIVE. I know, Netta.

NETTA. I don't know.

OLIVE. I know.

NETTA. I don't know.

OLIVE. *(Turns the lights on.)* Oh, my God, Aunt Lottie. Scare me to death. Sitting in here in the dark. Are you all right?

LOTTIE. Yes.

OLIVE. You should come into the kitchen and have something to eat.

LOTTIE. No.

NETTA. Has Sally come back to the house?

LOTTIE. No.

NETTA. She hasn't eaten a bite. I called her out back.

OLIVE. Maybe she went into town.

NETTA. Oh, Lord, I hope she doesn't hear from somebody in town!

LOTTIE. She'll be in soon.

NETTA. I know she's willful, but she's so strong and she sees so much at the army hospital. I just wish she was here. What were you doing in here by yourself?

LOTTIE. Nothing. *(She exits.)*

HARLEY. *(Entering from outside with Buddy and Eldon.)* I better call Mary Jo again, if I can use your phone.

NETTA. Sure, Harley, tell her we're fine. Now, there's a pie that Olive's made and there's coffee yet.

ELDON. Later on maybe.

HARLEY. *(On phone.)* Three-eight-O, please.

BUDDY. You bring it in, in a bit.

OLIVE. We will not, you'll come out and eat at the table after we've cleared up. *(She and Netta go.)*

HARLEY. *(On phone.)* Hi, toots, I'm still here. No, I won't be long. I'll tell 'em. You keep your seams straight. *(Hangs up phone.)*

BUDDY. Boy, I thought that girl was gonna start wrecking the furniture in here. Who the devil is she?

ELDON. From what she said, you know perfectly well who she is.

BUDDY. You're the one who was talking to her. Let me in here, I'd have handled it.

ELDON. Sounds like you've been handling it all along.

HARLEY. I don't know what happens with that kind of girl. They paint up what could be a pretty face, twist their behinds around. Can't be more than seventeen years old, already she's the worst whore in town. She is.

BUDDY. Hot number like that could be trouble.

ELDON. No, no, no trouble. She's going to be no problem.

BUDDY. No problem of mine.

ELDON. That depends on whose story you believe.

BUDDY. Shoot, every guy in town's been down to those woods. Maybe she got me mixed up with Timmy.

ELDON. No more of that.

BUDDY. No more of what?

ELDON. No more of that anymore. That's all over now.

BUDDY. What's over?

ELDON. You think everything you do is all right, if you can drag Timmy into it.

BUDDY. I never used Tim for anything in my life. There's not two brothers in town closer than—

ELDON. Fine, I know. I know.

BUDDY. Those doors are thick, but that girl wasn't talking all that private. You gonna lecture me about moral weakness and character? Like Granddad?

ELDON. That's enough.

BUDDY. *(Easy.)* I remember all those lectures about moral fiber. I used to think you ought to order a couple hundred bolts, make you a new line of clothes outta moral fiber.

HARLEY. Shit. They wouldn't move. Sit on the shelves and go begging. *(Lottie enters.)*

BUDDY. Good Lord, Aunt Lottie. Thought you'd gone to bed.

LOTTIE. I don't go to bed, you know that.

ELDON. Are you all right?

LOTTIE. I swear to God, Eldon, I feel like I might glow in the dark.

ELDON. Is that good? I don't think that sounds—

LOTTIE. That's not good. No, that's not good.

ELDON. Lottie—Buddy. How are we supposed to take this? How do people take it?

LOTTIE. I don't know, Eldon.

ELDON. I can't get Netta to talk about it. I don't think it's really hit her yet. *(The radio has been turned on.)* No, Don't turn that on, damn fool thing, what do I care tonight what's happening with the war? I got my—one son here with me. My other, I don't even know where he fell. I just wish I knew that he got his man.

BUDDY. You can be damned sure Tim did.

ELDON. Ten for one, damn them, and they keep fighting. That's what the paper says, ten Japs for one Yank.

HARLEY. You can be damn sure Timmy got his limit, Eldon.

ELDON. I know that; enough of that, now. Enough of that. Has Sally come in?

LOTTIE. I haven't heard her.

ELDON. She still doesn't know. Well...we've got Buddy here.

BUDDY. Yeah, I wish I was here for good.

HARLEY. We'll have you back down at that plant before you know it.

BUDDY. Oh boy. Maybe I'll stay in Italy.

HARLEY. See, he's seeing the world, he starts getting ideas.

ELDON. How you gonna keep them down on the farm? Huh? After they've seen—well, Rome, I guess it has to be.

BUDDY. Naw, I'm like Granddad. I'm not stuck on that factory.

ELDON. I know; I've never forced it on you.

BUDDY. No, sir. Come home from Princeton with a degree in business administration; in a week I'm fixing sewing machines.

HARLEY. Still the best repairman we've had down there.

ELDON. I seem to remember it wasn't long before you were working at the bank.

BUDDY. You know it.

ELDON. Hell, I own what, a quarter of that bank. I never could stand it.

BUDDY. To each his own. I can't believe I'm back. No wonder they don't want us coming home on leave. If it wasn't for Timmy, this would be…*(He nearly cries, recovers, tries to continue heartily.)* Boy! I tell you, after last winter, I'm trying to convince Olive to live in a desert somewhere. California or Arizona. I mean it rained—and cold.

ELDON. I always imagined Italy to be warm.

BUDDY. Yeah, sunny Italy, what a load of fertilizer that is. Hell, when the ground froze, at least you could walk on it. You've never seen so many kids in your life. We learned to say to them, *"Buon giorno, ragazzo,"* and they're supposed to say, *"Bene grassi, signor."* You know what they say?

HARLEY. What's that?

BUDDY. Got any gum, chum?

ELDON. Sounds like Clark balled up Italy as much as Nimitz did the Pacific.

BUDDY. I don't know what else General Clark was supposed to do. I just counted myself lucky to be in out of the rain. *(Talley enters from the office, dragging a large, half-filled mailbag.)*

ELDON. I thought you were in your room.

TALLEY. *(Lucid.)* No, no. Kenneth.

BUDDY. Sir.

TALLEY. Harley. Good evening. I'm surprised you're showing your face, Eldon.

ELDON. Did the women get you something to eat?

TALLEY. Yes, thank you, I've had sufficient. Is Emmet Young back yet?

ELDON. I didn't know he'd gone someplace.

TALLEY. Kenneth, bring along that big sack full of papers to the kitchen.

BUDDY. Yes, sir.

ELDON. Dad, we should go through anything that's important together.

TALLEY. Now listen here—if I have to talk to you. There's some papers nobody's business but mine—long useless to anybody but me—that I intend to burn in the kitchen cook stove. If that's all the same to everybody. You just tend to your sewing machines, that's always suited you fine, and suited me fine.

ELDON. Dad, you might destroy something that…

TALLEY. Sir, that's all, sir. *(He exits.)*

ELDON. *(Sotto voce.)* What got his dander up?

LOTTIE. He's just covering his tracks like a good fox.

TALLEY. *(Coming back.)* I think you'll find a fox doubles back on his tracks, he doesn't cover them up, Charlotte. *(To Buddy.)* Go on, then, and poke those a few at a time into the stove there. *(Buddy exits.)*

HARLEY. Buddy.

TALLEY. Mind you don't get yourself burned.

HARLEY. Well, hell.

ELDON. I'd like to go through those things with you.

TALLEY. You been digging through everything in there like a dog for a mole. Nothing that would interest anybody but me, thank you. *(Starts to go.)*

HARLEY. Old love letters. Maybe.

TALLEY. *(Turns.)* No, sir, I left the loving everybody except my wife to your father, Mr. Campbell. And my son, here. And you see where that's got us. Small mind in business and adulterous in his marriage, and everybody in the state knows it.

ELDON. There's no call to speak to that now, Dad. *(Sotto voce.)* Boy, I can't take this tonight.

TALLEY. How many girls—

LOTTIE. Not tonight, Dad.

TALLEY. —was it you came to me about before you was shipped off to school? Who was the New Jersey lawyer sent here to sue you for parentage? He didn't know who he was dealing with, I can tell you. Sent him packing.

ELDON. And used it as an excuse to pull me out of school two months before I graduated.

TALLEY. Set you up, sir, in business down there—only place I knew of where I wouldn't have to lay eyes on you.

ELDON. And I took that two-bit outfit and made it into something you should be proud of.

TALLEY. Pride goeth before the fall, sir. I was your age exactly when the Great War came. I saw it coming. You looked at Europe, you looked at the Pacific, said it wouldn't happen again. Anybody could have told you better and did. With that son-of-a-bitch Democrat cripple in the White House playing king, roughshodding over every good man in the country till he decided he needed them to fight his war.

HARLEY. All that's changing now; things aren't going to be that easy for him.

TALLEY. I saw what was coming in 1914. You stuck you head in the sand.

LOTTIE. You bought everything the war was gonna use and sold it back to them for double, didn't you, Papa?

TALLEY. Yes, I did, and treble and four times, and it bought you the college education you never used and the food in your mouth and the shirt on your back, young man, and don't you forget it.

LOTTIE. I'm not a young man anymore, Papa.

TALLEY. Well, Lottie, if you didn't tell them, there wouldn't be nobody who'd know the difference.

LOTTIE. At this point, if I recall the last time he was quasi-coherent, he begins on how frail and beautiful Momma was and his disappointment in me. Very reminiscent of Eldon's lament over Sally. *(She stands up, is dizzy, and is forced to sit back down.)* Well, so much for the grand gesture. I was intending to sweep from the room.

TALLEY. That's the only sweeping you'd know how to do, Charlotte. Fine children I raised. You and what's-his-name both. If Stuart had lived, then you'da seen something—

ELDON. That's fine, Dad, don't get excited.

LOTTIE. You had one die and two that were stillborn, Daddy, and none of us asked for the favor of having you for a father.

ELDON. That's enough, Lottie.

LOTTIE. *(Lower.)* I never could understand why he kept trying if he was so unhappy with us.

ELDON. *(Low.)* Maybe he wanted to keep at it till he got another one he was satisfied with.

LOTTIE. Well, Momma, bless her, didn't live that long. Doctors told him she wasn't strong enough; it's not like we're Catholic. Didn't they have rubbers back at the turn of the century?

ELDON. Lottie, for God's sake.

LOTTIE. I don't know why I'd expect you to know—you're apparently completely unacquainted with them.

TALLEY. Eldon.

ELDON. Dad?

TALLEY. Who? I don't want to be in this room.

ELDON. Are you O.K.?

TALLEY. Blamed! Where's the boy? Where's Eldon?

ELDON. I'm right here.

TALLEY. Where?

ELDON. Who? Goddamn it, now he's got me doing it.

TALLEY. The boy.

ELDON. Kenneth is in the kitchen, where you sent him. *(Pause.)* Dad? What's wrong?

TALLEY. *(After a moment, crushed.)* My God, sir, what I've come to…

ELDON. You're better than last week—if you'd take care of yourself. You shouldn't be trying to do all this. If you'd let me help.

TALLEY. Where?

ELDON. Where's what?

TALLEY. Your boy.

ELDON. You had Buddy take a sack of papers to burn in the cooking stove that hasn't been connected for twenty years. Nora cooks on an oil range now.

TIMMY. Then we'll take them out to the barnyard, sir. *(Exits. Pause.)*

ELDON. And there's no barnyard either.

HARLEY. He starts in with the "sirs" and "thank you's" you know you're in trouble.

ELDON. I hope he's not burning anything important—you never know with him.

HARLEY. Well, before I go, you know what I'm going to say.

ELDON. Not tonight, Harley.

HARLEY. Eldon, I was willing to wail till Timmy got back.

ELDON. Not tonight.

HARLEY. It's not going to be any easier tomorrow.

ELDON. I know that, thank you.

HARLEY. Buddy's here, you're here.

ELDON. You want to explain it to Dad? And why we're not waiting for Timmy? You want to tell him that?

HARLEY. Anything to do with that plant, you don't need him. You got power of attorney.

ELDON. Well, that wasn't my idea, that was the government's idea. I'd never use it. It isn't funny, Lottie.

LOTTIE. Government man came down here to tell Dad how good Talley & Son was doing and Dad kept calling the factory a chicken farm.

ELDON. He was pretty bad that year.

HARLEY. *(Laughs.)* Told the inspector to pick out a pair of hens to take home for himself.

ELDON. Now look at him; the man has nine lives. No disrespect. His father died at thirty. Built this house and didn't live a year in it. I think Dad lived out his dad's life and then his own. And then mine.

OLIVE. *(Entering.)* Now, it's absolutely against my principles to indulge you men like this, but Mother says if you come into the kitchen and get your coffee, you can bring it back in the parlor. We're not finished in the kitchen yet. Aunt Charlotte, there's a good apple pie…

BUDDY. *(Entering.)* Dad

ELDON. Anything important in those papers?

BUDDY. I don't think so.

OLIVE. No, no, don't come in without your coffee, and there's pie. Get it in the kitchen and bring it in here.

HARLEY. What kind of service is that? We're trying to talk in here. I thought you'd bring it in on a fancy tray.

OLIVE. We happen not to have a maid anymore, like you do Harley. And I'm not going to volunteer. Wouldn't I look cute—I'll get me a little hat and sew a little ruffle around my apron.

HARLEY. I remember when you had a maid and a girl to help Nora out.

OLIVE. Well, that was before my time. Try to find a colored girl now with the wages they're getting down at your factory. Aunt Lottie, you're going to go straight to H-E-double-tooth-picks with those cards.

LOTTIE. Oh, kiss my ass.

OLIVE. Well, you'd enjoy that, wouldn't you! Why are you so hateful to me?

BUDDY. Honey.

ELDON. Ladies. Olive, Lottie isn't well tonight.

OLIVE. Eldon, I understand sorrow and tension. I told Lottie she looked upset and tired; she should go to bed.

ELDON. She hasn't been sleeping.

LOTTIE. I've never slept. Maybe I'm bored, not tired.

OLIVE. Well, I don't understand that as something to be proud of.

BUDDY. Olive.

OLIVE. Well, don't "Olive" me, dernit. I don't understand being bored and I don't understand not being able to sleep. I understand getting up early and working hard and getting things done and being tired and going to sleep and sleeping.

BUDDY. Honey?

OLIVE. And getting up early and working hard and getting things done and being tired and going to sleep and sleeping. There's too much to do to be bored, and there's too much to do not to be tired, and there's too much to do not to sleep. I'm sorry, that's the way I am. It's the way I am. That's the way I am.

ELDON. Come on.

BUDDY. Honey!

ELDON. Come on, sweetheart. *(She exits. Buddy and Eldon follow.)*

HARLEY. Buddy. Eldon. *(He exits, leaving Lottie and Timmy onstage.)*

TIMMY. Dad said he didn't even know where I fell. That official "fell." Like a lotta people he gets very—not just correct, but formal—under pressure. Hell, "fell" isn't half of it. Splattered is more like it. Didn't feel a thing. Shock and whatnot takes care of that. I felt a force all against me and suddenly I've got a different angle on the terrain. I'm looking up into the trees instead of out across the jungle floor. I thought, How am I looking at that? Then I thought, Oh, sure, I'm flat on my ass looking up. Some squawking parrot up there looking down at me; gonna drop it right on my face. I figgered, all right, this part is easy. I just lay here till some corpsman comes up and does his job. You get very philosophical. Then the corpsmen come and, oh, Daddy, I knew from the look on their faces that this is bad. This young recruit, couldn't be sixteen, turned around and I thought he was gonna puke, but he flat our fainted before he had the chance. You could tell he'd enlisted in this thing ten minutes after seeing *To the Shores of Tripoli*. Then all of a sudden I'm on a stretcher and they're rushing me off to somewhere. You understand, you don't feel the stretcher under you, you just know they're rushing you to somewhere. You're looking up into the sun; some guy is running along beside you, trying to keep his hand over your eyes, shade them from the sun; you'd kinda rather see it. And all the corpsmen are still looking so cut-up I said, "Hey, do you raggedy-asses think I don't know you're razzing me? I got a pass to go home, you're trying to make me think I won't get there." Or, actually, I thought I said that; then I realized nothing had come out. I thought, Well, hell, if this isn't a lousy predicament. You always wondered if it comes will you fall all to pieces, and now it's come and I'm doing fine and damned proud of it and nobody is gonna know. *(Talley enters from the kitchen and exits out the front door.)* Granddad Talley would say, "Pride goeth before a fall, sir." Should have known it. Of course, you do know that the body is doing what the body does. You can feel—barely, a little bit—that your body is urinating all over itself and your bowels are letting go something fierce. You try to get ahold with your mind of the muscles down in your belly that you use to hold it off, but your mind can't find 'em. *(Pause.)* If those guys hadn't looked so bad, you might have gone all to pieces, but they're so torn up, you feel somebody has got to take this thing lightly.

NETTA. *(Off.)* Eldon.

ELDON. *(Enters; Netta following.)* I wish you wouldn't hound me tonight, damn it.

NETTA. I just want to know what that woman was doing here. I wouldn't put it past her to take something from the house.

ELDON. I don't know who you're talking about.

NETTA. That Viola Platt. I don't want her coming around.

ELDON. She's been doing the wash here for fifteen years—

NETTA. And I've never liked it a minute and I've never trusted her a minute. I'd rather do the washing myself or, God knows, there's any number of colored women into Old Town who need the money more than she does. Her husband just drinks it up and gives us all a bad name.

ELDON. I want to say right now that I've had it with this hysterical attitude you and Olive have tonight— We're all upset, but there's no call for this.

NETTA. There is call and I'm calling, and Olive is with me in this. Now, I'm just shaking like a leaf, this has got me so upset.

ELDON. Please get it through your head that it means nothing to me who does the washing here.

NETTA. Then we understand each other fine. But can you tell me why she's come back here again three times now in one day?

ELDON. Where? What's she doing here?

NETTA. Emmet drove her to the front of the house; your father went out personally to—

TALLEY. *(Entering with Emmet and Viola.)* In here. Here. If you please. I asked Mr. Young if he would be so kind as to fetch Mrs. Platt here. I want to thank the both of you for coming by at this hour.

ELDON. Dad, not tonight. I'm sorry, Mrs. Platt, we've had some bad news here—

TALLEY. Mrs. Platt, Mr. Young, I think you're acquainted…?

VIOLA. I know who he is, I guess; we ain't acquainted.

NETTA. Mr. Talley, I'm about at the end of my patience here. I want you to please explain to—

TALLEY. This is a family thing that we can have you join us for or not. If you'd rather, you can please shut the door behind you. *(Netta looks at Eldon and leaves, shutting the door.)* This won't be but a minute.

ELDON. Dad, no. Whatever you're up to. Not tonight.

TALLEY. I heard you the first time, sir. You can sit over there and attend or join the women in the kitchen. I imagine these two people want to get home.

VIOLA. It sure ain't my preference to be hauled out of the house in the middle of the night.

TALLEY. Now, the past is the past and we're not going to talk about that. I think we know why we're here. Now, Viola, your daughter—her name is…?

VIOLA. Avalaine?

TALLEY. Speak up, Platt; say what?

VIOLA. Avalaine, Mr. Talley.

TALLEY. Avalaine.

VIOLA. I thought she'd runned off.

TALLEY. Well, it's turned out that that is not the case. Now I am a man who has always been direct and fair, anybody will testify.

LOTTIE. God save us!

TALLEY. Charlotte, you look terrible. You should be in bed.

LOTTIE. Not on your life.

VIOLA. Avalaine said she come up here and got slapped in the face for her trouble. I tried to talk to Mr. Eldon, but you being so busy—

TALLEY. Your daughter stated a slander in this house this afternoon, which won't happen again.

VIOLA. Avalaine most often says what she likes. *(There is a commotion in the hall.)*

AVALAINE. *(Off.)* You just get your damn hands off me—*(Opening the door.)* Is Ma in here?

OLIVE. *(From doorway.)* Mr. Talley is in a private—

AVALAINE. I said somethin's going on, goddamn it, and I'm gonna know what it is.

OLIVE. Mr. Talley, Mr. Eldon—

AVALAINE. Are you talking about me?

ELDON. I don't want this commotion, now.

AVALAINE. It don't much matter what you want. Mom, what're they saying here?

NETTA. Eldon—

TALLEY. That's fine.

ELDON. That's fine, Dad said. I don't know what—

TALLEY. Miss Platt, I thought you'd be contrite and embarrassed, or I would have asked you to join us. *(Pause. Avalaine looks at him.)* Maybe she is.

AVALAINE. I don't know what you're talking "embarrassed." You got some-thing to say, say it.

ELDON. You're opening a can of beans you've no—

TALLEY. Eldon, shut the door if you would. *(Avalaine flinches when Eldon approaches.)*

ELDON. I'm not going to hit you. *(He closes the door.)*

AVALAINE. *(To Emmet.)* What the hell are you doing here?

EMMET. Would you just shut up.

AVALAINE. We's supposed to go to the picture show.

TALLEY. Now, one thing has to be understood. Avalaine Platt, you stated a slander in this house this afternoon; that won't happen again.

AVALAINE. I didn't say nothin' that wasn't the—

EMMET. Why don't you listen once?

TALLEY. We don't have to worry about you repeating it, as that would be actionable by lawsuit.

AVALAINE. Bullshit.

TALLEY. The Jeff City jails aren't so full they can't take a few more; not just you, but whoever in your family is spreading this libel. I don't have to go into that. As it happens, I've been talking to Mr. Young here for some time. Mr. Young is intimately acquainted with Avalaine, which I assume you know.

VIOLA. I guess if that means what I think it means, I ain't surprised. It's no business of yours.

TALLEY. Say what?

VIOLA. I know she likes the soldier boys.

TALLEY. Mr. Young is very much a civilian.

AVALAINE. He's got asthma.

EMMET. I've got flat feet.

TALLEY. Now, I've asked that he join us here because Mr. Young applied for the job of cutter at the factory last month, wanting, as he said, a position that had more of a future. Inside, out of the weather. Mr. Young is an ambitious man. Now, my son had thought of hiring another applicant, but tonight we've made the decision that Mr. Young is the right man for that position. Now, I think you wanted to say something.

EMMET. It's been put to me that Avalaine and I should be married.

AVALAINE. In a pig's eye.

TALLEY. I think that would be the honorable thing for the young Mr. Young and Miss Platt to do. And I'm happy that we'll be giving you the means to do the honorable thing. I don't see any other way we could accept them into our home.

EMMET. I understand that, sir. Sirs. *(To Avalaine.)* What'd I tell you?

TALLEY. Then I think Eldon will agree that you can start at the factory as a wedding present. The day after the marriage takes place. I feel it's the least I can offer, Miss Platt, and, if you understand me, it's the most I can offer.

AVALAINE. Oh, it ain't difficult to understand. It just ain't enough.

VIOLA. If that's all you wanted, you should have asked Avalaine here to begin with.

ELDON. It's not necessary, Dad.

VIOLA. I ain't asked nothin' from nobody, I want that understood.

ELDON. I know that, Viola.

VIOLA. I tried to tell you.

ELDON. I know.

VIOLA. You people don't owe us.

AVALAINE. Like hell they don't—

VIOLA. You don't have to do nothin' you don't want to, Avie. You can just as easy go to Springfield.

AVALAINE. On what?

TALLEY. Thank you very much. With Miss Platt here, I think we'll do fine.

VIOLA. If I tell you, you just do different out of spite.

TALLEY. Thank you very much. *(Pause.)* Thank you very much.

LOTTIE. That means he's finished with you, honey.

VIOLA. Is that what that means? Avie don't have to do nothin' she don't want.

LOTTIE. No, she doesn't.

AVALAINE. I ain't said nothin'—one way or another—

VIOLA. Well, none of that work is gonna finish itself. *(Eldon gets up.)* Don't bother, Mr. Eldon. I know the way out of this house. *(She exits.)*

TALLEY. Mr. Young, congratulations. Eldon, she said she can find the door. I know we none of us will have to think about this again.

AVALAINE. I ain't said nothin', I said.

EMMET. Will you listen once?

AVALAINE. Will you jump in the lake.

EMMET. He could have you in jail in a minute.

AVALAINE. Like hell he could.

EMMET. The hell he couldn't.

AVALAINE. And have his name in the paper?

EMMET. They wouldn't print it, nobody'd know. *(They argue in violent whispers.)*

TALLEY. I think we can expect Mr. Young to put it to Miss Platt; he seems inclined that way.

AVALAINE. *(To Emmet.)* What's to prevent it?

EMMET. Excuse me, sir, but we got no guarantee.

AVALAINE. We sure ain't.

TALLEY. Harley; Eldon, yell for Harley.

ELDON. Emmet, get Harley.

EMMET. *(Opening the door.)* Mr. Campbell, Mr. Talley wants you in here.

NETTA. *(In the doorway.)* Has she left?

ELDON. I'm sure you saw her go.

NETTA. Eldon, I want you to tell me why she was up here. Is that girl gone?

AVALAINE. No, I ain't gone.

HARLEY. *(Entering.)* Yes, sir. *(Buddy and Olive appear in the doorway.)*

TALLEY. Mr. Young—Mr. Campbell.

HARLEY. I know Emmet.

TALLEY. Mr. Young will be working alongside us down at the plant.

HARLEY. What do you mean "us"? I haven't seen you down there in twenty years.

TALLEY. Beside you and Eldon. Soon as the wedding's over. I just wanted you to meet here in this house, to start you two boys off on the right foot. Now, these two young people have to run along.

EMMET. Of course, the job of cutter isn't much of a—

ELDON. Bribe.

EMMET. —incentive.

AVALAINE. Cuttin'-room foreman might be more attractive.

HARLEY. You're joking. Cutter takes home over two hundred bucks a week. That's more than me or Eldon, either one draws. *(Pause.)*

AVALAINE. Mr. Talley? Cuttin'-room foreman?

TALLEY. For your first anniversary present.

ELDON. Dad, Harley's the man who does the hiring and firing—

TALLEY. Sir. You never admit when you've been outsmarted, and I do.

EMMET. If that could be in writing.

AVALAINE. I want to see all you said in writing. I can read.

TALLEY. Tomorrow morning. You get married tomorrow, I see no reason you can't start work the day after. Now, is that agreeable, Miss Platt?

LOTTIE. That's nothing you have to accept, Avalaine.

AVALAINE. Oh sure, you don't want nobody to have nothin', 'cept you. That's agreeable all except "inviting us into your home." Don't expect me to be spending much time up here.

TALLEY. Whatever you want. Now I'm tired.

LOTTIE. I don't wonder.

EMMET. I want to thank...

TALLEY. No thanks, no thanks. That's something you'll earn. And everything that comes after. Both of you.

AVALAINE. Can we leave here now?

TALLEY. Eldon, you want to see these people home.

AVALAINE. Emmet's got a car.

EMMET. Thank you. Good night.

LOTTIE. Good luck.

EMMET. Mrs. Talley.

NETTA. Good night.

EMMET. *(To Eldon.)* Dad. *(Emmet and Avalaine leave, squealing as soon as they are out the door.)*

OLIVE. *(Entering.)* Look at the way he dresses. Drives that fancy car. Everyone rationed to three gallons a week, I don't want to think where he gets the stamps for gas.

LOTTIE. You're really slick, huh, Dad?

TALLEY. Heck, it wasn't even fun. Shooting fish in a barrel. *(To Eldon.)* You stick it to a sow, you shouldn't be surprised to have a pig offspring; whatsoever a man soweth, that shall he also reap.

LOTTIE. If that was true, Daddy, I don't want to think what you'd be also reaping.

TALLEY. I'm glad you're not my judge, Charlotte.

LOTTIE. I'll be somewhere lobbying, Daddy.

ELDON. I hope you're happy now, Dad.

TALLEY. I've wiped your nose for you for the last time, sir.

ELDON. I could have taken care of it.

NETTA. What do you mean by that? *(Talley exits into office. To Eldon.)* Do you want to explain that? Do you want to tell us what you could have taken care of.

OLIVE. Dad, do you think—

ELDON. —I'm not joking about you two and your hysterics now.

NETTA. Do I look hysterical to you, Eldon? Because if you don't know what I'm saying, I'm perfectly willing to spell it out. Now you are walking on thin ice through a field of wild oats here and you better watch your step.

LOTTIE. I swear to God, Dad is the craftiest son-of-a-bitch I ever encountered.

NETTA. Yes, he is, Lottie, all of that. He doesn't care what he makes Eldon look like.

ELDON. Hell, that's the only reason he did it.

NETTA. Of course Eldon didn't care what he made us look like.

HARLEY. You think that man can learn the job?

ELDON. Don't you give me a hard time now. What's so difficult about pushing a cutting saw around a line?

HARLEY. You mess up, you're cutting twelve dozen legs at one go. That could get pretty costly on a narrow profit margin like we're running.

ELDON. Please don't tell me how the cutting room is run, I've cut enough—

HARLEY. You think he's foreman material?

ELDON. We can find something for him to do.

HARLEY. That's my partner who cares so much about the quality of the Talley & Son product.

ELDON. Goddamn it, Harley, we can find something.

HARLEY. I just wanted to know you felt good about it.

ELDON. It'll work out. Don't worry about it.

HARLEY. 'Cause I don't. I guess I'm not stupid. I know what's happening, but I'm damned if I feel good about it. You may think we can find a place for him; I don't think we can.

TALLEY. *(At the office door.)* Here, Netta. Where's that pie?

NETTA. Olive, see what Mr. Talley wants.

TALLEY. Where is the pie?

OLIVE. I'll get it for you, Granddad. Is there any left?

BUDDY. Sure. *(Olive exits.)* Better get some of that before it's gone. Harley? *(He and Harley exit.)*

NETTA. It's a great pleasure washing dishes with Olive out in the kitchen talking about getting a new flag for the window with a gold star for Timmy and a blue one for Buddy.

ELDON. Come on, now. None of that talk.

NETTA. I don't want it; I don't want either one of those stars in the window anymore. And I don't want a military funeral with a flag on the casket.

ELDON. *(Quite hot.)* That can wait till they send our son home. *(He exits to kitchen.)*

NETTA. Don't run out when I talk to you.

OLIVE. *(Bringing in the pie.)* Granddaddy! *(She knocks on office door; Talley takes the pie and slams the door.)* You said you wanted it. Mother. *(Netta exits; to Lottie.)* I don't mean to be angry, Lottie. It's not easy for me sometimes.

LOTTIE. Don't pay any attention to me, honey. *(Olive exits.)*

TIMMY. Lottie, she's coming up on the porch.

HARLEY. *(Off.)* I know, I know. All I'm saying. *(Sally enters from the door and starts up the stairs.)*

ELDON. *(Off.)* There's no need to raise your voice now—	LOTTIE. Sally! *(Sally hasn't heard.)* Sally!

HARLEY. *(Off.)*— not to make too big a fuss about it; all I'm saying is we're doing damn important work down there, and turning a pretty penny doing it. I don't want some green field hand—some mechnic—

SALLY. *(Listening to Harley and Eldon.)* I started to say I can't believe they're still yelling, but I should be used to it by now.

ELDON. *(Off.)* There's no call to get angry. If we can't talk—

HARLEY. *(Off.)* Sure, sure, fine. I don't want a wrench thrown in it, Eldon, is all I'm saying.

LOTTIE. Matt Friedman was down at the boathouse, wasn't he?

SALLY. Yes.

LOTTIE. I knew that's where he'd go. Soon as they said his car was alongside the road. I swear to God, I've been straining my ears so hard I'm damned near deaf.

SALLY. We're going to drive down to Springfield, junk that Plymouth, and take the bus up to St. Louis. I want to tell them I'm leaving.

LOTTIE. No. You're not going to stay another minute here. All hell is breaking loose here tonight.

SALLY. Well, a little more from me'll be good for them.

TIMMY. Don't let her go in the kitchen.

LOTTIE. I won't allow you to go in there. You go in there and I swear to you, Sally, everything will change. You won't be able to get on that bus.

SALLY. I thought you knew me better than that.

LOTTIE. Sally, I been keeping alive to hear this and you aren't going to spoil it for either one of us now.

SALLY. I swear you'd think it was you running off.

LOTTIE. It is, it is me. I been courting that crazy person all winter long. Now I'm running off to St. Louis and getting married.

SALLY. I have no bitterness, Aunt Lottie. They can't touch me tonight.

LOTTIE. If you got no bitterness, then you got no need. You— Oh damn, what did Mrs. Platt tell Avalaine? She didn't have sense enough to do it. You got sense, I hope.

TIMMY. "Fly away on."

LOTTIE. She told her, "You fly away on," so now I'm telling you: "You fly away on."

SALLY. I don't know how fast a Trailways bus is gonna fly.

LOTTIE. Fast enough. High enough.

HARLEY. *(In hallway, to Buddy.)* You just finish your pie and come on in here.

SALLY. I have to pack some things. If you don't want me to see them, then I better go.

ELDON. I'd as soon thrash all this out tomorrow.

LOTTIE. Sneak up quick. Run upstairs.

HARLEY. The old man's here, you're here, Buddy's here.

ELDON. I know.

HARLEY. I'm not going back to the telegraph office anymore. I tell you. I'd rather it'd been anybody on this earth come to you with that news than me. *(They open the front door and step out.)*

SALLY. What?

SALLY. There isn't anything happened, has there? What's happened?

LOTTIE. Oh, Sally. Your brother...

TIMMY. Don't you dare.

LOTTIE. He's just been raising hell. You know how Buddy... Nothing you have to hear tonight. Run upstairs. You call me tomorrow and I'll tell you everything.

SALLY. You tell them where I've gone. *(She gives Lottie a hug.)*

LOTTIE. Oh, I'll tell them, don't think I won't. *(Harley and Eldon come back in.)*

HARLEY. They've started the Fourth of July celebration down by the river.

LOTTIE. Go go go go go go go go. *(She opens the double doors and pushes Sally, as Eldon and Harley come in the other double doors.)* Oh I could just dance a jig. I could just dance a jig. Damn me for never learning how to dance a jig.

ELDON. You look like the cat that ate the canary.

LOTTIE. Do I look like that? I got to admit that's the way I feel. I chopped down the cherry tree and I ate the canary. Sweetest little thing I ever et. Tasted like lemon-meringue pie. Everybody knew they tasted like that, there wouldn't be a canary left in this town.

BUDDY. *(Entering.)* Harley!

HARLEY. Sit down, sit down. We should just go over the Delaware proposal step by step, I guess.

OLIVE. *(Entering.)* I didn't know if you'd need these brochures or not.

TALLEY. *(Comes from office, pie in hand.)* Harley, before you go. *(Hands the pie to Olive.)* Here. This ain't got no taste.

OLIVE. I beg your pardon. I put a full teaspoon of nutmeg and two teaspoons of cinnamon in that pie. *(Netta enters.)*

HARLEY. Good to see you so fit, sir, but all due respect, I'm the man does the hiring down there, and I'm not so sure you're recruiting the right man for the job.

TALLEY. Never had any intention of that fool working down there. I wouldn't have him around. Now, sir. This is the note and this is the partnership agreement signed by me and your dad. This is the certificate of ownership on that factory. *(To Olive.)* That say ownership?

ELDON. That's what I thought he was up to all along.

OLIVE. Yes, sir, it does.

TALLEY. Now, tomorrow after that baboon and his concubine get married, you call up your Delaware people and you tell them to go ahead with that takeover. After they move that equipment down to Baton Rouge, Mr. Young can do all the cutting and all the foremanning he wants. Let *them* find out what they got. But he ain't working one day for me. Now I'm going to bed.

HARLEY. You don't sell the plant because you got someone working for you you don't like.

NETTA. You do if you want to get rid of a scandal. You send 'em to a town that never heard of the Talleys.

TALLEY. I've never been blackmailed and I won't be. Not by some whore of Whistler's here.

NETTA. Of Eldon's, you mean,

ELDON. I think you'll find the Talley share of that factory is mine, and that decision is mine.

TALLEY. You try not to talk, 'cause I'm making an effort to make sense—we know how I get. I went into that office and prayed for the soul of my grandson, Timothy Everett Talley, who isn't coming back from the Pacific.

LOTTIE. Dear Jesus.

TALLEY. Those two were going to get it all. Now there's just one and he don't want no part of it and never did, and I don't either and never did. Now, Harley, are you for that takeover; yes or no?

HARLEY. If we can work it out.

TALLEY. Good. Here, what's-your-name, vote on the takeover. Yes or no.

Move it out or keep it here. The Talleys are voting on what's going to happen to their share of that pestilent place.

BUDDY. We've been talking about it, sir; I've just been listening.

OLIVE. Buddy, honey, come here a—

TALLEY. You're no namby-pamby; if you are, you grow up now.

BUDDY. There's a lot of things I'd rather do.

OLIVE. Buddy.

BUDDY. You know my interest in the bank, sir.

TALLEY. Speak your mind, what there is of it.

ELDON. Don't let him badger you, Son.

BUDDY. It means a lot to Dad, sir. You better sit down.

TALLEY. Takeover, yes or no, if you want your share. Otherwise I'll give the blamed thing to what's-his-name. Yes or no? Yes or no?

BUDDY. Yes.

OLIVE. Darn it, Buddy.

TALLEY. So. We've had a democratic vote like a family. I vote for them, Kenneth votes for them, you vote for yourself and lose. Two to one. Now, Harley, you know what we think—you do what you want about it.

BUDDY. Dad, I'm sorry, I've never wanted to work here.

TALLEY. Don't be sorry.

OLIVE. Mr. Talley, sit down.

TALLEY. Sorry is for people who know they're doing the wrong thing while they're doing it. You ask Eldon about sorry.

ELDON. Yeah, I could tell you a lot.

HARLEY. If the factory is worth somebody wanting it, it's only because of the standards you've—

ELDON. I'm glad you understand that.

HARLEY. We'll thrash this out tomorrow. It's your decision really, not... (Nods to Talley.)

ELDON. I know it is. Dad doesn't know it. I guess Buddy doesn't either.

BUDDY. What's that?

ELDON. Olive knows though, don't you? I have to say, Buddy, I'm a little surprised.

BUDDY. Dad, I'd like to be down there with you like Timmy was, but...

ELDON. No, you always liked going off with your grandpa to the bank.

BUDDY. I did, sir.

ELDON. And you expect a position to be waiting there for you when you get out, I know. You remember back when my momma died, she left, what was it, thirty percent of the bank to Dad and thirty to me?

BUDDY. Yes, sir.

ELDON. She wanted to be sure I had something, I guess. I've never seen Dad so mad in my life. Remember that, Dad? Tried to get a lawyer to overthrow the will.

OLIVE. Don't get him upset, Dad, he's just burning up.

ELDON. You have what, Harley—twenty-two percent of the bank?

HARLEY. Last time I looked.

ELDON. Now, I figure it's worth about half of the Talley share of that factory, right?

HARLEY. About that, maybe a little more.

TALLEY. No, sir. That factory cannot be touched. Not by you.

ELDON. *(To Harley.)* I know I'll be taking a punishing loss, Harley, but if you're willing, I'd just as soon swap your share in the bank for the Talley half of that factory.

BUDDY. Dad, now…

HARLEY. I couldn't let you do that, Eldon.

TALLEY. Not yours to give and not yours to deal, sir.

ELDON. No, Dad, for over two years I've had power of attorney.

TALLEY. You got no power of nothin' over me.

ELDON. I never dreamed I'd use it. Never dreamed it.

TALLEY. No lawyer on this earth—

ELDON. Dad, damn it, the government man came here to talk to you about increasing production down there, you told him if the hens weren't laying to wring their necks.

LOTTIE. He told you to put more girls on the line, you said you'd put twenty of 'em to set on a dozen eggs each.

ELDON. Then you went around the house crowing like a rooster for two weeks. Harley, swap me your part of the bank.

BUDDY. Dad, we'd be losing our shirts on a trade like that.

HARLEY. You'd want a considerable piece of change, Eldon, I'm not that liquid right now.

ELDON. Thank you, no, not a nickel. With Timmy gone I've got no further interest in the garment business. We'll just shake on it and draw up the papers tomorrow. Yes or no?

HARLEY. You're putting me on the spot here.

ELDON. Yes or no? It's the only way. Your part of the bank for our part of Talley & Son.

OLIVE. That doesn't seem really—

ELDON. That's all right, Olive.

OLIVE. Well, it isn't fair to us, is it?

ELDON. Everybody's all of a sudden worried about what's right and fair. Harley, I've never known you to hesitate over a bargain. You gonna start waffling? Where's that natural greed, boy?

TALLEY. That's my bank down there.

ELDON. No, Dad, it was part mine and part yours; now it's going to be all mine. Harley?

HARLEY. I'll go along with you, Eldon, if that's what you want.

ELDON. Good. I'll see you in the morning then.

OLIVE. I tried to tell you, Buddy.

HARLEY. Good night, Mrs. Talley.

NETTA. Good night, Harley.

HARLEY. Uh…well, listen, Buddy…uh…good to see you…uh…you take care of…uh…good night all. *(He exits.)*

ELDON. I'm sorry, Buddy. I'm sorry, Dad. I know what that bank meant to you two.

OLIVE. *(To Buddy.)* Honey, give me a hand with these cups.

ELDON. You and Buddy were going to hear the band.

BUDDY. Not tonight.

ELDON. No, you go on—let your wife show off her soldier in his uniform.

OLIVE. We've got tomorrow night. Mr. Talley?

TALLEY. Face is burning up. Seeing two of everything. Blamed. Seeing two Lotties, two Eldons, two Olives, enough to give a man a heart attack.

BUDDY. Get him a washrag. *(Olive exits.)*

TALLEY. I'm fine, sir. I'm fine.

BUDDY. You're gonna lose thousands of dollars on that deal, just out of spite.

ELDON. Well, I can't think of a better way to spend money. You didn't want to get your hands dirty with me and Timmy down at the factory, now you don't have to worry about it. *(Olive comes in with a washcloth. Talley wipes his face.)*

BUDDY. That's enough about Timmy. I'm a little sick of hearing that tonight.

ELDON. Timmy was there. I could count on him. You were never on my side in your life.

BUDDY. Oh, bullshit. All Tim ever did was whatever you wanted, so you'd maybe pat him on the head—which you never did. Timmy was his father's little puppy dog, just like you are.

ELDON. Enough.

BUDDY. God knows, I tried to shake some sense into him. Now the son-of-a-bitch's even died for you. *(Eldon slaps him across the face. The blow is blocked, but Buddy staggers back.)* Maybe you'll finally give him credit for doing something.

ELDON. Buddy, you want to work down there at the bank, you better pick up an application tomorrow. There's a lot of good men already ahead of you.

TALLEY. Got no business with that bank, sir.

ELDON. Dad, why don't you go to hell. At least go to bed. You've done enough for one night.

TALLEY. I'm fine, sir.

BUDDY. Let me help you to bed. Come on.

TALLEY. I'm fine, sir.

BUDDY. Come on. Olive, give me a hand. Up you go…down you go…*(He helps Talley out. Olive follows.)*

ELDON. *(He takes the washcloth from where Talley left it, wrings it out in the potted fern. Unconsciously wipes off face. There is a pause.)* You just wonder why you did any of it. Not for Buddy, he was never interested in anything I wanted.

NETTA. I always thought you were doing it for yourself. You knew Buddy didn't like it; I don't think Timmy wanted it either. No point in lying to yourself about it now.

ELDON. I thought they'd see its value when they got older.

NETTA. You didn't care if they did or they didn't as long as you got a day and a half's work out of them. Where the devil has Sally got to?

LOTTIE. I imagine she's around. She'll be here before long.

NETTA. Lottie, don't stay up all night now, you try to get some sleep. *(She is by the window, takes down the flag with two stars.)* I don't want this display in the window anymore. I don't want that. And you take down the one that's in the window at the factory, and the one at the bank. I'm going to sleep in Tim's room tonight. Day after tomorrow I'll move my things in there. I'm not getting out of bed tomorrow. I don't want anyone mooning over me; I just want you to know I'm not coming downstairs.

ELDON. There'll be people come tomorrow to pay their respects—

NETTA. I'm not coming downstairs tomorrow. And you tell Buddy I'm not going to the train to see him off, and I'm not writing any more V-mail letters to him in Belgium or France or Italy or wherever they send him. When he comes home, fine, but until he comes home I consider that he's gone, too. I'm not going to sit home and hope he'll come back. *(Pause.)* And I want you to lock up the house tonight.

ELDON. *(Finding his voice.)* Now, no need for that…

NETTA. *(Still level.)* I want the house locked tonight.

ELDON. There's never been a door locked in this town.

NETTA. You shut these windows and you find the keys, wherever they are, and you lock the house. Now I'm going to bed. *(She goes upstairs.)*

ELDON. If I lock the doors, I'll lock Sally out.

LOTTIE. I'll be here. *(Eldon would like to say something, but can find nothing to say. He exits to the office as Sally starts to sneak down the stairs. To Sally.)* Wait! *(Sally goes back up the stairs. Eldon re-enters. He goes to the French windows and locks them. He and Lottie have been shutting off lights as he goes.)* Don't forget the windows in the dining room.

ELDON. *(Mumbling.)* What a bother. *(He goes.)*

LOTTIE. *(Calling up the stairs.)* Sally! *(Sally sneaks down the hall.)*

SALLY. We'll have you up to visit us in St. Louis soon as we can.

LOTTIE. No, don't worry about me…

SALLY. And we'll be down for a visit next spring. I don't know how the family will like that.

LOTTIE. They'll just have to lump it. *(Eldon re-enters and stops when he sees Sally and Lottie. Sally turns to him.)*

SALLY. I'm going to St. Louis tonight.

ELDON. You going to live with that man?

SALLY. I'm going to marry Matt Friedman, yes.

ELDON. It's not like you to run away without telling the family off.

LOTTIE. That was my idea.

ELDON. You sure you're doing the right thing?

SALLY. Oh, I'm sure.

ELDON. Sometimes you think you're doing the right thing but it doesn't work out that way.

SALLY. It'll work out.

ELDON. I hope so, Sally. *(They embrace.)*

LOTTIE. Sally. You call me tomorrow and I want to hear that operator say I have a collect call for Charlotte Talley from Sally Friedman.

SALLY. Good-bye. *(She exits.)*

ELDON. She'll call you tomorrow?

LOTTIE. Yes.

ELDON. Someone has to tell her about her brother.

LOTTIE. I'll do that. *(She takes the keys.)*

ELDON. Well…Good night, Lottie.

LOTTIE. Good night, Mr. Talley. *(Eldon stands for a moment, then exits. Pause. Lottie and Timmy look out the window.)* Dad's right about one thing; everything's gone to the dogs. The house has needed painting for four years.

TIMMY. Yeah, it's beginning to show it. The garden's pretty bad.

LOTTIE. There's no one now to take care of it. *(She unlocks the French windows.)*

TIMMY. It's a nice old house. It's a lot smaller than I remember.

LOTTIE. *(Opens the French window—a distant band is playing.)* The band's playing down across the river. Oh, that's wonderful. *(A deep breath.)* Oh, that's wonderful. What is it, honey?

TIMMY. America won the war today. We all go off; by the time they get back, the country's changed so much I don't imagine they'll recognize it.

LOTTIE. I know. *(Timmy walks outside and off. Lottie stands alone in the room, listening to the distant band, wondering if she imagined Timmy was there. Then she realizes she is quite alone. The music continues as the light fades.)*

END OF PLAY

A TALE TOLD

Fritz Weaver and Helen Stenborg in the Circle Repertory Company production of *A Tale Told.*
Photograph ©1981 by Gerry Goodstein.

ORIGINAL PRODUCTION

A Tale Told was first produced by Circle Repertory Company, in New York City, during their 1980–1981 season. It was directed by Marshall W. Mason and the production stage manager was Fred Reinglas. The cast was as follows:

Viola Platt	Nancy Kilmer
Olive	Patricia Wettig
Netta	Helen Stenborg
Lottie	Elizabeth Sturges
Eldon	Michael Higgins
Buddy	Timothy Shelton
Emmet Young	Lindsey Richardson
Harley Campbell	Jimmie Ray Weeks
Mr. Talley	Fritz Weaver
Avalaine Platt	Laura Hughes
Timmy	David Ferry
Sally	Trish Hawkins

CHARACTERS

MR. TALLEY, eighty-five. Sometimes senile or nearly, sometimes not. Very much the head of the Talley family.

LOTTIE TALLEY, forty-five. His daughter.

ELDON TALLEY, fifty-four. Talley's son

NETTA TALLEY, Eldon's wife, about the same age.

KENNETH (BUDDY) TALLEY, twenty-nine. Eldon's son. In the uniform of an army Staff Sergeant.

OLIVE TALLEY, twenty-eight. Buddy's wife.

TIMMY TALLEY, twenty-five. Eldon's son. In Marine fatigues.

SALLY TALLEY, thirty-one. Eldon's daughter.

EMMET YOUNG, a handyman, silent with shifty eyes.

VIOLA PLATT, thirty-five, but looking older. The washerwoman, worn and exhausted but with fiber.

AVALAINE PLATT, seventeen, looking older. Her daughter.

HARLEY CAMPBELL, thirty-one. Eldon's business partner. Positive and sentimental.

A Tale Told

ACT ONE

The living room of the Talley place, a large and elegant farmhouse con-
structed in 1865, just outside Lebanon, Missouri. On the Upstage wall is a
fireplace with imposing double doors to the front hall on either side. We can
see the stairs going up and, perhaps, across the hall a set of matching doors—
going into another parlor or the dining room. Front door is visible at one end
of the hall. At one side of the living room there is the door to a room used as
Mr. Talley's office. Opposite the office large French windows open onto a sur-
rounding front porch. In one of the windows is a two-star flag indicating the
family has two sons in the war. The time is sunset, July 4th, 1944. The liv-
ing room is empty.

VIOLA. *(Off. Calling loudly.)* Mr. Eldon? Anybody to home? Mrs. Talley? Yo-
   hoo. Anybody to home?—
OLIVE. *(Upstairs, stage whisper; overlapping.)* Mrs. Platt. Hush up. Oh, my
   goodness.
VIOLA. *(Continuing.)* —Mr. Eldon? Anybody to home here? Miss Talley?
OLIVE. *(Continuing.)* Oh, good lord, would somebody shut that woman up.
   (As Netta appears from the back hall.)
OLIVE. Mother, I just got June to sleep. She's gonna wake her right up.
   (Tim walks from somewhere into the middle of the room. He is wearing
   clean fatigues. He looks about the room, wandering from one side to the
   other.)
NETTA. *(Hurrying past the door, to the front door.)* I was back in the kitchen
   with Nora, I didn't hear her. *(Opens door.)* Here, let me help with that,
   Viola. I was all the way in back.
VIOLA. *(Still too loud.)* I come by for the wash, I saw the car gone, I didn't
   know if you was all over to the park or if somebody was home.

OLIVE. *(Off. From "park".)* Oh, good lord, woman, shush! That woman, I swear, yelling through the house to wake the dead.

NETTA. Lower your voice, Vi, and come on into the back with me. Olive's just got the girl to sleep. If we wake her up we'll be in for it all night. *(They pass by the front door.)*

VIOLA. I figgered I'd best come by and talk to Mr. Eldon.

NETTA. *(They appear at the back door.)* I couldn't even tell you where he's got to. Buddy came back on furlough yesterday and we're all upside-down. I haven't near got the laundry together.

VIOLA. I'm running late myself this evening.

NETTA. *(Slowing down a bit.)* That was a fine turnout for the service for your brother, Vi. I guess he was quite a hero.

VIOLA. Thank you, Mrs. Talley, I appreciate it.

LOTTIE. *(Appearing from the back.)* Is that Vi?

NETTA. Well, have you decided to come out of hibernation?

LOTTIE. I'm not speaking to you. I'm very angry with all of you.

NETTA. Lottie, I don't want the whole family upset again. I would like this to be a normal evening if that's possible. *(Sotto voce.)* Nora and I are trying to cook supper for ten people with Olive running in and out of the kitchen and that's enough for me to deal with, thank you. I'll get the laundry together, Vi.

VIOLA. I can do that.

NETTA. No, we don't want any more people in the kitchen; it's all upside down. *(She exits.)*

LOTTIE. Reverend Poole preached a remarkably restrained service for Vaughan.
(Timmy walks out the French doors, leaving the house.)

VIOLA. If they thought we was any of us gonna be mortified, they got another think comin'.

LOTTIE. They mean well by it.

VIOLA. All that "This is the first Platt ever to be laid away in the church cemetery," like we wasn't good enough for 'em. The reverend's wife bawling like the Noah's flood. All that show is just for them. The army paid for it.

LOTTIE. I'd think that was the least they could do.

VIOLA. Preacher didn't know Vaughan. Had to ask momma what the boy's name was. Momma said "It don't matter to me, you call him what you want."

LOTTIE. Did you see Sally when you came up the road just now?

VIOLA. I didn't, but I wasn't looking. Did you lose her? Maybe it's something with the weather, 'cause I think my girl's runned off.

LOTTIE. Who has? Avalaine?

VIOLA. Yeah, I think she's took off.

LOTTIE. Where would Avalaine go, she's got nowhere to go.

VIOLA. Who knows, she just took off, off and took. It don't matter, just
means more work, but I gotta talk to Mr. Eldon.

LOTTIE. I heard my brother come home from town, but I couldn't tell you
where he is.

VIOLA. I'll have to come back later, 'cause I got to see him.

LOTTIE. Can't it wait till tomorrow? You look done in.

VIOLA. No, it better not.

OLIVE. *(Entering, brisk whisper.)* I thought you'd slipped a cog and was talking to yourself. Don't be too loud, I got June to sleep and Buddy's taking a nap. Mrs. Platt, can you do these antimacassars? Oh, lord, with Mr.
Talley practically breathing his last to talk of a thing like doilies, but I
think momma Talley must of done that work. Did your mother do
these, Lottie?

*(Lottie does not answer, she's not speaking to Olive either; Olive makes the
best of it.)*

OLIVE. Look how fine that work is. You heard my Buddy came home on
leave yesterday? Does this room smell? I aired it out last night, I've had
the windows opened in here all day, I think it still smells. I say you heard
my Buddy came—

VIOLA. Mrs. Talley said.

OLIVE. Have they gone all yellow? I hope that comes out. My eyes, I swear,
in this light. They have to be pinned down to dry.

VIOLA. I know 'em, they're a blamed nuisance.

OLIVE. Don't try to take an iron to them, you'll stretch them all out of kelter.

VIOLA. Fine workmanship like that, if you want to do 'em yourself, I'll
understand.

OLIVE. Well, do what you can. They're the awfullest bother. It seems wrong
to be rejoicing at Buddy coming back and his grandfather's condition so
questionable, but we have to go on, don't we? He's only got a three-day
leave, but my prayer is that the war ends right this week and he doesn't
have to go back to Italy at all.

VIOLA. Is that where he's been stationed?

OLIVE. He was at the wheel of General Mark Clark's car last month when
they drove the Krauts out of Rome. We wired him that his granddad was

failing, General Clark wrote an order for him to come home, right on the spot. Then, he'd hurt his arm, too, so he couldn't drive.
(Lottie snorts.)

OLIVE. He doesn't let on, Lottie, but you can tell he's in pain.

LOTTIE. He's Clark's chauffeur, and he fell down a flight of stairs.

OLIVE. They were under fire all winter, thank you; slugging through that mud, they had casualties everywhere; darn near driven back into the sea, the papers said. They only liberated Rome!

NETTA. *(Entering with the laundry.)* If there's something I'm forgetting, it can just wait till next week.

OLIVE. Should these be starched, mother?

NETTA. Olive, I'm sorry, don't call me mother, it just makes me jump. I can't visit, Nora and me are turning the goose.

OLIVE. I'm sorry, I know. Should these be—well, do what you want. Did your mother put up any blackberry jam this year? That's the first thing Buddy asked for—could you bring back a couple of glasses?

VIOLA. That's all gone by now.

OLIVE. Blackberry season's hardly over, I don't imagine you've had—

VIOLA. We sold all that. I'll get these back soon as ever.

OLIVE. I wanted them for today but there's just so much—we'll have to have them by tomorrow. I want Buddy to see the place looking nice before he has to go back. He should have that, don't you think…?

VIOLA. You want 'em for tomorrow, you best do 'em yourself. Ain't hard, just pesky bothers.

OLIVE. Well, do what you can. Don't step there, honey, with those rubber shoes, I'll be down on my hands and knees again all night.

VIOLA. I spec I'll be back afore long; you tell Mr. Eldon for me that it's important I talk to him. Tell him I said that.

OLIVE. *(Overlapping some as Viola exits.)* Don't yell in the hall, Mrs. Platt; don't go out that front you'll…
(Door slams.)

OLIVE. In my born days I have never seen such a lack of the most basic social graces in my life. That woman has all the class of a draft mule. Not one word about poor granddad, and she knows the condition he's in.

LOTTIE. That was last week. He's strong as a bull today.

OLIVE. Not a syllable about Buddy being home. That whole stupid, squalid family of them is dumb as cattle. I heard they descended on every blackberry patch in Leclede county and just stripped it like a plague of locusts

and she says they already sold it. This furniture needs recovering, does-
n't it?

LOTTIE. Not this evening.

OLIVE. Lottie, there is no call for you to be catty.

LOTTIE. I'm not talking to you, Olive. Vi's brother Vaughan was killed in
Cherbourg last week; they buried him three days ago. She said her
daughter Avalaine has run away, she has worries enough.

OLIVE. I will not believe that Viola Platt is so narrow that she can't rejoice
in another's fortune even in the midst of her own sorrow. That family is
vindictive, ignorant, low and distrustful, but I refuse to believe she's
unfeeling. *(Sotto voce.)* And Avalaine Platt has been seen with these eyes
out with Emmet Young and I wouldn't repeat the condition they were in.
(The door opens, Eldon enters.)

OLIVE. Oh, good lord, I thought I'd seen a ghost. I didn't even know you
had a key to that office, dad. The washerwoman was looking for you, I
think I got rid of her.

ELDON. I see you're opening the parlor.

OLIVE. Mother and I thought we'd air it out. It seems so callous, but we
all—

ELDON. Good idea.

OLIVE. Oh, dad; that door opened, I couldn't imagine. My hand is just
shaking like a leaf.

ELDON. Should have gone in the office ten years ago.

OLIVE. What does he keep in—well, it's no business of mine. I don't want
to know. I'm fixing up a little surprise for supper so I better get busy.
(She exits.)

ELDON. I've told Olive a hundred times not to call me dad. My sons don't
do it, I don't see any reason for one of their wives to. Netta got four letters from Timmy this morning. Has she read them?

LOTTIE. I don't know.

ELDON. I was hoping we could have both the boys home at the same time,
so the whole family could be together this once.

LOTTIE. They're in her apron pocket, I don't know if she's had the time to
read them.

ELDON. The old man must have his system of filing things, but I swear I
can't figger it out. Piles of paper and deeds. Stock certificates for companies that have been out of business for fifty years.

LOTTIE. Did you see Sally on the road when you were coming back from
town?

ELDON. I didn't see her; why, is she lost?

LOTTIE. The Talley family has been acting up to its usual standards of hospitality this evening.

BUDDY. *(Coming down from upstairs.)* Oh, lord, all I have to do is stretch out on that bed and I'm gone to the world. Ollie, have you seen my—

ELDON. Well, there's another country heard from.

BUDDY. *(Looking in the room.)* Hey, Eldon, when did you get back from town?

ELDON. Looks like someone's been taking a cat nap.

BUDDY. All I have to do is stretch out on that bed and I'm gone. Did Lottie tell you we had our fireworks around here early this fourth. You missed it.

NETTA. *(Entering from kitchen.)* Eldon Talley, have you been in here all this time since you got home?

BUDDY. He missed the fun.

NETTA. I'll fun you. I swear you have an absolute talent for leaving the house when you're going to be needed.

BUDDY. You remember that Jew you said Sally dragged to supper here last year? Well, I had the pleasure of making his acquaintance this evening.

ELDON. The hell you did.

BUDDY. He came by here from St. Louis to see her.

NETTA. If he'd stayed ten minutes more, Sally would have drove up while he was standing right there on the porch.

BUDDY. I'd liked to have seen that.

NETTA. Well, now, everything is back to normal. I don't want the whole family getting upset again.

ELDON. What'd he want here?

NETTA. I couldn't make out what he wanted. Buddy and Harley finally got rid of him.

BUDDY. Took out that old shotgun; he started shaking like a hound shittin' razor blades.

NETTA. *(Loving it.)* I won't have that army barracks talk in here. That man would have turned around and gone right back to his car if Lottie hadn't deliberately tried to entice him into the house. I just think your sister has a lot of explaining to do.

ELDON. That's what you're talking about the Talley hospitality?

LOTTIE. I said I wasn't discussing Matt Friedman with anyone in this family, and I'm not.

OLIVE. *(Entering.)* Honey, did Mrs. Platt wake you up, yelling for dad?

BUDDY. I woke up because I started smelling Nora's Christmas goose and baked turnips. I could almost see the snow falling.

ELDON. You said you wanted to have Christmas in July.

NETTA. They're buttered they're not baked and supper is at least two hours yet.

BUDDY. I think I've missed Nora's cooking about as much as I've missed—

OLIVE. —Don't you? Did you have a good nap?

BUDDY. I slept like the dead once I got the chance.

OLIVE. *(Thrilled.)* Oh, don't say that! Oh! You! Oh!

NETTA. What are you napping about? I don't know why you baby him like that. Napping, in the middle of the afternoon.

BUDDY. I was babyin' her, she wasn't—

OLIVE. *(Playful to instant serious.)* Oh, you! None of that! Mother, do you think Granddad is strong enough to come to supper tonight?

NETTA. I'll look in and see.

ELDON. He was up this morning, and dressed.

NETTA. He ate enough dinner to last him a week. I haven't seen him that strong in over a year.

OLIVE. He's so remarkable. Buddy, I wrote you, if you could of seen him a week ago. We did, we all thought it was the last.

LOTTIE. You might have counted on him.

NETTA. I'm amazed he didn't wake up with the ruckus that—Friedman person was causing.

BUDDY. Aunt Lottie, if you're looking for that—jerk he's long gone.

LOTTIE. I'm wondering where your sister has gotten to. After the way you and Netta were talking to her.

NETTA. Lottie, Sally is over thirty years old and able to take care of herself, to say the least.

ELDON. Sally's *never* home if she can help it. Between that volunteer nursing—

LOTTIE. Nurse's aide.

ELDON. Well, whatever it is she does and I'm not saying it isn't necessary, but she's never here, if she can help it.

LOTTIE. She came home tonight and everybody lit in on her like she—

NETTA. I am still her mother, I hope. And I know as well as I'm standing here that she brought that—man home last year just out of spite. I can't understand a word he says, I swear I think he's a communist.

LOTTIE. You have no call treating anybody in that manner.

ELDON. Lottie, I don't know what gets into you.

NETTA. The man is a crazyperson. He liked to scare Olive half out of her wits.

OLIVE. I went to the door; I saw him standing there—I couldn't even speak.

ELDON. The man is crazy, I think.

NETTA. He *is,* he's a maniac. Chasing after Sally like that.

BUDDY. Fat chance of anybody getting her interested.

NETTA. No, she's got no interest in him, she told me so. He won't take a hint. The man has written her a letter every blessed day since he was down here last summer. He's just got no sense at all.

BUDDY. I hope he writes better than he talks.

NETTA. Every blessed day. I don't think Sally even reads them. The man is a madman.

BUDDY. I've fought alongside the Poles and the Canadians, and the English and the French, not to mention some of the GIs, but that character takes the cake.

NETTA. I told Olive to call the sheriff, nobody could find you.

ELDON. No need to bother Cliffy with Buddy and Harley here.

LOTTIE. I hope they're proud of their behavior, too.

BUDDY. Oh, we gave him a fine reception.

NETTA. If he wasn't so hopeless I'd be scared silly of him.

BUDDY. No, he's harmless.

ELDON. What was Harley doing here when he's coming to dinner tonight?

BUDDY. Oh, we had a good talk. He's lost some weight; you must be working him down at the factory.

OLIVE. No business, now.

NETTA. I notice you're not getting any thinner. They can't be starving you.

BUDDY. It's an education the things a person can gain weight eating. Did you find those house shoes?

NETTA. I looked, Buddy, I think they might be gone.

BUDDY. They aren't gone, I've been dreaming about those shoes all through Central Italy.

OLIVE. Well, if we can't find them we can surely buy you a new pair.

BUDDY. I don't want a new pair. I want my damn house shoes. I told you to send them to Rome.

OLIVE. Well, they've taught you a few new words.

NETTA. We haven't got any of your mail from Rome yet.

BUDDY. I been dreaming about those shoes.

OLIVE. I don't know as I even remember what they look like.

ELDON. Did Harley tell you about Delaware Industries proposition?

BUDDY. Yeah, and he wrote me. It sounds interesting.

ELDON. I'm sure from his point of view.

BUDDY. Interesting, I said.

NETTA. No business talk, now. You know how you two are.

BUDDY. Harley gets pretty het-up sometime.

ELDON. I think Harley has pipe dreams of being on the board of directors of some big corporation, sitting back on his can smoking a cigar, doing nothing.

BUDDY. Pipe dreams about smoking a cigar—listen, as long as it pays.

OLIVE. There's coffee, honey, on the stove…

ELDON. Oh, it pays, they got money to burn, as long as the price of the Delaware Industries stock goes up on the stock exchange. That's what they're offering us; stock in their company.

BUDDY. It's interesting, I said. You turn out a good product; you've attracted some attention; you should have been looking out for it.

NETTA. Eldon, have you—

ELDON. We turn out good work; so they take over our name and sell what they please under it.

OLIVE. Are you going to put on your shoes or you going to go barefoot?

BUDDY. I was hoping to be able to put on my damn house shoes.

NETTA. Just don't be getting so free with that talk.

LOTTIE. Oh, shit. Everybody knows Olive burned those shoes last April.

OLIVE. Lottie Talley, when I do—I could even say, more than my share, I can't remember during Spring cleaning, with so much, if I might have accidentally thrown out—

NETTA. (Overlapping above.) Now, I don't know where they are, Lottie. Olive had no way of knowing Buddy'd be asking for those slippers.

BUDDY. It's OK, it doesn't matter. Good lord.

OLIVE. If something happened to them, I'm sorry, though I'm sure if they're so important then they're still around. Now, there's coffee on the stove. There's going to be no shortage of coffee for you.

NETTA. And there's sugar.

ELDON. They've saved up their stamps for the last month.

OLIVE. And I'm planning a treat, but you're just going to have to be hungry till supper-time. Mother's planned a feast is what she's done.

ELDON. She's killed the fatted calf.

NETTA. We've killed the fatted goose and I'm not joking; I've never seen so much grease in my life.

BUDDY. Coffee doesn't sound like a bad idea. I heard the Italians made such good coffee; I hadn't had coffee in a month, they gave me a cup, I had to spit it out on the ground. Wooo! Tasted like they burned it; god knows what they did to it.

ELDON. You won't spit this out.

(Olive and Buddy exit to kitchen.)

NETTA. Buddy, don't get in Nora's way in there. *(Sotto voce.)* She's about to run out of patience with Olive, I'm not joking.

ELDON. Well, he doesn't keep records, I don't know what it is he keeps. Every time I ask him about anything he goes senile on me. That's his new trick. Lottie could remember some of these people if you tried. You knew the Sapers, I didn't.

LOTTIE. Dad didn't tell you about his transactions, and I didn't want him to tell me. You let me in there, I'll burn the office and its contents.

ELDON. You and Sally, I don't know where you got your attitude.

NETTA. Sally wouldn't be caught dead in there.

LOTTIE. No, we'd have a gay old time. You just be sure you keep it locked.

NETTA. Well, not to keep you out.

ELDON. Oh, Olive wouldn't be surprised at anything you find in there, you can bet.

NETTA. I'm sure nothing as piddlin' as a strong Yale lock ever kept that one out of—well, nobody wants to hear mother-in-law talk.

OLIVE. *(Entering.)* Did granddad come through here, mother?

NETTA. *(Jumps a foot.)* Oh! Lord! Olive! Scare me out of ten years growth.

OLIVE. Did he go to the bathroom?

ELDON. I haven't seen him.

OLIVE. I went in to see if he wanted to come to supper tonight, he isn't there. He's not here. He isn't strong enough to go upstairs, is he?

NETTA. I looked in after dinner and he was dressed and sitting up. Told me to get out so I got.

ELDON. He's full of vinegar today.

LOTTIE. You could have counted on him coming back to life out of contrariness.

NETTA. Lottie, *(Going off, yelling.)* Mr. Talley?

BUDDY. *(Entering.)* He's not around to the side.

NETTA. *(Off.)* Well, this is absurd. Mr. Talley?

ELDON. He couldn't hear you if you yelled that right in his ear.

LOTTIE. Don't kid yourself.

ELDON. Well, so he lets on when it's convenient.

OLIVE. *(Off and back on.)* Did you park the Packard in the drive when you came back from town?

ELDON. I took the pickup.

OLIVE. Well, where'd you leave the Packard?

ELDON. Same place I've always—

OLIVE. Cause unless someone's moved it, I can't see it out there.

ELDON. It's right in front of the pickup.

OLIVE. Well, I'm sorry, but it isn't.

ELDON. Don't fly off crazy, Emmet's probably washing it around behind the barn.

OLIVE. Emmet Young is sitting on his duff like he always is, whittling a stick.

ELDON. *(Yelling out the window.)* Emmet! Emmet, come in here.

OLIVE. If ever anyone holds a contest for stick whittling, I'm going to enter that man and make my fortune.

NETTA. Oh, good lord, he couldn't have got up and taken that car off.

ELDON. He doesn't even know how to drive it; he doesn't know the shift.

NETTA. He couldn't do that. He's out to the barn to look at the horses.

ELDON. There's no insurance on that car with him drivin' it.

BUDDY. There's not been a running horse on the place since I was a kid.

NETTA. You tell him that, and tell him they don't skate down on the millpond anymore.

OLIVE. Tell him the church burned down.

ELDON. He remembers what he wants to.

(Emmet enters.)

ELDON. Have you seen dad since dinnertime?

EMMET. Not since this morning. I been down to the pump house.

ELDON. You hear the car drive off? You see it?

EMMET. I had that auxiliary pump goin', I wouldn't a heard nothin'.

ELDON. Well, look around and see if you can see the Packard. Damn it all.

(Emmet leaves.)

NETTA. I better call Cliffy. Good lord. *(Exits.)*

ELDON. What does he think he's up to?

BUDDY. I'll take the pickup and go along the road; don't bother Cliffy, we'll catch him.

OLIVE. Dad can do that. Or Emmet can go in his own car. *(Chasing him out.)* Buddy, we have to go up and look in on June; well, I'm coming along.

BUDDY. You're helping mother cook supper, I thought.

OLIVE. Buddy Talley, I swear; you just got home, honey, you're only on leave for seventy-two hours. Honey!

(Everyone has left except Eldon and Lottie.)

ELDON. I knew dad was half senile, but I *(Pause. He notices that Lottie is standing frozen, in pain.)* Are you in pain? *(Pause.)* I wish you'd let the others know you're sick. *(Pause.)* I wouldn't think it would be so painful. *(Pause.)* Is there…?

(She shakes her head. Catches her breath.)

ELDON. Is it passing?

LOTTIE. *(Nods.)* Oh, damn.

ELDON. Better?

LOTTIE. *(Blissfully, breathlessly.)* Oh! Gone! Gone completely. Blessed relief. Oh, I'm walking on air. Nothing left of it at all.

ELDON. I wouldn't have thought it would hurt so much.

LOTTIE. Oh, who knows anything about it. Oh, I feel lovely. Oh, my. It certainly is taking it's time, isn't it?

ELDON. Enough of that.

LOTTIE. Oh, it's only pain, after all…Oh, wonderful!

ELDON. When do you go back to see the doctors?

LOTTIE. I think they've lost interest. All the other girls have kicked the bucket except five of us that they know about. One of those is about to go, poor thing. The other four of us are holding out on them. The doctors would like to close the books, publish their reports. We're not going to let them. We're in a race to the *(Laughing.)* well, I was going to say to the finish. That's the truth!

(Phone rings.)

LOTTIE. That's for me.

NETTA. *(In the hall.)* I got it, Lottie.

LOTTIE. I'll get it. You know better than that.

(Standing in the hall, within sight. Netta is out of sight.)

NETTA. *(Off.)* Hello.

LOTTIE. Who is it? Is that for me?

NETTA. *(Off.)* Hello, Cliffy.

LOTTIE. Is that for me?

NETTA. *(To Lottie.)* It's Cliffy. *(Phone.)* Well, how is he, we've been worried sick.

LOTTIE. I don't want you tying up that phone tonight.

NETTA. He's fine he says. They're bringing him back. Harley is. *(Phone.)* What say?

ELDON. *(As Lottie comes back into the room.)* You're quick enough when that phone rings.

LOTTIE. If that's my one pleasure, I don't want it denied me.

ELDON. Who's the secret admirer?

LOTTIE. I have my enjoyments.

ELDON. You haven't been talking to someone for Sally's benefit have you?

LOTTIE. If I had I wouldn't discuss it.

ELDON. Who was it?

LOTTIE. Dad's alive, I guess. It was Cliffy, in town.

ELDON. What's the sheriff doing calling here? Is dad OK? He didn't have a wreck?

NETTA. He's fine, he said. *(Exits.)*

LOTTIE. With Olive sprucing up the parlor for a funeral so the old boy can be laid out in style, it looks like the least dad could do is oblige everybody by dying.

ELDON. I don't want to hear that, Lottie.

LOTTIE. I never understood martyrs, Eldon.

ELDON. So you became one.

LOTTIE. Me? Shit. If that company hadn't gone out of business, or gone under cover, I'd sue them for every dime they have. Make a bundle. Leave it to…whom? *(Playing solitaire.)* Disperse it to the Talley victims.

ELDON. There's no such animal.

LOTTIE. We could never talk about that. Well, I don't know anything about it.

ELDON. No, you don't. Dad was the—is the—best businessman Southern Missouri ever saw. I'm no match for him.

LOTTIE. No, you're not, to your credit. You take after mom; I think I must take after dad.

ELDON. I don't know how he did it.

LOTTIE. I'm the schemer between the two of us. When did old Marie Curie kick the bucket? Ten years ago, bless her, or I could bring a suit against her. Little wisp of a thing, I saw a photograph once. 'Course Old Marie didn't tell us to point our brushes with our tongues.

ELDON. Oh, don't.

LOTTIE. Give you the willies? Everyone of us did it. Had a little pot of radium paint to paint the clock dials with. Point the brush on our tongues, dip it in the paint, paint a number, point the brush on our little tongues. What did we know? Nobody knew anything about it. The foreman told us not to. Thought it was unsanitary. They gave us little wet sponges for the purpose. Only one girl used it that I know of. Didn't like the taste. I couldn't tell it had any. She went too—years ago—cancer of the bone. Whole arm dried up, hair fell out. Poor baby. Well, that's the rewards of a delicate palate.

NETTA. *(Entering.)* They're pulling up out front. Harley brought him back. Buddy didn't get to the road even, Harley turned into the drive.

ELDON. Where the devil had he got to?

NETTA. He did, he took the Packard. Harley's driving him back in it.

OLIVE. *(Entering.)* He could be hurt, anything could have happened.

ELDON. No sense worrying about—

(Netta and Olive exit to hall.)

BUDDY. *(Off.)* We're back. He must be OK, he's walking almost by himself. I never saw anything like it.

NETTA. *(Off.)* Come on, back up, here we go.

HARLEY. *(Off.)* I tell you, he is a cuss!

TALLEY. Wooo! Oh, boy.

HARLEY. Forward, wooo, I bet! You should a seen it. I was— *(Entering with Talley, Netta and Olive and Buddy.)* just driving by, I saw the car run into a ditch up at the hill. I thought—

ELDON. Is he alright?

HARLEY. I thought what the hell's going on—excuse me, Netta. Oh, he's fine. Old man Talley's got more guts than an army mule. Ain't ya?

TALLEY. Who?

HARLEY. He's been sayin' that all the way. I parked my car, got out, and there he was up on the hill—dressed for the middle of winter, standing up in the middle of the graveyard. Caretaker—

(Netta and Olive say—"Oh, my lord," etc.)

HARLEY. —said he'd been taking up a spot and looking around, then moving to another spot. Admiring the sunset, I guess.

BUDDY. Selecting his site, maybe.

NETTA. Oh, his place is all laid out.

HARLEY. Well, maybe he decided he doesn't like it no more.

ELDON. He's right by momma.

TALLEY. Who? Say who?

NETTA. He's overexcited.

OLIVE. You don't want to stay here, Mr. Talley. You want to go into your room?

TALLEY. Here, you! Blamed woman. Let me be. Who? Say who?

NETTA. What, Mr. Talley?

TALLEY. Who?

HARLEY. Sounds like a goddamned owl.

NETTA. *(Smiling.)* Harley, I don't want talk like that, and don't be disrespectful. This is still Mr. Talley's house.

OLIVE. I've never seen him so rambunctious.

TALLEY. Who?

NETTA. He doesn't hear. Darlin', would you want to go? You want to go to your room?

OLIVE. Mr. Talley? You want to go?

TALLEY. Blamed woman. Get her off me.

ELDON. He's not hurt none.

HARLEY. Shoot no, try to hurt him.

ELDON. What kind of shape is the car in?

HARLEY. I didn't look, it drives good. That's the miracle. I don't think he knows where the brake is on it.

ELDON. He doesn't know how to drive it at all; he doesn't know the shift.

HARLEY. Run it into a bank to stop it; might be scratched up.

(Eldon exits.)

NETTA. The important thing is he's not hurt.

TALLEY. Fine house. Fine room. Chair. Chair.

NETTA. He wants a chair, Buddy.

OLIVE. Here you go, Mr. Talley.

TALLEY. Get me to sit down. What? Who?

BUDDY. Looks like he's happy enough with himself.

NETTA. I don't know what causes his mind to just snap like that. This morning he was sharp as a tack. He went into his office.

HARLEY. It's good to see old Buddy, ain't it! All dressed up like a soldier. I thought you'd be in civvies for one day at least.

OLIVE. Harley. You're always in service. You're always on call. You know better than that.

HARLEY. I didn't know I was going to be impressed, or I'd have prepared myself.

OLIVE. Uncle Sam may need you at anytime night or day.

BUDDY. And he ain't the only one.

TALLEY. Who? Oh, boy. *(Smiles, grunts.)* Oh, boy. *(Smiles, grunts.)* Oh, boy.

NETTA. What's that? Mr. Talley? Oh, no. No, papa, not here. Oh, dear, Olive, help me get him into the bathroom—Oh, Mr. Talley. Oh, no.

HARLEY. Wooooee! Oh, boy for sure.

BUDDY. Well, momma said. It's his house.

HARLEY. Netta, you said do you want to go and he went.

BUDDY. I guess he's just following orders.

OLIVE. Both of you, now.

NETTA. Don't you laugh.

HARLEY. Never in my life seen a man so pleased with himself.

NETTA. *(She and Olive have moved Talley almost to the door. They stop.)* Mr. Talley? No? Well, come on. Wait. Don't you laugh, you'll be like this someday. I think that was a false alarm. Do you want to go to the bathroom?

(He sits.)

NETTA. He's fine. He's been gassy is all. Don't you laugh.

ELDON. *(Entering.)* Whole side of the car is scratched from front to back. Must have gone against a tree, but there's no real damage to it.

NETTA. Don't you want to take off your coat?

OLIVE. Are you too warm?

TALLEY. Who?

NETTA. What does he think I'm saying?

HARLEY. I haven't seen a coat of that quality in twenty years. That must have cost a hundred dollars.

NETTA. Oh, he was always a dresser.

OLIVE. Weren't you, Mr. Talley?

TALLEY. *(As they take off his coat.)* Hey, hey. Let me go! Blamed. Blamed.

OLIVE. Aren't you too warm?

BUDDY. Look at that suit material.

OLIVE. Well, it wouldn't hurt you to have one good suit.

HARLEY. He's always been pretty classy.

OLIVE. And you, too, Harley, when you own the garment factory in town you might as well dress like it.

HARLEY. Shiii—nothing like that ever came out of Lebanon. Imported wool, made by hand in St. Louis. Him and dad both thought they was hot stuff. Only good it did dad was give him something fancy to be buried in.

NETTA. It isn't all just show.

HARLEY. You wait till you see me tonight. I'm gonna put on the dog for you.

OLIVE. I tried to air out the room, but it still has a smell.

NETTA. That's the coal furnace; the room's been closed up since last winter, it still has that coal smell.

ELDON. I remember when I was a boy they heated with wood. The whole house, when you came into it smelled like a smokehouse. You opened the door in the wintertime, that smell was everywhere.

TALLEY. No, sir.

ELDON. What say, dad? I think he's calmed down.

NETTA. What say, darlin'?

TALLEY. Said coal.

OLIVE. What's he saying?

TALLEY. All coal heat. Steam heat into the radiators, fired by a coal furnace. Bought and paid for it myself. No different from now. School was coal, church was coal, city hall was coal. Me and Elijah Scott bought a half interest in the delivery service. Talley place got a new furnace, with radiators, everybody in town had to have one.

ELDON. Well, then, what am I remembering?

TALLEY. You're remembering courting one of your girlfriends out in her daddy's smokehouse.

LOTTIE. Yes, he's calmed down to normal.

HARLEY. I think.

TALLEY. You're thinking of some roadhouse speakeasy. *(To Harley.)* Sit down, Mr. Campbell. I can't look up.

HARLEY. That old boy used to scare the tar outta me. He was somethin'.

ELDON. I don't know what he's saying.

NETTA. To see a mind as sharp as his used to be…

BUDDY. Looks pretty fit to me.

TALLEY. Contracted for the school delivery and contracted for the Municipal Building delivery—

BUDDY. Eldon pulled every string he knew; General Clark put me on a plane to get me back because granddad was—

NETTA. We should just count our blessings, Buddy.

BUDDY. —on his last leg; I get here and look at him. Strong as an ox.

HARLEY. That Jew's Plymouth is parked down the road.

ELDON. The hell you say.

HARLEY. Looks like he run outta gas and pushed it off the road.

ELDON. If I thought he was still on the property I'd go out hunting. And be within my legal rights, too.

BUDDY. Hell, he's long gone. That one won't hang around.

HARLEY. Buddy took out that old shotgun; you shoulda seen him hightail it. You heard what happened night before last down at the Eagle's Hall? You know Windy Pine? The milkman?

OLIVE. What kind of name is Windy Pine?

ELDON. Well named, too. Get him started the milk could sit there and clabber.

HARLEY. Well, now, his granddaughter got herself married Sunday; the Eagles was throwing them a dance. Old Windy Pine was out on the dance floor doing his Balling-the-jack, fell over dead in the middle of the floor. Ain't that the way to go?

ELDON. I heard that this morning in town.

OLIVE. Oh, no, Harley.

HARLEY. That's the way I want to go. None of that having cancer or being paralyzed and laying abed for ten years, depending on somebody.

OLIVE. How old a man was he?

HARLEY. You know Old Windy Pine?

OLIVE. I beg your pardon, how am I going to know the milkman?

HARLEY. How did you get such a stuck-up wife? I thought Mary Jo was high-toned.

OLIVE. Oh, you!

ELDON. Windy must of been seventy-five if he was a day. Didn't look it.

HARLEY. Hell, no; excuse me. didn't look it at all.

NETTA. And his daughter was just getting married?

BUDDY. There's hope for Sally, yet.

(Lottie shuffles the cards.)

HARLEY. His granddaughter was getting married, Netta.

(Lottie back-shuffles the cards.)

NETTA. Well, I thought. Of course we don't go to any of those dances.

OLIVE. Lottie, you're going to go right to "H-E-double-toothpicks" with those cards.

LOTTIE. Every step of the way.

TALLEY. Windy Pine. Yes, sir. There he was.

HARLEY. Mr. Talley knew him.

NETTA. Don't say anything then, I don't want him upset.

TALLEY. Goin' a blue streak.

OLIVE. Are you going to be hungry? Do you want to have supper with the family this evening? Harley, you might as well stay now you're here again.

HARLEY. I got a dozen things to do first; I got to go to the draft board yet; this stop wasn't on my schedule; I'm about to spend the whole day and night here. I still haven't had a chance to go home and change my clothes; wash up.

NETTA. You look fine.

HARLEY. No, I said. A big dinner like you got planned, Mary Jo would have a fit if we didn't dress up and turn out.

ELDON. We're not used to these fancy late supper parties; I'm about starved.

NETTA. You'll just have to wait like everybody else.

OLIVE. Buddy missed Christmas with the family, so we're having it now.

HARLEY. So how about that Delaware Industries offer? You read those brochures I left with you?

BUDDY. I looked at some of the pictures.

ELDON. Thought you didn't know about it.

BUDDY. I don't.

NETTA. No, now, no business talk and none tonight or the women will just leave you sitting at the table.

HARLEY. I think it's pretty sound. 'Course I don't know the first thing about it to hear Eldon.

BUDDY. I'm always willing to listen.

OLIVE. She's not joking, now. You two.

HARLEY. OK, OK. *(Lighting a cigarette, gives Buddy one.)*

OLIVE. Harley Campbell and Kenneth Talley! You two, if you want to smoke a cigarette, you step outside and do it or step into another room. You know better than that. Mother'll have your hide.

HARLEY. Son of a gun, I clean forgot.

OLIVE. Oh, I'm sure. I'm not kidding with you, now.

HARLEY. I know, I know. Come on. What a bossy woman. I don't know how you put up with her.

BUDDY. Oh, I need it. Keeps me in step.

(They move out the French doors.)

OLIVE. You can't tell me Mary Jo allows you to smoke in the parlor, I don't care how modern you are.

TALLEY. Windy Pine. Right there. Going a blue streak.

NETTA. I hope Harley hasn't started him going. I don't think he wants to move. He's OK here.

OLIVE. He's all right. *(Olive exits.)*

NETTA. She's going right back to that kitchen. Nora is going to flat quit on us.

TALLEY. Windy Pine. All gone. Everyone of 'em gone.

NETTA. How does he know that? Eldon, now, don't talk business this evening. I don't want you and Buddy in an argument. Nothing should be decided without Timmy here anyway.

ELDON. Timmy has always gone along with anything his big brother told him to do.

NETTA. You heard what I said. I'd like it to be peaceful. *(She exits.)*

ELDON. I know. Dad? You look like you're in pretty good shape. What did you think you were doing? Up on the hill? *(Beat.)* Dad?

TALLEY. Had a drive, sir. Had a walk around.

ELDON. We're here to drive you around anytime you want to go out.

TALLEY. Looked around; see a mile.

ELDON. From up there at the cemetery? I'd think you can see twenty miles; you can see into Greene County. *(Beat.)* Dad, I've been going through your office, trying to sort things out for you.

TALLEY. Say who?

ELDON. *(Gives up; looks to Lottie.)* Did you know dad owns half the Basset farm?

LOTTIE. I don't know anything about what he owns.

ELDON. Well, I didn't either. But the income from forty percent of the Basset Farm has been coming to him for twenty years. He doesn't write it down, just keeps a stack of notes—"Basset Farm, 1942, earned three thousand net, forty percent: twelve hundred dollars." With a paperclip in the corner, I guess where there was a check attached.

LOTTIE. Cash. The Bassets don't use a bank.

ELDON. I can't find anything says we own it, but the money comes in.

LOTTIE. Dad's probably got something on Leslie Basset.

TALLEY. Place has gone to the dogs.

ELDON. The Basset Farm? Looks pretty good to me.

TALLEY. Talley place, I say. Look at this room. Wouldn't invite a dog in here. All going to the devil without me.

ELDON. Dad, with the war on, everything is run down. *(Low, where Talley can't hear.)* And you are very much with us.

TALLEY. What account are you? Keeping books is all you're good for. Start out keeping books, sir, you end up keeping books.

ELDON. *(Low.)* We can do without that tonight.

TALLEY. You. Sally. Answer up when you're spoke to.

ELDON. That's Lottie, dad.

TALLEY. We all of us got to go, young lady. You scared of going?

LOTTIE. *(Beat.)* Well, I'm hoping not to see you there; wherever it is.

TALLEY. I ain't. Ain't anxious, ain't scared.

ELDON. Do you believe that? And he doesn't even know about you.

TALLEY. I ain't scared. Come and take me. I've lived a good, clean, Christian life in my time.

LOTTIE. If there's a heaven, daddy, you'll burn in hell.

ELDON. That's not called for.

TALLEY. Charlotte, besides painting clocks what have you done? Run off to be independent, come hang-doggin' it back ten years later— Done nothing.

LOTTIE. Thirteen. And if there had been another place to go—

ELDON. She got sick, dad.

TALLEY. Stood there with her college degree in her hand and told me I was a curmudgeon. Said she was going off to work amongst the poor people. Ended up painting clocks. That place closed down and where did you go? Speak up. Chicago. Working in some socialist outfit. Working with the colored children; guess she couldn't stomach them, cause first thing you know—

LOTTIE. I spent nine years in Chicago, before I started feeling weak, and it's the only time I've been of any use to anybody at all.

TALLEY. And what you got to show for it? Come hang-doggin' it back, looking for the curmudgeon to feed you. Fine family I raised; fine children, the two of you.

ELDON. I don't know what more I was supposed to do.

LOTTIE. I'm not going to have a conversation with you, daddy; I choose the people I talk to.

TALLEY. Comes a time in a man's life, he totals it all up; adds it all up. I go and the place goes to blazes.

ELDON. *(Low.)* We'll just have to do the best we can if we're ever given the chance.

LOTTIE. Amen.

ELDON. He's never made a will, he never kept a book. He's never confided anything to a lawyer. Used a different lawyer for every transaction he made. Didn't trust them. Can't say I blame him.

LOTTIE. He's not afraid of going because he doesn't think he will.

ELDON. He may not, Lottie, he may not.

TALLEY. Use your head.

ELDON. Yes, well, I'm sure you've still got every deal you ever made stored away somewhere in yours.

TALLEY. Look at you with that paper. You go in that office with all those papers, you know what you'd do? Sir? You'd alphabetize them.

ELDON. I'd like to pitch out most of it. What does that signify? Can't even read it. Carl Saper, December, 1913. What's funny?

(Talley smoothes the paper out, laughs.)

ELDON. Is he laughing or is he crying?

TALLEY. Well, sir. Old Carl Saper had thirty acres wildland. Had eighty-five black walnut trees on it. Wasn't worth nothin'.

ELDON. What's he talking about?

LOTTIE. But you took it away from him anyway, didn't you, daddy?

TALLEY. No, lady, no sir. Loaned him a bundle, mortgaged the land. Nine thousand dollars for fifteen years. Damn fool tried to raise geese. Didn't know the first thing about it. Feathers everywhere. Said he couldn't pay that year. Couldn't pay the interest, couldn't pay the principle; said don't take the land away, leave the land in my name and take the walnuts. Well, sir, I went down there, looked the place over, said, "Next year you pay, this year what I can get off those walnut trees is mine." Wrote it out, notarized by Norma Ann Comstock. Black walnuts sellin' for forty cents a gunnysack, hulled. Had the colored boys from Old Town pick 'em up, haul 'em to the exchange, called a company in Minneapolis, Minnesota, came here, cut down the walnut trees for fancy lumber. Made veneer out of 'em. Made eleven thousand dollars off that no count wildland in 19 and 13. Told Old Saper, now you got good pastureland. I should charge you for clearing it. Fool tried to sue me. Hadn't read the paper. Read what you sign, I tell him. Use your eyes. Know the worth of a thing. *(Laughs.)*

LOTTIE. *(Without looking up.)* Is he laughing or crying?

ELDON. He was always the one for a bold strategy.

TALLEY. Wouldn't sell to me, lady. Dern fool sold at a loss not to sell to the Talleys. See what's happening and happen first. Eldon never looked up from his bookkeeping. Start keeping books, you end up keeping books.

ELDON. Don't start in on me, damn it; Dad, I've done pretty well with what you've allowed me to do. I'm not a steward to some—

TALLEY. Only thing you ever did on your own was run gin to St. Louis during prohibition; thought I didn't know how you was enhancing the Talley name. Fine children. Get me up. Up. Won't have it. Fine children.

ELDON. Just when I think his mind is back it leaves again; when I think it's gone it's back. Here, don't go alone; wait and I'll help you.

TALLEY. Up. Up. Get me to my room, blamed. Blamed.

VIOLA. *(Entering.)* Excuse me. Mr. Eldon. Everybody was around to the kitchen, so I came to the front.

TALLEY. And if you had any gumption you'd have Harley tell those Delaware boys to jump in the creek; got no gumption.

ELDON. You don't know anything about that.

VIOLA. I knocked, I couldn't get nobody to hear. I didn't want to wake up the baby again.

LOTTIE. You can come into the room; don't worry about it.

TALLEY. Who?

VIOLA. Mr. Eldon, could I have a minute of your time?

ELDON. *(Moving Talley to the door.)* I can't talk now.

VIOLA. This is important to you, Mr. Eldon.

TALLEY. Me and Elijah Scott got a furnace, everybody in town had to have one...

VIOLA. If I could just—

ELDON. Fine, come to the factory on Friday or next Monday, talk to Mrs. Willy.

VIOLA. It's important to you, Mr....

(Eldon and Talley are gone.)

VIOLA. Well...I guess I been put in my place. The Talleys was always good at that... *(Beat.)* I got them antimacassars put to soak in Purex. I ain't promising to get them white.

LOTTIE. I have no interest. Momma didn't make them. Momma was a knitter she didn't crochet. Throw 'em out for all I care.

VIOLA. They're a botherin' nuisance but they protect the furniture.

LOTTIE. Sit down, Viola, before you fall.

VIOLA. I walked from the house; one of the boys took the truck. Is that Eldon's boy out there with Mr. Campbell? He looks good in his uniform. The other boy, Timmy, is a sailor ain't he?

LOTTIE. Timmy's in the marines; over in the Pacific.

VIOLA. All them sailors over fighting in their white uniforms, I wouldn't want to do their laundry.

LOTTIE. It's enough we're paying the bill. No, he's in the marines.

VIOLA. I'm trying to remember that one's name. I liked Timmy. This is the older one, ain't it?

LOTTIE. That's Kenny.

VIOLA. That ain't what I remember.

LOTTIE. Buddy. His name's Kenny, they call him Buddy.

VIOLA. That's who he is. *(Sighs, sits.)* No, Lottie, I tell you, I'm plum might worn frazzled this evening. I didn't get no sleep. I was up with the twins.

LOTTIE. I don't remember you having twins.

VIOLA. Oh, god help me, that's all I'd need. Mrs. Niewonker's two. I'm taking care of them while she's at the hospital having another one. This morning at dawn Mrs. Pine sends to have me wash every sheet in the house. All the curtains and towels, tablecloths. Her old man dropped dead at their granddaughter's weddin' yesterday. She couldn't wait to clear out the house. All the kids was there grabbin' at everything. Avalaine wasn't with me and I couldn't get my boys to go.

LOTTIE. That's not men's work, I know.

VIOLA. Hell, ain't nothing men's work to hear them tell it.

LOTTIE. I can't imagine Avalaine leaving for good. She'll be back soon enough.

VIOLA. No, she's off, I think. Seventeen years old, looks like twenty-five. There's no controllin' her. Talking back to her brothers, and them twice her size. She was hanging out down to the roll-arena, and around the Blue Line.

LOTTIE. The what?

VIOLA. The Blue Line. Roadhouse. Cars parked around it a mile outside of town, just like before the war. That many people find it so important to use up their gas coupons, there must be somethin' goin' on there.

LOTTIE. I've lived my whole life in this damned town except thirteen precious years, I don't know the first thing about it.

VIOLA. They ain't your type if Avvie liked them. Well, she went there and up to the roll-arena. Not gettin' home till all hours. Her daddy whipped her fit to kill her, she took the strap away and licked him back. She's a hellion, I mean it. But she didn't come home at all last night, so she's more than likely gone.

LOTTIE. It doesn't sound like she's been much help lately.

VIOLA. No, just last month she and me washed down the whole Farley house. She was my first. Her brothers ain't no good. All they do is hang around the filling station talking war. I spec they'll enlist soon as ever. Don't matter, ain't no good. Even the army couldn't make one useful man outta the both of 'em.

LOTTIE. Avalaine'll be back in time; she was only gone one night.

VIOLA. Oh, hell, Lottie. I told her to go. I said, you fly away on. Fly away on. There ain't nothin' here. Don't talk to me about opportunity. It's all the same. You're workin' for the Talleys or you're working for the Campbells or you're working for the Farleys. You fly away on and don't slow down to say I'm leavin'. *(Laughing.)* And I guess she didn't.

LOTTIE. I guess not.

VIOLA. Can't blame 'em for doin' what you told 'em to do.

HARLEY. *(Off. Coming to the door.)* I said five hundred a week was a livin' wage, considering you do nothing to earn it.

BUDDY. *(Off.)* I'd guess so.

HARLEY. *(Entering.)* I swear if it don't look like it's gonna rain like pourin' piss out of a boot. Oh, lord, excuse me, ladies, I didn't know you was in here.

VIOLA. *(Beat.)* Well, none of that work is gonna finish itself.

HARLEY. Mrs. Platt, I thought the service for Vaughan was very well handled. He deserved it.

VIOLA. Thank you, Mr. Campbell. I appreciate it. And thank you for coming by personally with the telegram. Mom appreciated it.

LOTTIE. I'll tell Eldon.

VIOLA. No, don't trouble him about me. I'll come by the office like he said. I should of known not to come up to the house. You all have a nice evening, now.

LOTTIE. You, too, Vi.

(Viola is gone.)

HARLEY. I was down at their place, you never seen people living in conditions like that; the place is clean enough, but all the windows wide open to the outside; flies thick as the freckles on a turkey's egg.

LOTTIE. You're a rich man, Harley, you ought to send them some screen wire if you're so concerned.

HARLEY. Old man Platt would have it sold and drunk up before nightfall. I was the one took the telegram to her mother, said her son was killed. I had to read it to them; that ain't easy.

BUDDY. Who was that?

LOTTIE. Vi's brother, Vaughan.

HARLEY. Vaughan Robinson; older than you, worked at the garage. Used to pitch for the softball.

BUDDY. I don't think I know him.

HARLEY. Lord, I'll tell you, I'd rather be over there fighting than back here bringing the word.

BUDDY. It isn't anything you have to do.

HARLEY. Yeah, it is. It's just something I started doing. I figure if I'm on the draft board helping to send you all over there, then when the telegram comes I'm the one who should take the responsibility for bringing it to the family. I wouldn't feel right about it if I didn't. I don't know. I started doing it, now people expect it. I'd a whole lot rather be fightin'.

NETTA. *(Has come in to hear this last.)* Your mother has lost enough, Harley. She needs you here. Harley has taken it on himself to be the one—

HARLEY. Come on, now, enough of that.

BUDDY. He was just saying. I'll tell you it's different from what it looks like from home; half the GIs, if they had the guts would go AWOL. So— how's the garment business? Are we still well off?

HARLEY. Oh, Buddy, I just don't sleep anymore. I just don't sleep. You gotta see the books to know what's happening. We can't keep up with it. Even considering that the cost of everything has gone right through the ceiling, we can't keep up.

(Eldon enters.)

HARLEY. *(Continued.)* Between trying to pitch in at the draft board and trying to keep the lines moving, I just don't sleep. Well, Eldon can tell you; he's down there twelve hours a day.

BUDDY. Nothing new in that.

ELDON. Yeah, but it's getting a little out of hand there.

HARLEY. We have a difference of opinion over that. Nothing we can't settle.

ELDON. Come on, we don't want to talk shop. Anything we have to talk about we can do after dinner tonight.

BUDDY. For my money it can wait till Timmy gets back here, if you're going to ask me, might as well include the kid.

ELDON. We don't know when he'll be back or I would.

BUDDY. Hell, telegraph Admiral Nimitz; tell him we need my kid brother for a couple days. I'd like to see him.

ELDON. I don't imagine he's a personal friend of his commander like you are.

BUDDY. Dad has this illusion Timmy cares a damn what's going on down at the factory.

ELDON. As a matter of fact it is Tim's concern as well as yours if either of you know it or not. You worked down there and you earned it.

BUDDY. Boy, did we.

ELDON. The Talley interest will be divided equally between the two of you—or the three of you if Sally changes her mind.

BUDDY. The sooner Sally just waltzes on out of here the happier everybody will be. I come home, talking last night about Anzio, she didn't even stay to listen. "Welcome back, heard you sprained your arm falling down the Spanish Steps."

HARLEY. Is that what you told the family?

BUDDY. Just calm down, now.

HARLEY. It had to be a sprain, hell they got x-rays now they can tell if it's broke or not.

BUDDY. It was sprained, it swelled up—maybe not as bad as I let on. I don't exactly expect Clark to give me a medal.

ELDON. Sally sees enough at the Veteran's hospital.

BUDDY. I'm just sayin' for my money, the sooner—

ELDON. I'm not disagreeing. She isn't any happier about staying than I am about her having to stay. Especially with the sort she's been hanging around with lately.

(Lottie leaves the room.)

ELDON. I think the Talleys got to have one in every generation.

NETTA. You know how she is about Sally. She's tried to influence that girl since the day she was born. *(Netta exits.)*

BUDDY. Timmy's not gonna give a hoot about the factory either. Timmy's gonna be a farmer, if you let him have his way.

ELDON. If he thinks he wants to work for a while at the University's experimental agricultural station—

BUDDY. That's all he ever talked about—working down there—before he went off to the University of Wisconsin. All day long. He couldn't wait to graduate from High School.

ELDON. He should be in on any decision to merge with some other company—or be taken over, is closer to what they're trying to put over.

HARLEY. They're not trying to put anything over.

BUDDY. What are we talking about is all I want to know. Who did you say these people are?

HARLEY. Delaware Industries.

BUDDY. I never heard of 'em.

HARLEY. You know their products, you know everything they make. I can't think of one right off the bat.

ELDON. Country Oven Bread.

HARLEY. Country Oven Bread.

ELDON. Baked in Pittsburgh.

HARLEY. They started out as an insurance company.

ELDON. That should tell you right there how far they can be trusted.

HARLEY. Used to be in Delaware, now they've moved down to Baton Rouge.

ELDON. That's interesting, too. Delaware Industries, Baton Rouge, Louisiana. Man said they had a company that baked bread, baked breakfast rings, whatever they are, said they made springs, had a company that made coils for a car, made brakes, owned natural gas in Kansas and Oklahoma. Had a chemical plant making plastic paint whatever that is, wanted to get into the garment factory trade. Trying to get into road-building.

BUDDY. Roadbuilding might interest Timmy—get him up on one of those Caterpillars. He'd like that.

HARLEY. They're a big operation. They're trying to diversify.

ELDON. Trying? That's about as diversified as I'd ever hope to get. I said to the man, "It used to be a fellow was in the business of making something. All you management guys, what do you say when someone asks what business are you in? When someone asks me what business I'm in, I say I'm in the business of making army uniforms. Before the war, I was in the business of making work pants. What business do you say you're in?" And that man says, "Well, then, we say we're in the business of making money."

HARLEY. Nobody told me we weren't interested in turning a profit down there.

ELDON. In the business of making money. That says it as far as I'm concerned. What say? Harley, I love you like a son but I'm not going to get into this argument with you now.

BUDDY. Where did these guys come from?

ELDON. They got a finger in our pie the same way they got all their other companies. They're a commercial insurance company, insure businesses. Soon as a company gets in trouble they buy them out, reorganize—

BUDDY. Nobody told me we were in any kind of trouble.

HARLEY. That's not right at all, Eldon.

ELDON. No, not us, OK. They got some two-bit garment outfit they subcontracted flies to us. Where did they come from? Subcontracting. Which I was against from the beginning.

HARLEY. Well, as far as I'm concerned, it's what saved us. You remember the pants' flies? Three years ago—those two girls over in the corner making pants' flies, well, those were for Delaware.

ELDON. And then they subcontracted an order of fatigues, and they got so much pull in Washington suddenly they get this contract for damn near all the uniforms in the country—they're keeping us so busy we can't see. One hundred percent, everything we do is subcontracted from them. And they have a dozen other factories our size working on the order.

HARLEY. Only they're beginning post-war production plans, and they figure—

BUDDY. Woooa. Reverse that. They're what? I love being home; it's everything they say it is.

HARLEY. Well, that might sound funny to you, but—

BUDDY. Listen, I'm glad they believe in us. More power to them.

HARLEY. People who don't look ahead will be—

BUDDY. I see it. We get the magazines; Olive and I write each other—planning what we want in our house; everybody's looking ahead, you'd be a fool not to.

HARLEY. There won't be a single sewing machine we got that isn't out of date a year after the war. We've seen the prototypes. Delaware is buying our machines for a year, eighteen months, just to get the jump on the competition.

ELDON. That's not what they're wanting to take us over for, they're wanting to take us over for an order form is what they're wanting.

HARLEY. I think that's the only thing he gives me credit for.

ELDON. You know better than that. Harley put in an order for three hundred bolts of Nylon.

BUDDY. I didn't imagine you could get it.

HARLEY. I think the Du Ponts needed the money if you can believe it, and we had it that week. Three hundred bolts every four months for five years, soon as the war's over. So we got in on the ground floor. Now you can't get near an order, even if you are Delaware Industries. So one thing that interests these guys in us—

ELDON. If you can't buy the nylon, you buy the company that has it, next best thing.

BUDDY. Hell, better.

HARLEY. *(As Netta enters.)* Hell yes, excuse me, Netta. The fact remains it's better money and less work.

ELDON. It's not work at all. They don't want us.

BUDDY. They're wanting to move the plant to Louisiana?

HARLEY. The machines, sure, use the building here for a warehouse, stock.

NETTA. What would happen to all the girls who work down there? Where would they go?

HARLEY. Oh, good lord, Netta; they'd go to Louisiana. Hell, excuse me, damn it, they're—excuse me—riffraff anyway. Divorced women, unmarried mothers. The town would be better off without them.

NETTA. Now you're sounding like Mr. Talley.

HARLEY. Well, it's about time somebody did.

ELDON. Please, mother.

HARLEY. I personally think this is the best time we could get out. They've been working time-and-a-half for three years, they got a taste of money, they're just going to want more and more. They're going to try to organize again, you know it.

ELDON. I wondered when we were getting to that—we took care of them before and we will again.

HARLEY. It's going to be nothing but headaches. And we can't appeal to their patriotism after the war. You try to get them to stay after eight at night without double time after the war.

ELDON. There wasn't anything patriotic about it.

HARLEY. Well, for me there was.

ELDON. If you need it to help you deal with them, fine. You're too soft-hearted, is your problem.

BUDDY. Dad, I don't see your point and I'm trying to see it.

HARLEY. He thinks they're going to turn out crap.

ELDON. I do, yes, among other things; I do. And it may be old-fashioned to be concerned with the product that has your name on it, but that's my concern. I've seen their projections and I've seen their intentions—

HARLEY. He doesn't like their figures.

ELDON. Nobody could make the kind of profit they're projecting with any kind of quality control. They got tables of profits, projected for fifteen years from now. They're talking 1959.

HARLEY. I can't make it clear to him that the way he does it isn't the only way.

BUDDY. Sounds familiar.

ELDON. What business are you in, we're in the business of making money.

TALLEY. *(Entering.)* Blame it, blame it.

OLIVE. *(Tailing him.)* Mr. Talley, don't you want to lie down?

NETTA. What's he doing up?

OLIVE. He came through the kitchen, I thought he was trying to head back to the car.

ELDON. Well, maybe he was hungry.

NETTA. He said he wanted to go to his room.

BUDDY. Olive.

OLIVE. Well, is he all right?

TALLEY. Blamed woman. Stop houndin' me.

HARLEY. I know you like putting in twelve hours down there, but I'm ready for a little rest.

OLIVE. Buddy, mother's fixing all the Christmas trimmings and every—

BUDDY. Not now.

ELDON. I don't doubt we've both earned it, Harley.

OLIVE. Harley, you got to get home and get changed and pick up Mary Jo.

HARLEY. Eldon, I tell you, I'm tired. I tell you, well, you know, we buried dad, I went right from the graveyard to the factory without changing clothes and cut pants till after midnight, was back on the job at six the next morning—thirteen years ago and I haven't let up yet. Didn't even have time to order a marker for dad's grave. Now, it killed him, but it's not going to kill me.

ELDON. Maybe we all should take a month off after the war; start treating ourselves.

NETTA. There's a stone now, on your dad's grave.

ELDON. Mother.

HARLEY. What say? Oh, I know. I went back five years later, somebody had put up a stone. Must of been mom. Looks cheap as hell. Made for the both of them, her birthday already cut into it I haven't said anything about it. She's all the time afraid someone might say they had to spend a nickel on her. Thinks we're still living in the depression. I gotta go.

NETTA. She's a good—

HARLEY. I didn't work any harder than Eldon did, but I'm about due for that vacation.

ELDON. You go with Delaware and you retire completely. They don't want us.

OLIVE. I thought they offered you a job as a—

ELDON. A position on their—what is it? Board of directors or board of—

HARLEY. Advisory board.

ELDON. Which means our names in a list on their stationery. For what it's worth, Olive, that place has been my life.

NETTA. Eldon.

ELDON. Well, mother, what else, except for my family, have I had?

OLIVE. You have to think about Buddy's future, of course, and Timmy's future.

HARLEY. Hell, Olive. Tim plans to be a farmer. He doesn't want to work with us.

BUDDY. Agronomist. Agronomist.

HARLEY. Is that what they call it now?

BUDDY. Timmy says when they give you a degree for it you have to fancy it up.

ELDON. Do you want to live in Louisiana?

BUDDY. I'm just listening.

ELDON. I don't know how a company can pull gas, make automobile brakes, and bake bread.

TALLEY. Raised horses, raised hogs, finger in the bank, finger in the factory. Finger in the coal trucks.

NETTA. Don't let him get started on the horses again.

BUDDY. He have a finger in the horses did he?

ELDON. Dad, you were one man, everything you did went in one pot—this outfit has got so many pots they're going to end up without a pot to—

HARLEY. It seems to be working for them; and they aren't the only ones.

ELDON. I'm just saying the floor is going to get wet, if you understand me. They want to own a piece of everything in the country, I think.

TALLEY. Me and Whistler gave that riverland for a park to the city. Gave it free and clear.

HARLEY. Yes, sir, and you've had the whole town by the gonads ever since.

TALLEY. Yes, sir. Knew it at the time. So did they. Harley, my boy. You'd do well, sir, to remember who the head of the Talley household is.

ELDON. You hear that? He's as lucid as a windowpane when he wants to be.

HARLEY. How can you assume that these people aren't interested in making a quality product?

ELDON. Look at the budget. Have you ever seen anything like it? One quarter nearly of their expenditures is for advertising. Now, how can you justify that?

HARLEY. You don't believe in people is your problem. You think people will buy anything they're told to like sheep. You can't make people buy an inferior product. There is no possibility of staying afloat.

ELDON. Their outlay for thread is for an inferior tension.

HARLEY. How do you know what synthetics have been developed? You don't realize the size of the purchases. Not five times what we're used to ordering: five hundred times. The discount is amazing. You know what's eating you is all? You've been a big fish in...

(Eldon repeats OK, OK, OK, to his next line.)

HARLEY. A small pond for so long, you're just afraid to be a little fish in a big pond, is all it is.

ELDON. Twelve percent of their entire budget is on legal advice and fees.

HARLEY. Hell, patents, leasings...

ELDON. Lawsuits, antitrust actions; ask dad about lawyers, he didn't trust one of them.

HARLEY. Laws have changed since Talley made his bundle; you couldn't get away with half his shenanigans today.

TALLEY. Never did care. Never did. No interest in that factory. Tell you why.

HARLEY. It'd take a committee of about fifty to get away—

TALLEY. Sir, when I'm talking—tell you why. Moral corruption. Never trusted those women. Broken homes, and moral weakness just like others I could mention. They're a bunch of no-goods making pants for another bunch of no-goods who are somewhere making shirts for the first no-goods. Scum of the earth.

OLIVE. The girls who work there or the people who wear the clothes?

TALLEY. Same people. Both of 'em. Blamed women.

HARLEY. What's galling him is the government loaned them the money for the plant; Delaware will take in all these little companies, put them in one plant and after the war they'll buy the whole factory for a song. He just wishes he'd thought of it. Don't think General Motors is gonna quit making trucks in their new plant; that the government damn near bought. Don't think Ford won't.

ELDON. And with the same slapdash assembly line that—

BUDDY. It's a hard working truck; those little eight-cylinder jobs. They better keep making it; I intend to get me one.

ELDON. Turning out, the paper says, over a thousand trucks a month.

BUDDY. Well, I beg to differ—they're damn handy on the supply line, over there.

ELDON. Very well, I don't know what I'm talking about.

BUDDY. Well, in this instance—

OLIVE. Honey—

ELDON. Fine.

BUDDY. I've driven them through the damn Italian mud; half over the axle, and I don't imagine you have.

ELDON. I have not; they don't make them for civilians.

HARLEY. People have management teams now, not two owners like us—trying to do it all.

ELDON. Delaware doesn't know what people are going to want in fifteen years and nobody else does.

TALLEY. Everybody wants what the rich man's got.

ELDON. Well, then that's the answer.

TALLEY. They don't want what the good man has. They got that. It's no use to them.

ELDON. Right, dad, the Talley place gets it, everybody else wants one. Do you want to go to your room?

HARLEY. Boy, am I late for everything. Listen I got to go to the draft-board people, I'm miles late now. I can't stay around; back before you know it.

BUDDY. They'll be closed by now.

HARLEY. Hell, the telegraph office doesn't close now till eleven.

NETTA. You be back here by eight and don't forget.

HARLEY. I'm gonna be busier than a cat with two tails till then, let me tell you.

BUDDY. I'll run you into town.

OLIVE. Buddy.

BUDDY. It'll only take five minutes to drop him at the Laclede Hotel and be back.

OLIVE. We have to check on June, remember?

BUDDY. The telegraph office still at the hotel building?

HARLEY. No, no, I'll borrow your pickup, if that's alright.

ELDON. Sure thing.

BUDDY. No problem.

OLIVE. Buddy!

BUDDY. June's alright. Oh. Maybe I better.

HARLEY. Yeah, you check on little June.

BUDDY. And maybe put in a little time toward getting her a little brother.

HARLEY. A little Buddy, Junior.

ELDON. We'll thrash this out; you'll see the light.
    (Eldon walks Buddy and Harley to the door.)

TALLEY. Never trusted a blamed lawyer further than I could pitch him.

OLIVE. You want to set down tonight with the family? I'm going to set you a place.

TALLEY. Woman, stop. Blamed.

OLIVE. Buddy, you want to go with me now to look at June?

BUDDY. Yeah, we better. Maybe better think of checking up on Buddy, Jr. while we're at it, like Harley said.

OLIVE. Oh! You! I'm not thinking that.

ELDON. *(Returning.)* Buddy, I'm expecting your support in this.

BUDDY. I know, sir.
    (Buddy and Olive exit.)

TALLEY. Windy Pine. Old Windy. Up on that hill.

NETTA. What's he talking about?

ELDON. The graveyard, I guess. He was up there. Had an adventure, didn't you?

TALLEY. Yes, sir.

ELDON. Dad, do you think you can come into the office and tell me—

TALLEY. Pine, Windy Pine. Whistler too.

ELDON. Boy, he hears what he wants to hear, doesn't he?

NETTA. Yes, it's windy; there's a breeze up there when you'd swear there wasn't a breath in the county. He'll be alright.

ELDON. Sure.

NETTA. Eldon, don't get so involved you don't come to supper when you're called. And it wouldn't hurt you to wash up before.

ELDON. I will.

(Netta exits.)

ELDON. Dad?

TALLEY. Windy Pine. Still going. Going at it. Talking a blue streak. Going on.

(Eldon looks at Mr. Talley, then goes into the office leaving Talley onstage alone. The French windows open slowly. Avalaine Platt steps into the room.)

AVALAINE. Mr. Talley. Is Mr. Eldon in?

(Pause. She realizes he isn't going to speak. She moves into the room. She walks to the front hall door, listens. There is a noise from the kitchen. Avalaine goes past Mr. Talley to the back door and listens.)

TALLEY. Windy won't shut up.

(Avalaine whirls around and looks at him.)

TALLEY. Dead and buried, still won't quit yammering.

(Avalaine looks around the room; Talley does not seem to know she is there. After a second she sits across the room from him, staring.)

TALLEY. Old Whistler up there whistling, Old Windy goin' on; telling his tales. Can't hear yourself think. No, sir.

AVALAINE. *(After a long pause.)* There you sit, you petrified old stick. You don't have a brain left in your evil old head, do you? You'd think the devil would come and collect his own before you became an embarrassment. *(Beat.)* Who is it that's going to tell the mayor and the Town Hall how to run their business, now? *(Pause.)* I used to think you went stalking through Old Town at midnight stealing babies to eat for breakfast. *(She stands.)* You're just a dried-up old stick ain't ya? *(She walks to him.)* Ain't ya? Just a dried-up old horse. *(She tickles him on the ear.)* Ain't ya? Huh? *(Talley has sat still for a moment. Now with one swift move he slaps her across the bridge of the nose, knocking her flat to the floor.)*

TALLEY. There! Got ya! Ha!

AVALAINE. You son of a bitch!

(She yells in pain. From several places throughout the house people call "What's going on." Eldon opens the door from the office, says. "Jesus Christ" and heads for the back door closing it in Netta's face as she arrives.)

NETTA. What in the deuce is going on?

ELDON. *(Overlapping.)* Never mind, I'll take care of this. This isn't for you.

(Closes door.) You better go on down the road to your mother, Avalaine, she's been missing you.

AVALAINE. You think you got her and everybody else under your thumb, don't ya? Nobody dare say nothing.

OLIVE. *(Arriving with Buddy.)* Dad, what's going on.

ELDON. Just close that door there and never mind.

(They do.)

ELDON. I'm not going to call Cliffy, because you're going to go home now.

(Avalaine holds her hand to her face. Her nose is bleeding.)

AVALAINE. That son of a bitch broke my nose.

ELDON. You just go on, now, you can go across the fields.

AVALAINE. Well, I'll tell you, Mr. Eldon, I've stayed with my mother's family for seventeen years; I got to thinkin' it's time I moved up here to live with my daddy.

ELDON. It wouldn't do for you to say anything against the Talleys, Avalaine.

AVALAINE. You thought ma wouldn't tell me.

ELDON. I wouldn't want you to be starting rumors; nobody could profit from that.

(As the door opens and Netta says, "I said what's going on.")

ELDON. Just stay out there.

AVALAINE. As it happens, since Buddy Talley practically raped me last time he was home and since he come by the house last evening to ask me to go into the woods with him—

ELDON. I don't want to hear anything against Kenny. I've heard all I'm listening to.

AVALAINE. My ma thought it was best to tell me as how Buddy Talley was my part brother.

ELDON. *(To outside.)* Never mind, in a minute.

AVALAINE. She thought she'd better let me know so's I didn't conceive no two-headed bastards, both of us being your kids.

ELDON. I won't have you interfering with Buddy's life, and you're not going to interfere here with the Talleys.

AVALAINE. I tell you what, papa. The Talleys are well treated in this town. I come up the hill to get my own. I figger you owe me my piece of all this. That bastard liked to kill me.

ELDON. Avalaine Platt. The entire town knows you're a whore for sale to any buyer. Our own handyman, Emmet Young has as much as told me—

AVALAINE. No more, no more, papa, no more. I done what was necessary, but it ain't necessary no more is it?

ELDON. With your reputation do you think anyone in this town would believe anything you said?

AVALAINE. I'm as good as any of you.

ELDON. You better just go back down the hill and I won't call the sheriff on you for breaking in the house.

AVALAINE. The door was wide open.

ELDON. *(As the front door opens.)* Just stay out a minute—

HARLEY. *(Appearing in the door.)* Eldon— *(He can say no more. He carries a telegram, hardly sees Avalaine; stands frozen a few feet inside the door unable to speak.)*

ELDON. Harley, you didn't have to bring the pickup back tonight; we have a problem here, I'm taking care of something right now.

AVALAINE. You can call in the whole damn town as far as I'm concerned. I didn't steal nothing from you.

HARLEY. Eldon, I'm sorry.

ELDON. Is it Timmy?

HARLEY. I'm sorry.

(Olive, Netta, and Buddy come in from the other door.)

NETTA. I don't know what you're thinking screaming at this child when she should have an ice pack on that face.

OLIVE. *(Overlapping half.)* Was she looking for her mother? What is that girl doing up here?

ELDON. Buddy, Olive, not now.

NETTA. Eldon, I want to know why that girl isn't taken care of. She could have her nose broke.

OLIVE. Not now, mother.

NETTA. What's the matter? Have I said something? Well, why are you looking at...what is it? Harley?

ELDON. It's all right, mother.

NETTA. *(Looking at Harley. He holds out the telegram.)* That isn't true. That isn't true. *(Beat.)* Harley... *(She takes a few uncertain steps toward Harley and faints, falling to the floor.)*

END OF ACT ONE

ACT TWO

Evening. Lottie onstage unseen. Lights only in the hall. The living room is dark.

NETTA. *(Off.)* I don't know why you say I fainted. I didn't faint.

OLIVE. It doesn't matter, mother.

NETTA. Olive, please don't call me that.

OLIVE. I know, I'm sorry. Should you be up?

NETTA. *(Appearing in doorway.)* I'm fine. I can't just lay there.

OLIVE. *(In doorway.)* You rested some. You had a little nap.

NETTA. I didn't go to sleep. I couldn't sleep, now. How could I sleep?

OLIVE. *(As Buddy comes in other door.)* Is that Buddy? Buddy? Don't hang around here in the dark, honey.

BUDDY. *(In dark.)* I'm not.

OLIVE. *(Joining him, Netta has gone to kitchen. Sotto voce.)* Buddy, I can't take it here. We have to get a place of our own; a place in town.

BUDDY. I know, we will.

OLIVE. I try, I really do, but you see what it's like.

BUDDY. Not now.

OLIVE. I know, honey, but we can't even talk.

BUDDY. I know.

OLIVE. The prices are just going to keep climbing. We might as well do it now as some other time.

BUDDY. I know they are. When I get back.

OLIVE. Would you agree to a place if I find one? We can't have a minute to ourselves here.

BUDDY. Not out in the Hayes addition or the Hough addition.

OLIVE. What do you think I am?

NETTA. *(Entering.)* Don't stand in the dark in here, you two.

BUDDY. Are you alright, mom?

NETTA. I wish everyone would quit asking me that. I have never blacked out in my life. For some reason I thought there was a chair right behind me. I know there isn't a chair there, but I thought there was and I put my hand back to steady myself, and there wasn't a chair there and I went over. I certainly fell down, but I didn't faint. I've never fainted in my life.

OLIVE. Your eyes were rolled back in your head, and you went down like a sack of potatoes, mother.

BUDDY. Olive, good law.

OLIVE. Are the shades pulled down in here? Can we turn on a light?

NETTA. Come on back into the kitchen with me and Eldon. Don't hang around in here by yourselves. Buddy?

BUDDY. How's dad?

NETTA. *(Sotto voce.)* He's taking this very bad. Oh, lord. Don't say anything; Olive, don't let Eldon see you crying. And don't say anything, or, I don't know. I don't know.

(She goes. Buddy follows.)

OLIVE. Buddy, honey?

BUDDY. Come on into the light. Dad's in the kitchen all alone.

OLIVE. Harley's with him, and mother.

BUDDY. Come on into the light.

(He goes and in a second Olive leaves. The room is still for a moment. When Tim speaks we have not noticed him before and cannot see him now. After a moment he moves into a swatch of moonlight.)

TIM. We won the war today. Flat out and did it. Won the war and didn't even know it. It'll be August next year before anybody knows, but we did it. We took the first of the Marianas, speck of land called Saipan. You could put twenty of 'em into Laclede County, and it's over. You can see the writing on the runway. Marianas. Some dogface Lieutenant said they were named for some Nip's Wop whore. I told him it was the Spanish Jesuits named 'em for Mary and they were a tough band to try to tangle with. He was pissed beyond all proportion. It's amazing the pride some people have in their ignorance. Course he was already renaming them the Eleanor's. He was getting all misty about it. He thought that sounded real sweet; we told him Eleanor wouldn't want 'em after we got through, but he was all sozzled on patriotism. Well, half patriotism, half this cache of Nip beer; which considering the Nips made it, isn't half bad.

For a person studied Agriculture, never been farther away from home than the University of Wisconsin, walked all my life through the woods here 'til there isn't a plant I'm not on intimate terms with, I want to let you know it's disconcerting to be flat landed on a place where there is not one living thing familiar, plant or animal. Central Pacific. Boy oh. You say hold on, we got us a snail here. There's a shell just ordinary brown and normal; that's sure as hell a snail like any other. And his head comes peeking out and it's purple; and his horns are orange curving things like bicycle handlebars with little blue grips on the end of them, and you say well, I'll be a little piece of shit if you're any snail I've ever made the acquaintance of.

But just when you know there's not one island gonna be anything but a tangle of jungle and mangos, all of a sudden one morning you're off Saipan, and you turn your glasses to look at Saipan's little sister, Tinian. I thought, I've been witched. I thought, Timmy Talley, you're home. You're looking at Ohio. You go six miles any direction from Lebanon, Missouri, you're gonna find fields of sorghum squared off neat next to fields of beans and barleycorn. If you could fly over it and look down at it, Tinian would be a five by ten mile America. They just floated one of those flat, fertile Iowa counties out to sea and tied it up three miles off Saipan. They pulled up a little half-mountain on one end and built four airstrips; but that's all they did to disguise it. Didn't fool any-body.

The marine objective, of course, being the airfields. Especially old Ushi off Ushi point in the Northern Sector of Tinian. That's your num-ber one airstrip in the Pacific. Way off here on this tiny Ohio island. From Ushi the new bombers can hit Tokyo and get back to base again. And it's over. They know it. We know it.

Course we first have to take Saipan and put the Saipan runway in operation. Oh, brother. Saipan you can have; some wiseacre said it'd take three days to knock it off. Shit. They didn't get to Tinian for a month. It would a took one good look at the terrain to know it; the information we get on these islands is pathetic. You could of guessed and come closer. Saipan's got these wild-assed razorback ridges running down it; ruggeder than hell, like the Arkansas back hills only more so. Big old limestone cliffs honeycombed with caves, some of 'em really good and dry. And with these caves for a start, I mean to tell you those damn Nips have done one piece of work on that terrain. One of the prettiest jobs you ever saw. Those bastards have been at that island like a hill a ants. Spider holes dug in, backed up by earthworks, blockhouses, pillbox walls five feet thick—you never saw such a job of work. But that's up in the hills. The airstrip is down on the flat and they damned near abandoned it. Taking the runway was a cakewalk. The Nips all pulled up to their holes. We spend three days bombing the shit out of the airstrip, then we go in and make it serviceable; extend it to a big coral forty-seven-hundred-foot runway. Coral, but nothing you'd want to wear around your neck. Build a runway. Sounds easy? Oh, daddy; you're right back in the jungle. I knew better the minute it was out of my mouth three years ago; "Sure,

I've had experience on a bulldozer, used to dig ponds down home"—
Timmy Talley, shut your mouth—you're in South Saipan with a Seabee
kid off a New York City construction crew and he is lost, I mean lost—
he can't walk on the ground without a sidewalk—you're beating down
the bushes, leveling the ground, filling the holes, knocking down
some—what is it?—red-flowered thing covered with insects—don't ask
what *they* are either—they think this red thing is clover. You'd of supposed they'd be hot after this yellow-flowered bush cause it's so sweet-
stinking, you almost faint from it—who knows what it is either—the
bugs won't have anything to do with it. Oh, daddy, Saipan, Agraham
and Guam. Breadfruit, Coconuts, who-knows and sugarcane. A peren-
nial—I don't know how that works, I guess you hack it down and up it
pops again—not sorghum, an annual, and something I understand. But
either one, one hundred percent guaranteed to put you on insulin, and
rot your teeth. Coconuts, sugarcane, who-knows; breadfruit and those
yellow-flowered anybody's guesses that smell so sweet and cloying that
you could up your C-Rations. Which would be no great loss.

ELDON. *(Off.)* I don't want anything said in front of dad. If you ever got
him to understand, it'd probably kill him.

NETTA. *(Off.)* I know, Eldon, nobody's saying anything.

ELDON. *(Off.)* He put great stock in that boy. Aren't you eating?

NETTA. *(Off.)* I don't want anything, no. I'm fine. Eldon, come into the living room, now, you want to listen to the radio while me and Olive clean up.

ELDON. *(Off.)* I don't know that I do.

NETTA. Of course you do.

TIM. Dad's taking this really hard. He went out to the barn and leaned up
against the cattle stanchions and cried like I've never seen. When I was
eight—I went running to that same room, leaning up against that same
stanchion when my hamster died. Course dad came and found me there,
so he maybe was remembering that too.

NETTA. *(Entering.)* You come on now, and let me and Olive clean up. You've
hardly eaten a bite, Harley, that's not like you.

HARLEY. *(Off.)* Another time I'll make you proud.

(Olive joins Netta.)

NETTA. Can you hear what they're saying?

OLIVE. I don't know what to do with them.

NETTA. Eldon can't take this sort of thing, Olive.

OLIVE. I know, he put such stock in—

NETTA. He's got no bounce; he's not resilient like we are.

OLIVE. Everything will be fine, mom.

NETTA. And I think Mr. Talley knows—he stood and looked me in the eye—looked right through me. Then he turned around and went in the office.

OLIVE. Eldon said not to tell him.

NETTA. I think he knows.

OLIVE. *(Turning the lights on.)* Oh, my god, Lottie. Scare me to death. Sitting in here in the dark, are you alright?

LOTTIE. Yes.

OLIVE. Shouldn't you eat something?

LOTTIE. No.

NETTA. Has Sally come back to the house?

LOTTIE. No.

NETTA. She hasn't eaten a bite. I called her out back.

OLIVE. Maybe she went into town.

NETTA. Oh, lord, I hope she doesn't hear from somebody in town!

LOTTIE. She'll be in soon.

NETTA. I know she's willful, but she's so strong and she sees so much at the army hospital; I just wish she was here. What are you doing in here by yourself?

LOTTIE. That's my trouble, I don't have anything to do; I was planning a career, trying to imagine something I'd be useful doing.

OLIVE. Anything you set your mind to, Lottie. Bright as you are.

LOTTIE. Bright, am I?

OLIVE. Well, you're considerably brighter than me and I've worked. You're good with figures, aren't you? You could keep books.

LOTTIE. Dad says you start out keeping books, you end up keeping books. I don't think I'm quite here tonight. I'm not sure you're here; I think I'm seeing things. I could be the assistant of some traveling botanist; ride a horse, take notes. That's a Dipsophilla ruba. *(Writing.)* Dipsophilla ruba. Catalog the flora of some unexplored province in Canada, go up through Montana into Saskatchewan bundled in fur blankets at night; horses flogging through the mud from the thaws; up before dawn, frying salmon for breakfast; fold the blankets, off at the first light; that's an undiscovered species of Polypodus, Miss Talley, that I'll dedicate to you, Polypodus Charlottii. How do you collect ferns?

OLIVE. Would you *enjoy* cooking? I wouldn't think that would be too taxing. *(Lottie leaves.)*

OLIVE. Well, for goodness sake. I cook for her, I don't see why…

HARLEY. I better call Mary Jo again, if I can use your phone.

NETTA. Sure, Harley, tell her we're fine.

(As Buddy and Joe enter.)

NETTA. Now, there's a pie that Olive's made and there's coffee yet.

ELDON. Later on maybe.

HARLEY. *(On phone.)* 380 please.

BUDDY. You bring it in in a bit.

OLIVE. We will not, you'll come out and eat at the table after we've cleared up.

(Olive and Netta go.)

HARLEY. *(On phone.)* Hi, toots, I'm still here. No, I won't be long. I'll tell 'em. You keep your seams straight.

BUDDY. Boy, I thought that girl was gonna start wrecking the furniture in here. Who the devil is she?

ELDON. She seemed to think she knew you pretty well.

BUDDY. You're the one who was talking to her. Let me in here, I'd have handled it.

ELDON. Sounded like you've been handling it all along.

BUDDY. You're the one she wanted to talk to, looked like.

HARLEY. I don't know what happens with that kind of girl. They paint up what could be a pretty face, twist their behinds around. Can't be more than seventeen years old, already she's the worst whore in town. She is. Eldon hired her to work for us.

BUDDY. That was friendly.

ELDON. And promptly had to let her go.

HARLEY. Guess he felt sorry for her.

ELDON. Waste of time.

HARLEY. She's flirting with everything in pants the minute she comes in.

ELDON. Didn't show to work half the time. When she did show, she didn't work.

BUDDY. That kind can still be trouble.

ELDON. No, no, no trouble. Now, I don't want to hear anymore about her.

HARLEY. Looked like somebody damn near broke her nose for her.

BUDDY. She was tickling him on the ear he said. So he popped her one.

HARLEY. Too bad for her own good that he didn't do her some permanent damage.

ELDON. Well, she's going to be no problem.

BUDDY. No problem of mine.

ELDON. That depends on whose story you believe.

BUDDY. If she's talking about me, must have me confused with someone else. Maybe Timmy knew her. Looks like about his type.

ELDON. No more of that.

BUDDY. No more of what?

ELDON. No more of that anymore. That's all over now.

BUDDY. What's over?

ELDON. You're not going to be blaming Timmy for your weaknesses anymore.

BUDDY. I never used Tim for anything. There's not two brothers in town closer than—

ELDON. Fine, I know. I know well.

BUDDY. Those doors are thick, but that girl wasn't talking all that private. You gonna lecture me about moral weakness and character? Like granddad?

ELDON. That's enough. Everybody's on edge.

BUDDY. *(Easy.)* I remember all those lectures about moral fiber. I used to think you ought to order a couple a hundred bolts, make you a new line of clothes outta moral fiber.

HARLEY. Shit. They wouldn't move. Sit on the shelves and go begging.

ELDON. If you heard so good you know that she seemed to think she knew you—

BUDDY. She was just excited. Liable to say anything.

ELDON. You get involved with that kind you gotta expect them to try every way to get something out of you.

BUDDY. You ought to be telling yourself that, it sounded like.

ELDON. Anything she said about her mother, is just that girl's wild fancy.
    (Lottie enters.)

BUDDY. Good lord, Aunt Lottie. Thought you'd gone to bed.

LOTTIE. I don't go to bed, you know that.

ELDON. Are you alright?

LOTTIE. Tonight that's all relative. Everyone is asking everyone that tonight, aren't we?

ELDON. You look terrible.

LOTTIE. I swear to god, Eldon, I feel like I might glow in the dark.

ELDON. Is that good? I don't think that sounds—

LOTTIE. That's not good, no, that's not good.

ELDON. Lottie—Buddy. How are we supposed to take this? How do people take it?
    (The radio has been turned on.)

ELDON. No, don't turn that on, damn fool thing, what do I care tonight what's happening with the war? I got my—one son here with me. My other, I don't even know where he fell.

BUDDY. Don't get out those maps. Last time I was here, that's all we did was trying to figger out on what godforsaken island Timmy—he's got a code, he tells 'em where they're sending him, they don't know if they got it right or not. All those islands are named in some Mickey language; nobody ever heard of one of those places.

ELDON. I need a better atlas. No, I know. He said he was going to the Marianas. Papers have been full of nothing but Saipan Island. Trying to make it sound like it won't be another Torawa. I wish I knew that he got his man.

HARLEY. You can be damned sure Tim did.

ELDON. Ten for one, damn them and they keep fighting. That's what the paper says, ten japs for one yank.

HARLEY. You can be damned sure Timmy got his limit, Eldon.

ELDON. I know that; enough of that now. Enough of that. Has Sally come in?

LOTTIE. I haven't heard her.

ELDON. Well…we've got Buddy here.

BUDDY. Yeah, I wish I was here for good.

HARLEY. We'll have you back down at that plant before you know it.

BUDDY. Oh, boy. Maybe I'll stay in Italy. I don't know how that sounds.

HARLEY. See, he's seeing the world, he starts getting ideas.

ELDON. How you gonna keep them down on the farm? Huh? After they've seen—well, Rome, I guess it has to be.

BUDDY. Naw, Olive and me have been writing; you know, I'm like grand-dad. I'm not wild about the factory.

ELDON. I know; I've never forced it on you or Timmy either one.

BUDDY. No, sir. Come back from Southwest Missouri State University with a degree in Business Administration and in a week I'm repairing sewing machines.

HARLEY. Still the best repairman we've had down there.

BUDDY. God, I can't believe I'm back. No wonder they don't want us coming home on leave. If it wasn't for Timmy, this would be… Boy! I tell you after last winter, I'm trying to convince Olive to live in a desert somewhere. California or Arizona. I mean it rained; you've never seen troops trying to maneuver in mud like that. And cold. Even in Clark's quarters.

ELDON. I always imagined Italy to be warm.

BUDDY. Yeah, sunny Italy, what a load of fertilizer that is. Hell, the ground froze, at least you could walk on it then. My feet never got dry once, all winter. You've never seen so many kids—we learned to say to them, *"Bon giordno ragazzo."* and they're supposed to say, *"Bene gracias senor."* You know what they say? "Got any gum, chum?"

HARLEY. We followed you: sounded about as balled up as every other operation.

BUDDY. Well, I heard that, I don't know what Clark was supposed to do; it wasn't his command. He's amazing—I don't think he's spent a day out of the army since he was born.

HARLEY. Yeah?

BUDDY. Hell, he was at Antwerp. Course, you understand, they all think the world of themselves. Awful fond of the photographers.

HARLEY. Why don't you lean into some of those pictures, we wouldn't mind seeing your mug in the papers.

BUDDY. I just counted myself lucky to be in out of the rain. Anyway, I can't talk Olive out of living anywhere but here; we're thinking about building someplace in town, soon as I get back. One of those one-story jobs, maybe with some of the appliances they say we'll have. Indoor refrigeration for the rooms.

HARLEY. Air-conditioning. Mary Jo got one for the bedroom; noisiest machine I ever had in the house. I had to turn it off.

BUDDY. Well, or electric heat, all that—then I been reading up about prefabrication for homes. The officers get all this literature.

HARLEY. Hell, Olive's gonna want something better than you could get with any of those prefabrications.

BUDDY. I'd be interested not so much in the buying viewpoint as in the selling. Vacation homes, things like that, up on the Lake of the Ozarks. God damn, there's a feeling—the second you come back to the States, people are ready to get up and move. They're not going to be sitting on their butts; people are going to be moving. Have you read about those house trailers.

HARLEY. He's going to be selling prefabricated housing trailers.

ELDON. That's what it's sounding like.

BUDDY. Well, I wouldn't have one, but you can feel it. Over there you can't think about after it's over—except when I'm writing Olive, cause she needs it—I just get restless. But back here, it's the first thing you feel. Get this damn war over and get a move on. Build some decent roads. Spend some of that money.

(Talley enters.)

ELDON. I thought you were in your room.

TALLEY. *(Lucid.)* No, no. Harley, good evening.

ELDON. Did the women get you something to eat?

TALLEY. Yes, thank you. Is Emmet Young back yet?

ELDON. I didn't know he'd gone someplace.

TALLEY. Kenneth, bring along that big sack full of papers to the kitchen.

BUDDY. Yes, sir.

ELDON. We should go through those papers together, Dad.

TALLEY. Now, listen here. If I have to talk to you. There's some papers nobody's business but mine. Long useless to anybody but me, that I intend to burn in the kitchen cookstove. If that's all the same to everybody. You just tend to your sewing machines, that's always suited you fine, and suited me fine.

ELDON. Dad, you shouldn't burn something that might…

TALLEY. Sir, that's all, sir.

ELDON. *(Sotto voce.)* What got his dander up?

LOTTIE. He's just covering his tracks like a good fox.

TALLEY. *(Has started to go, comes back.)* I think you'll find a fox doubles back on his tracks, he doesn't cover them up, Charlotte. *(To Buddy.)* Go on, then, and poke those a few at a time into the stove there. Mind you don't get yourself burned.

ELDON. I'd like to go through those things.

TALLEY. You been shuffling through everything in there like a dog for a mole. Nothing that would interest anybody but me, thank you. *(Starts to go.)*

HARLEY. Old love letters, maybe.

TALLEY. *(Turns.)* No, sir, I left the loving anyone but my wife to your father, Mr. Campbell, and to my son here.

ELDON. I wouldn't say…

TALLEY. Don't matter ever what a person says if they go ahead and do something other. Ask anybody in the state of Missouri who is trustworthy, moral, and upright. For my family and my father and my father's good name.

LOTTIE. I missed something there.

TALLEY. Then your son comes along to tear it all down. Small mind in business, and two-faced with his family and everybody in the state knows it.

ELDON. Dad, I don't believe there's any call to speak to that now.

TALLEY. How many girls was it you came to me about before you was even shipped off to school? Who was the New Jersey lawyer sent here to sue you for parentage? He didn't know who he was dealing with, I can tell you. Sent him packing.

ELDON. You couldn't complain about the way I've handled anything you've allowed me to run.

TALLEY. I was your age exactly when the Great War came. I saw it coming. You looked at Europe, you looked at the Pacific, said it wouldn't happen. Anybody could have told you better and did. With the sonabitch democrat cripple playing king, not president, roughshodding over every good man in the country—till he decided he needed them to fight his war.

HARLEY. All that's changing now; things aren't going to be that easy for him.

TALLEY. You and Harley could be buying up every garment factory in the Midwest if you're so interested in making coveralls. I saw what was coming in 1910, you stuck your head in the sand.

LOTTIE. You bought everything the war was gonna use and sold it back to them for double, didn't you, papa?

TALLEY. Yes, I did, and treble and four times, and it bought you the college education you never used and the food in your mouth and the shirt on your back, young man, and don't you forget it.

LOTTIE. I'm not a young man anymore, papa.

TALLEY. Well, Lottie, if you didn't tell them, there wouldn't be nobody who'd know the difference.

LOTTIE. At this point if I recall the last time he was quasi-coherent, he begins on how frail and beautiful mom was and his disappointment in me. Very similar to your reveries about your disappointment with Sally. *(She stands up, is dizzy, and is forced to sit back down.)* Well, so much for the grand gesture. I was intending to sweep from the room.

TALLEY. That's the only sweep you'd know how to do, Charlotte. The problem, sir, with getting something done legally is that it takes a lawyer to do it. That's the problem of getting something done legally.

ELDON. Yes, sir.

(Pause. Talley is staring vaguely into space with concern.)

ELDON. Dad?

TALLEY. Who? I don't want to be in this room.

ELDON. Are you OK?

TALLEY. Blamed! Where's that boy? Where's Eldon?

ELDON. I'm right here.

TALLEY. Where?

ELDON. Who? God damn, now he's got me doing it.

TALLEY. The boy.

ELDON. Kenneth is in the kitchen where you sent him.

TALLEY. My God, yes, what I've come to…

ELDON. You're better than last week—if you'd take care of yourself.

TALLEY. Where?

ELDON. Where's what?

TALLEY. Your boy.

ELDON. You had Buddy take a sack of papers to burn in the cooking stove that hasn't been connected for twenty years. Nora cooks on an oil range now.

TALLEY. Then we'll take them out to the barnyard, sir. *(Exits.)*

(Pause.)

ELDON. And there isn't a barnyard either. For fifteen years.

HARLEY. He starts in with the "sirs" and "thank yous" and you're in trouble.

ELDON. I don't suppose there's anything valuable in any of that paper.

HARLEY. Well, much as I'd like to I can't stay here all night.

ELDON. No, Harley, I thought we should settle this thing. While Buddy's with us.

HARLEY. Hell, excuse me Lottie, tonight, I'd just let you have your way; I'd be tied to that job for the rest of my life, better not talk now.

ELDON. God, I have to talk about something, Harley. Or I'll sit here thinking about—

HARLEY. Nobody's gonna be satisfied with any decision we make tonight.

ELDON. Well; I'll try to explain it to dad and see what we can get from him.

HARLEY. You better do that now, then.

ELDON. He's lucid, but he's in a mood. I've never known what he was gonna do; he's managed to fool me every turn.

LOTTIE. Days when I remember how he was when he was theoretically sane are scarier than seeing him totally senile.

ELDON. The man has nine lives. No disrespect. His father died when he was thirty. Built this house and didn't live a year in it. I think Dad lived his dad's life out and then his own. And then mine.

OLIVE. *(Entering.)* Now, it's absolutely against my principles to indulge you men and a—ladies like this, but mother says if you come into the kitchen and get your coffee, you can bring it back in the parlor. We're not finished in the kitchen yet.

HARLEY. Why don't you bring it in on a tray? What kind of service is that?

OLIVE. We happen not to have a maid anymore like you do, Harley; and

I'm not going to volunteer. Wouldn't I look cute—I'll get me a little hat and sew some lace around my apron.

(Buddy comes in.)

OLIVE. No, no, don't come in without your coffee, and there's pie. Get it in the kitchen and bring it in here.

HARLEY. I remember when you had a maid and a girl to help Nora out.

OLIVE. Well, that was before my time. Try to find a colored girl now with the wages they're getting.

(They are going.)

OLIVE. Lottie, you should eat something. There's a good apple pie.

LOTTIE. Oh, kiss my ass. *(She turns the lamp off.)*

OLIVE. Well, I couldn't miss it if I tried. Why are you so hateful to me?

BUDDY. Honey.

ELDON. Ladies. Olive, Lottie isn't well tonight.

OLIVE. Eldon, I understand sorrow and tension. I told Lottie she looked upset and tired; she should go to bed.

ELDON. She hasn't been sleeping.

LOTTIE. I've never slept, it's nothing. Maybe I'm bored, not tired.

OLIVE. Well, I don't understand that as something to be proud of.

BUDDY. Olive.

OLIVE. Well, don't "Olive" me, dernit. I don't understand being bored and I don't understand not being able to sleep. I understand getting up early and working hard and getting your chores done, and being tired, and going to sleep and sleeping; and getting up early and working hard and getting things done and being tired and going to sleep and sleeping. There's too much to do to be bored or not to sleep. I'm sorry, that's the way I am. It's the way I am. It's the way I am. That's what I understand.

(She exits, the others follow.)

TIM. Dad said he didn't even know where Timmy fell. That formal "fell." Like a lotta people he gets very—not correct, but official—under pressure. Hell, "fell" isn't the half of it. Splatted is more like it. Didn't feel a thing. Shock takes care of that. I felt a force all against me and suddenly I've got a different angle on the terrain. I'm looking up into the trees instead of out across the jungle. I thought why am I looking at that? Then I thought, Oh, sure I'm flat on my ass looking up. Some squawking parrot up there looking back at me; gonna drop it right on my face. You figger, alright, this part is easy. I just lay here till some corpsman comes up and does his job. You get very philosophical, very patient. Then the corpsmen come and, Oh, daddy, you know from the look on their faces that this is bad. This young recruit, couldn't be sixteen, turned around and thought he was gonna puke but he flat out fainted before he had a chance. You can tell he'd enlisted into this thing—gung-ho, ten minutes after seeing *To the Shores of Tripoli,* let me at those bastards, and he was having a hell of a time with it. The other guys are supposed to be hardened. I'm feeling nothing, you understand, I'm kinna full of it, in fact. I think some wise-acre attitude is called for. I say, "Hey, don't you Raggedy-Asses know you don't look at a guy like that? You guys are gonna scare him outta six years growth. You're supposed to be all reassuring." Or, actually, I thought I said that; then I realized that nothing had come out. I thought, well, hell, if this isn't a lousy predicament. You wonder if it comes are you gonna fall all to pieces; so it's come and you're kinna proud of yourself but you can't even put on your show. Nobody's gonna be able to see what a smoothy you are; and you are damn proud of your attitude. Granddad Talley would say, "Pride cometh before the fall, sir." Should have known it. Of course, you do know that the body is doing what the body does. You can feel—barely, a little bit—that your body is pissing all over itself and your bowels are letting go something fierce: there's no pinching it in. You try to get ahold with your mind of the muscles down in your belly that you use to hold it off, but your mind can't find 'em. And nothing smells worse on God's green earth than a C-Ration dump. Of course you've seen that so much you're not even embarrassed. You go under fire some non-com invariably says, "Keep a tight asshole," and, well, you didn't, but damn it, you're proud of your attitude. If those guys hadn't looked so bad you might have gone to pieces but they're so torn up you feel somebody has got to take this thing lightly.

ELDON. *(Off.)* I wish you wouldn't hound me tonight, damn it.

NETTA. *(Off.)* I just want to know what that woman is doing here.

TIM. Granddad sent the handyman, Emmet Young, to get the washerwoman and bring her back up to the house here, and mom is mad as a hornet. *(Beat.)* Nora, the cook, who used to be about my favorite person in the family, got so upset when they told her about me that she couldn't finish cooking supper. Dad had to drive her home. It's a good thing Olive made that pie.

NETTA. *(Following Eldon in.)* I thought I had said last week that I didn't want her or her family coming around. Eldon, now, you tell her. I'm sorry, I don't know what it is, but I just don't like that woman coming around; I wouldn't put it past her to take something from the house.

ELDON. I don't know who you're talking about.

NETTA. That Mrs. Platt. I don't like her coming around.

ELDON. She's been doing the wash here for fifteen years—

NETTA. And I've never liked it a minute and I've never trusted her a minute and I'm going to be listened to on this. I don't want her coming around. I'd rather do the washing myself or God knows there's any number of colored women into Old Town who need the money more than she does. Her husband just drinks it up and gives all of us a bad name. Now, I'll tell her to her face if you won't.

ELDON. I want to say right now that I've just about had it with this hysterical attitude you two have tonight—we're all upset but there's no call for this.

NETTA. There is call and I'm calling and Olive is with me in this, Eldon; we don't want that family spongin' off us, now and I mean it. Now I'm just shaking like a leaf this has got me so upset.

ELDON. Will you please understand that it means nothing to me one way or the other who does the washing here.

NETTA. Well, then why is she here?

TALLEY. *(Entering.)* In here. Here. If you please. I asked Mr. Young if he would be so kind as to fetch Mrs. Platt here. I want to thank the both of you for coming by at this hour. Charlotte, you look terrible, you should be in bed.

LOTTIE. Never mind.

ELDON. Dad, this is no concern of yours.

TALLEY. Mrs. Platt, Mr. Young, I think you're acquainted...?

VIOLA. I know who he is, I guess. We ain't acquainted.

NETTA. Mr. Talley, I'm about at the end of my patience here. I want you to please explain to—

TALLEY. This is a family thing that we can have you join us for or not. If you'd rather, you can please shut the door behind you.
(Netta looks at Eldon and leaves.)

TALLEY. This won't be but a minute.

ELDON. Dad, no action is called for by you.

TALLEY. I heard you the first time, sir. You can sit there and attend or join the women in the kitchen. I'm sure these two people want to get home.

VIOLA. I got a lot to do yet tonight.

TALLEY. Now, the past is the past and we're not going to talk about that. I think we know why we're here. Now, Viola, your daughter—her name is...?

VIOLA. Avalaine?

TALLEY. Speak up, Platt; say what?

VIOLA. Avalaine, Mr. Talley. I thought she'd runned off.

TALLEY. Avalaine. Well, it's turned out that that is not the case. Now I am a man who has always been direct and fair, anybody will testify.

(Lottie laughs; he doesn't hear her.)

VIOLA. Said she come up here and got slapped in the face for her trouble. I tried to talk to Mr. Eldon, but him being so busy…

TALLEY. Avalaine stated a slander in this house this afternoon, which won't happen again.

VIOLA. She most often says what she likes.

(There is a commotion in the hall.)

AVALAINE. *(Off.)* You just get your damn hands off me— *(Opening the door.)* Is ma in here?

OLIVE. Mr. Talley is in a private—

AVALAINE. I have a right to know what it is that's going on.

OLIVE. Mr. Talley, Mr. Eldon—

TALLEY. That's fine.

ELDON. I don't want this commotion, now.

AVALAINE. I want to know what is being done here.

NETTA. Eldon—

ELDON. That's fine, dad said. I don't know what—

TALLEY. Miss Platt, I thought you'd be contrite and embarrassed, or I would have asked you to come.

(Pause. Avalaine looks at him.)

TALLEY. Maybe she is.

AVALAINE. I don't know what you're talking about, embarrassed. I want to know what this is about.

ELDON. You're opening a can of beans you've no—

TALLEY. Eldon, shut the door if you would.

(Avalaine flinches when he approaches.)

ELDON. I'm not going to hit you.

AVALAINE. *(To Emmet.)* What are you doing here?

TALLEY. Now, one thing has to be understood. Avalaine Platt, you stated a slander in this house this afternoon, that won't happen again.

AVALAINE. I didn't say nothin' that wasn't the—

EMMET. Why don't you listen once?

TALLEY. We don't have to worry about you repeating it, as that would be actionable by lawsuit. The Jeff City jails aren't so full they can't take a few more; not just you, but whoever in your family is spreading this libel, I don't have to go into that. As it happens I've been talking to Mr. Young here for some time. Mr. Young is intimately acquainted with Avalaine, which I assume you know.

VIOLA. I guess if that means what I think it means, then I ain't surprised.

TALLEY. Say what?

VIOLA. I knew she likes the soldier boys.

TALLEY. Mr. Young is very much a civilian. Now, I've asked that he join us here because Mr. Young applied for the job of cutter at the plant last month, wanting, as he said, a position that had more of a future. Inside out of the weather. Mr. Young is an ambitious man. Now, my son had decided to hire another applicant, but tonight we've made the decision that Mr. Young is the right man for that position. Now, I think you wanted to say something.

EMMET. It's been put to me that Avalaine and I should be married.

TALLEY. I think that would be the honorable thing for the young Mr. Young and Miss Platt to do. And I'm happy that we'll be giving you the means to do the honorable thing. I don't see any other way we could accept them into our home.

EMMET. I understand that, sir. Sirs.

TALLEY. Then I think Eldon will agree that you can start at the plant as a wedding present. The day after the marriage takes place.

VIOLA. If that's all you wanted, you should of asked Avalaine here to begin with.

ELDON. I guess he thought you could present the proposition in a way that will make Avalaine understand,

VIOLA. She does what she pleases.

TALLEY. I feel it's the least I can offer, Miss Platt, and, if you understand me, it's the most I can offer.

AVALAINE. Oh, it ain't difficult to understand.

TALLEY. I'm a tired man and sick, and this is the only generous offer I can make. (He closes his eyes.)

ELDON. It's not necessary, dad.

AVALAINE. Is he going to sleep?

VIOLA. I ain't asked nothing from nobody. You people don't owe us.

AVALAINE. Like hell they don't—

TALLEY. Thank you very much. With Miss Platt here, I think we'll do fine.

VIOLA. If I told her, she'd do different out of spite.

TALLEY. Thank you very much. (Beat.) Thank you very much.

LOTTIE. That means he's finished with you, honey.

VIOLA. Is that what that means? Avvie does what she wants.

AVALAINE. I ain't said nothing—

VIOLA. I got work to attend to.

(Eldon gets up.)

VIOLA. Don't you bother Mr. Eldon, I know the way out of this house.

ELDON. Avalaine is pretty young to—

AVALAINE. How old was ma?

TALLEY. Mr. Young, congratulations. I know we none of us will have to think about this again.

AVALAINE. I ain't said nothing, I said.

EMMET. Will you listen once.

AVALAINE. Will you jump in the lake.

EMMET. He could have you in jail in a minute.

TALLEY. I think we can expect Mr. Young to put it to Miss Platt; he seems inclined that way.

EMMET. We got no guarantee.

AVALAINE. We sure ain't.

TALLEY. Harley! Eldon, yell for Harley.

ELDON. Harley, Dad wants you in here.

NETTA. Has she left?

ELDON. I'm sure you saw her go.

NETTA. Eldon, I want to know why she was up here. Is that girl gone?

ELDON. I don't want to hear this now.

AVALAINE. No, I ain't.

ELDON. Anything you want to do is fine by me.

HARLEY. Yes, sir.

TALLEY. Mr. Young—Mr. Campbell.

HARLEY. I know Emmet.

TALLEY. Mr. Young will be working alongside us down at the plant.

HARLEY. What do you mean "us"? I haven't seen you down there in ten years.

TALLEY. Beside you and Eldon. Soon as the wedding's over. I just wanted you to meet here in this house, to start you two boys off on the right foot. Now, these two young people have to run along.

EMMET. Of course the job of cutter isn't much of a—

LOTTIE. Bribe.

EMMET. —incentive.

AVALAINE. Cutting room foreman might be more attractive.

HARLEY. You're joking.

(Pause.)

TALLEY. For your first anniversary present.

ELDON. Dad, don't you think this is something Harley should be—

TALLEY. Sir. You never admit when you've been outsmarted and I do.

EMMET. If that could be in writing.

TALLEY. That's no problem. Not many people get such incentives; now mind you don't try to go too far. Simple respectability would have been enough.

AVALAINE. I want to see all you said in writing. I can read.

TALLEY. Tomorrow morning. Now, I'm tired—

EMMET. I want to thank…

TALLEY. No thanks, no thanks. That's something you'll earn. And everything that comes after. Both of you.

AVALAINE. Can we leave here?

TALLEY. Eldon, you want to see these people home?

AVALAINE. He's got a car.

EMMET. Thank you. Good night. Mrs. Talley.

NETTA. I'm sure.

(Emmet and Avalaine leave.)

OLIVE. Look at the way he dresses. Drives that fancy car; everyone rationed to three gallons a week. I don't want to think where he gets the stamps for gas.

LOTTIE. You're really smooth, huh, dad?

TALLEY. Heck, it wasn't even fun. Shooting fish in a barrel. (To Eldon.) You stick it in a sow you shouldn't be surprised to have a pig offspring; or so you sow, so you reap.

LOTTIE. If that was true, Daddy, I don't want to think what you'd be reaping.

TALLEY. I'm happy that you're not my judge, Lottie.

LOTTIE. I'll be somewhere lobbying, Daddy.

ELDON. You realize that no such compromise is necessary.

TALLEY. I want you to know that I've wiped your nose for you for the last time, sir.

NETTA. What do you mean by that?

ELDON. Not now.

BUDDY. Why does that baboon think she'd marry him?

NETTA. What does he mean by that? Wiped your nose for the last time. Do you want to explain that?

OLIVE. Honey, you come in with me, you help in—

ELDON. I'm not joking about you two and your hysterics, now.

NETTA. Do I look hysterical to you, Eldon?

HARLEY. You think that man can learn the job?

ELDON. What have I got to say about it?

HARLEY. You feel alright about him though.

ELDON. What's so difficult about pushing a cutting saw around a line?

HARLEY. Don't you give me a hard time, now. You mess up, you're cutting forty dozen legs at one go. That could get pretty costly on a narrow profit margin like we're running.

ELDON. Please don't tell me how the cutting room is run, I've cut enough—

HARLEY. I just wanted to be sure you felt good about him.

ELDON. I imagine we can put him on something.

HARLEY. You think he's foreman material? He's somebody you want to be working with?

ELDON. We can find something for him to do I said.

HARLEY. That's my partner who cares so much about the quality of the Campbell product.

ELDON. Goddamn it, Harley, we can find something.

HARLEY. I just wanted to know you felt good about it.

ELDON. It'll work out. Don't worry about it.

HARLEY. 'cause I don't. I guess I'm not stupid, I know what's happening, but I'm damned, begging you ladies pardon, if I feel good about it. You may think we can find a place for him, I don't think we can.

TALLEY. Here, Netta. Where's that pie?

NETTA. Olive, see what Mr. Talley wants.

TALLEY. Where is the pie?

OLIVE. It's in the kitchen, do you want to go out to the kitchen and have a piece of pie?

(He has left the room to go to his office.)

OLIVE. Is there any left?

BUDDY. Sure.

ELDON. Dad?

OLIVE. I better see. *(Light knock on door.)* Do you want some milk? You want me to heat up a glass of milk? *(She leaves.)*

ELDON. Wheeling and dealing makes him hungry.

BUDDY. Better get me some of that before it's gone. *(Exits.)*

LOTTIE. I swear to God dad is the cleverest son-of-a-bitch I ever encountered.

NETTA. Yes, he is, Lottie, all of that.

ELDON. That isn't clever, and it wasn't necessary. It's going to breed nothing but trouble. It's tantamount to admitting—what's that going to look like? He doesn't care a thing what he makes me look like.

LOTTIE. Oh, Eldon. I should have been the businessman in our generation. I should have been the politician.

ELDON. I'd damn near trade with you, Lottie.

NETTA. Did you care what you made us look like?

LOTTIE. I thought you knew dad by now.

ELDON. We have to keep our chin up, Netta.

NETTA. It's a great pleasure washing dishes with Olive out in the kitchen talking about getting a new flag for the window with a gold star for Timmy and blue one for Buddy.

ELDON. Come on, now. None of that talk.

NETTA. I don't want it; I don't want either one of those stars in the window anymore.

ELDON. I said I'm not going to listen to this tonight.

NETTA. And I don't want a military funeral with a flag on the casket.

ELDON. *(Quite hot.)* Not now, that's not for now. All that pain can wait till they've got our son back to us, mother.

OLIVE. *(Bringing in the pie.)* Mr. Talley. *(She opens the door.)* You said you wanted it.

HARLEY. I could use seconds, too. One for the road. *(Harley goes.)*

ELDON. Harley! Well, he'll cool off. Harley! *(He follows Harley to the kitchen.)*

NETTA. Don't run out when I talk to you! *(She leaves.)*

OLIVE. Mother? *(To Lottie.)* I don't mean to be upset, Lottie.

LOTTIE. Neither do I.

(Olive exits.)

TIM. "I, Timothy Everett Talley, do solemnly swear I will support and defend the Constitution of the United States against all enemies foreign and domestic; that I will bear true faith and allegiance to the same, that I will obey the orders of the President of the United States and the orders of officers appointed over me according to regulations and the Uniform Code of Military Justice. So help me God." Oh, boy. That's just out of your mouth and you feel proud as a peacock and scared shitless simultaneously. That is the cousin of, but a real grown-up development from, "On my honor I will do my best to do my duty to God and my country and to obey the Scout Law," let me tell you. Or, "I pledge my Head to clearer thinking, my Heart to greater Loyalty, my Hands to larger service and my Health to better living." *(Beat.)* And my balls to Uncle Sam. *(Beat.)* Which he collected in spades on Saipan, for what good they did him. Ever since I turned my field glasses to that farm island Tinian I was anxious to see what they were growing so neat. I didn't quite make it. I wouldn't have seen much if I'd got there 'cause Tinian became our Experimental Station, a place where we could try out all the fancy stuff that they were developing and we fairly tore the shit out of that place. Guy came up from Harvard with a new bomb, half-gasoline, half-soap so when it splatters on something it sticks to it like a tick and burns for about a day and a half. Daddy oh. Some of that stuff splatters on some-*body* instead of the vegetation that it was designed for and it's Torch-Man Time. But what the hell, it's a new toy, we don't have anything better to do, squirt some of that juice at Tinian. Clear the Nips outta the sugarcane and there goes Ohio. That place was green one day, bright blue and yellow and all those unfamiliar colors of a chemical fire all night, and the next morning smoking black. Hide in that, you son-of-a-bitch, and good-bye, Iowa. Too bad, barleycorn, but we're in a hurry. The scuttlebutt has it, see, that inside six months we'll get us a secret super bomb, and from Tinian the B-29s can reach Japan and, the scut-tlebutt runs, blow the Emperor's whole island right out of the ocean in one drop. So Tinian is the Amen. They're gonna raise a monument on this place. We're good at that. Then when we've all gone home the Nips'll come back and the Portuguese'll come back and start growing their fields of whatever-it-was again right up to the base of the marker. Which, you know, is inevitably what happens, and should happen, whatever field you're talking about.

So Nimitz is in a rush to win the war and everybody senses the end; even the celluloid boys, the Movietone moviemen are shooting double-time. Boy. *(Sings to "Da-da" the Movietone fanfare.)* Show all the moms and pops and all the guys and gals back home how we're beating the Japs. You talk about documented on film. Movie stars could have a respectable career and not spend as many hours in front of a camera as we do. And besides the Movietone boys they're photographing training films, living history or dying history, to show the troops in the next one, or if this goes on, the new recruits coming up, how it's done—or how it's not done, 'cause this is a one hundred percent logistical snafu. You feel it. As you do something asinine you know there's four cameras recording your fuck-up for posterity. See me run, see me fall over my own feet, see me dig a hole in the coral and take a sandy crap. See me step on a land mine or whatever I did. See me go. How am I doing, class?

Goddamn, but it is easy to get killed. This is what it takes. At a bright high noontime, half-drunk (you understand that everybody on both sides is half-drunk half the time and has been down through history, so that's just a given). I'm working alongside of the New York City Seabee whose name I can never remember 'cause I can't pronounce it. We're hacking back some bushes and he's telling us a tale in an accent— accent, hell, language—that I'm almost beginning to learn. He's laughing with the sun in his face, the rest of us—five in all, counting the Movietone man, are laughing, and I look over to him and say, "So, OK, how does it end?" And his head blows right off his body. Holy Christ. We're on the ground, fucking it, not hugging it, taking cover, with I-can't-remember-his-name's blood everywhere. And we start crawling toward where whatever-it-was came from. Me, three other Raggedy-Asses now, and the cameraman. See me crawl, kids, covered with what's-his-name's blood. This is the way we crawl. See me—Oh, boy— *(Lowly, as though involved in it now.)* see me spot that sniper. *(Still low, almost sighting along the barrel.)* There he sat—up the hill a bit, the son-of-a-bitch. He's crawled down from the cliffs for a few potshots and he's taken cover behind a rock, expecting us to come the other way. See me get a bead on that bastard...and then he moves behind the rock.

Now what you do is stay put, stay under cover, ever on the ready. This is a turkey shoot, and what you mainly do in a turkey shoot is wait. I happen to be very good in a turkey shoot. You steady your M-one, "Excuse me, your camera is in my sight." And the man behind the camera says, whispered, professionally troubled. "I got that." "What?" "I got that guy's face blowing up. I'm on a morale detail for the Homefront; all I wanted was a shot of him laughing. Jesus, I can't use this." *(Beat.)* And that's how easy it is to get yourself killed. *(Beat.)* See me jump up screaming and go running toward, not the cameraman, not the Homefront, but the turkey. I was yelling like a rebel, I scared that fool turkey half out of his mind. He jumped up, I blew the bastard to pieces. So, hell yes, daddy, I got my man, what the hell do you think I am? Hell, I'm running, I'll have you know, just like John Payne in the movies, and hell, if it ain't on film then they're missing one hell of a Marine, shooting from the waist, yet, yelling like a banshee; "I can't use this. I can't use this. I can't use this. I'm working on a morale detail for the Homefront and I can't use this."

And that's how you do something that you've been drilled very patiently and at great expense not to do. That's how you present yourself as a target.

Dad should have listened to the news; it might have been on. "And now to the editorial room of the Jergen's Journal and Walter Winchell—'Good Evening Mr. and Mrs. North America and all the ships at sea. Let's go to press. Flash! On Saipan. Private Tim Talley had a Flash! about what's being fed to Mr. and Mrs. North America, saw red, stepped on a land mine and went Flash! and was seen by all the ships at sea.'" I almost—but not quite—wondered if it was a land mine or if it was a shell, but shock and whatnot lets you off the hook and you don't hear the one that hits you; like lightning. So you lay there looking at this parrot looking at you and the corpsmen finally come. You're being carried on a stretcher, they're rushing you along to somewhere. You understand, you don't feel the stretcher under you, you just know they're rushing you to somewhere. You're looking up into the sun, some guy is running along beside you, trying to keep his hand over your eyes, shade them from the sun; you'd kinna rather see it: looking up into the trees as they go by, seeing, behind the kid shading your eyes, another cameraman.

So you asked whatshisname, the Seabee from New York, how it ends and he told you: This is how it ends. Fully documented, boys. Watch us go. Bumping along on a stretcher, dying. I Timothy Everett Talley do solemnly swear that I have supported and defended the Constitution of the United States against all enemies, foreign and domestic; that I have borne true faith and allegiance to the same, that I have obeyed orders of the President of the United States and the orders of officers appointed over me according to regulations and the Uniform Code of Military Justice. So help me God.

I think this is something maybe the Movietone newsreel people can use to boost the morale of the Homefront. I think we can use this. Somebody comb my hair.

(Beat.)

HARLEY. *(Off.)* All I'm saying—

ELDON. *(Off.)* There's no need to raise your voice, now—

HARLEY. *(Off.)* —not to make too big a fuss about it, all I'm saying is we're doing damn important work down there, and turning a pretty penny doing it, and I don't want some green fieldhand—some mechanic—

(Sally enters and starts up the stairs.)

LOTTIE. Sally!

ELDON. *(Off.)* There's no call to get angry. If we can't talk—

HARLEY. *(Off.)* Sure, sure, fine. I don't want a wrench thrown in it, Eldon, is all I'm saying.

ELDON. *(Off.)* Harley—

LOTTIE. *(Whispering.)* Sally!

SALLY. I started to say I can't believe they're still yelling, but I should be used to it by now.

LOTTIE. Matt Friedman was down at the boathouse, wasn't he?

SALLY. Yes.

LOTTIE. I knew it. I knew it. When they said his car was alongside the road, I knew that was where he'd gone. I swear to God, I've been straining my ears all night long, trying to listen in; trying to hear if you was coming back up on the porch without finding him; I been listening so hard I'm damn near deaf.

SALLY. We're going to drive down to Springfield and take the bus up to St. Louis. I want to tell them I'm leaving.

LOTTIE. No. You're not going to stay another minute here. All hell is breaking loose here tonight, and it's just started.

SALLY. Well, I'll add some to it, then. A little more from me won't hurt anything.

LOTTIE. You don't care what they think or what they do.

SALLY. I swear you'd think it was you running off.

LOTTIE. It is. It is me. I been courting that crazy person all winter long. Now, I'm running off to St. Louis and getting married.

SALLY. I'll be right back and say good-bye.

LOTTIE. I won't allow it. I won't allow you to go in there. You go in there and I swear to you, Sally, everything will change. You won't be able to get on that bus. I swear to you it's true.

SALLY. I thought you knew me better than that.

LOTTIE. Sally, I'm only your aunt and I've never given you an order, and you wouldn't have done it if I did, and I'm not more than twelve years older, well, fifteen, but you're not going into the family. Sally, I been keeping alive to hear this and you aren't going to spoil it for either one of us now.

SALLY. I have no bitterness Aunt Lottie. They can't touch me tonight.

LOTTIE. If you got no bitterness then you got no need. You—Oh, damn, what did Mrs. Platt tell Avalaine? She didn't have sense enough to do it. You got sense, I hope. She told her, "You fly away on," so now I tell you, you fly away on.

SALLY. I don't know how fast a Trailways bus is gonna fly.

LOTTIE. Fast enough. High enough.

SALLY. I have to pack some things.

LOTTIE. Sneak up quick. Run upstairs.

HARLEY. *(Coming back from the kitchen.)* Eldon. I'm not mad. We'll thrash this out tomorrow or next day.

SALLY. If you don't want me to see them, then I better go.

ELDON. *(Off.)* I can't say that it still can't be undone.

SALLY. There isn't anything happened has there? What's happened?

LOTTIE. Nothing you have to know tonight. Not a thing. There's no time now. Run upstairs. You call me on the telephone tomorrow and I'll tell you everything.

SALLY. You tell them where I've gone. *(She gives her a big hug.)*

HARLEY. *(Entering.)* Maybe the old boy knows what he's doing.

LOTTIE. Oh, I'll tell them, don't think I won't. Go go go go go go.

(Sally is gone upstairs.)

LOTTIE. Oh, I could just dance a jig. Oh, I could just dance a jig. Oh, damn me for never learning how to dance a jig.

ELDON. *(Entering with Buddy. To Lottie.)* You look like the cat that ate the canary.

LOTTIE. Do I look like that? I got to admit that's the way I feel. I chopped down the cherry tree and I ate the canary. Sweetest little thing I ever et. Tasted like lemon meringue pie. Surprised me no end. Everybody knew they tasted like that there wouldn't be a canary left in this town.

ELDON. Harley, you know I thank you for coming by.

(Netta and Olive enter.)

HARLEY. I tell you, I'm not going back to the telegram office anymore. I'm not going to do that. I don't have to tell you I'd rather it been anybody on this Earth come to you with that news than me.

ELDON. You don't know how we appreciate it, Harley. It helps, I guess, to have somebody like you…

HARLEY. I won't be doing it again. I can't do it.

ELDON. Don't say that, what if the next one's Buddy.

HARLEY. Hell, he's too mean.

TALLEY. *(Comes from office, pie in hand.)* Thought everybody had gone to bed. *(Hands the pie to Olive.)* Here. This ain't got no taste.

OLIVE. I beg your pardon. I put a full teaspoon of nutmeg and two teaspoons of cinnamon in that pie.

ELDON. It's too rich for you, anyway. You know better than that.

OLIVE. And it's past your bedtime that's for sure.

HARLEY. I'm just leaving.

BUDDY. I'll come out, have another of your cigarettes.

OLIVE. Don't you stand out there all night you two. I know you when you start talking.

HARLEY. Good to see you so fit, sir, but with all due respect I'm the man who does the hiring down there, not Eldon. And I'm not so sure you're trying to recruit the right man for the job. There's pretty bad talk about Emmet.

TALLEY. Wouldn't trust that man farther than I could pitch him.

ELDON. He's going to take some watching.

TALLEY. Ambitious people are fools, Harley. You ought to know that. They're too busy to look around and see what's happening.

HARLEY. Busy like a fox.

TALLEY. Who?

HARLEY. Talking about Emmet Young.

TALLEY. Never had any intention of that fool working down there. A man's reputation lies in the people he hires to work for him. I wouldn't have him around. Now, sir. This is the note, and this is the partnership agreement signed by me and your dad. This is the certificate of owner-ship on that factory. *(To Olive.)* That say ownership?

ELDON. Where did he have that? I didn't see anything like that in there.

OLIVE. Yes, sir, it does.

TALLEY. Now, the day after that devil and his concubine get married, you call up your Delaware people and you tell them to go ahead with that takeover like you been wanting to do. After they move the equipment out, Mr. Young can do all the cutting and all the foremanning he wants. But he ain't working one day for you and me. Now, I'm going to bed.

ELDON. You don't sell the plant because you don't want someone working for you.

NETTA. He's done it before.

TALLEY. Damn fool should use his eyes. Look around you. I've never been blackmailed and I won't be. What would that look like; not that Whistler here cares.

ELDON. *Eldon.* And I do care. Dad, my name may not be on that paper, but that factory, the Talley share of it, is mine. That decision is mine.

TALLEY. You try not to talk cause I'm making an effort to make sense—we know how I get. I went in that office and I prayed for the soul of my grandson that isn't coming back from the Pacific. Those two were going to get it all. Now there's just one and he don't want no part of it and never did and I don't either and never did. Harley, Eldon tends to forget you own more of that place than I do—you could do what you want with it.

HARLEY. No, sir, I—

TALLEY. Now, are you for that takeover; yes or no?

HARLEY. If we can work it out.

TALLEY. Good. Here, what's-your-name, vote on the takeover. Louisiana, Delaware, whatever. Yes or no. Move it out or keep it here. The Talleys are voting on what's going to happen to their share of that pestial place.

ELDON. Dad, you're sick—

BUDDY. We've been talking about it, sir; I've just been listening.

OLIVE. Mr. Talley

TALLEY. You're no namby-pamby, if you are you grow up now; you got your mind made up and you know it.

BUDDY. There's a lot of things I'd rather do.

OLIVE. Buddy, he's not good, now, don't push him—

TALLEY. Speak your mind what there is of it.

BUDDY. It means a lot to Eldon, sir; you better sit down.

TALLEY. Takeover yes or no if want your share. Otherwise I'll give the blamed thing to what's his name. Yes or no.

BUDDY. Yes.

TALLEY. So we've had a democratic vote like a family. Buddy and you and me. I vote for them, Buddy votes for them, you vote for yourself and lose. Two to one. Now, Harley; you know what we think—you do what you want about it.

BUDDY. I'm sorry, I've never wanted to work there, Eldon.

TALLEY. Don't be sorry; start out being sorry, end up being sorry.

ELDON. Dad, sit down.

TALLEY. Sorry is something for people who know they're doing the wrong thing while they're doing it. You asked Eldon about sorry. *(He sits, blinking and confused.)*

OLIVE. Mr. Talley?

TALLEY. Face is burning up. Seeing two of everything. Blamed.

BUDDY. Get him a washcloth.

(Olive exits.)

HARLEY. Eldon, I know what the place has meant to you—

ELDON. No, no—

HARLEY. You've been the one that kept everyone on the ball. If that place is worth somebody wanting it, it's only because of the standards you've—

ELDON. I appreciate it, Harley.

HARLEY. We'll thrash this over tomorrow.

ELDON. No, no, you do what dad said. He's the boss.

HARLEY. You got to admit he's slippery.

ELDON. Yes you do, I know it. Good night, boy.

BUDDY. Night, Harley. See you tomorrow.

(Olive enters. Mr. Talley wipes his face with the washcloth.)

ELDON. You two were going to hear the band.

BUDDY. Maybe not tonight.

ELDON. No, you two go on—let your wife show off her soldier in his uniform.

OLIVE. No, we'll talk—we've got tomorrow night. Is Mr. Talley?

ELDON. He's fine.

(Buddy and Olive exit.)

ELDON. Dad? *(He takes washcloth from Mr. Talley, wrings it out in the potted fern. Unconsciously wipes his own face. There is a pause.)* You just wonder why you did any of it. Timmy was never interested in the garment plant; he wanted to be a progressive farmer, I guess. Buddy was never interested. I guess I was just kidding myself, wasn't I?

NETTA. I always thought you were doing it for yourself. You knew they weren't interested in it. That place was poison to them. You knew they didn't want it. No point in lying to yourself about it now.

ELDON. I thought they'd see it's value when they got older.

NETTA. Why should they? I never did. I don't think you thought they would either. You didn't care if they did or they didn't as long as you got a day-and-a-half's work out of them. Where the devil has Sally got to?

LOTTIE. I imagine she's sitting out back. She'll be in before long.

NETTA. Lottie, don't stay up all night, now, you try to get some sleep. *(She is by the window, takes down flag with two stars.)* I don't want this display in the window anymore. I don't want that. And you take down the one that's in the window at the factory. I'm going to sleep in Tim's room tonight. Day after tomorrow I'll move my things in there. I'm not getting out of bed tomorrow. I don't want anyone mooning over me; I just want you to know I'm not coming downstairs. And you tell Buddy I'm not going to the train to see him off, and I'm not writing anymore V-Mail letters to him in Belgium or France or Italy or wherever they send him. When he comes home, fine, but until he comes home I consider that he's gone too. I'm not going to sit home and hope he'll be back. *(Pause.)* And I want you to lock up the house tonight.

ELDON. *(Finding his voice.)* Now, no need for that…we've always—kept the—

NETTA. *(Still level.)* I want the house locked tonight. You shut these windows and you find the keys wherever they are and you lock the house. Now, I'm going to bed. *(She goes upstairs.)*

ELDON. If I lock the doors, I'd lock Sally out.

LOTTIE. I'll let her in.

(Eldon locks the windows by Lottie. He would like to say something, but can find nothing to say. He takes a large ring of keys, finds one, goes to the French windows, locks them and goes out the door toward the kitchen. Sally sneaks down the stairs as he comes back through the house. He has been shutting off lights as he goes.)

LOTTIE. *(Sotto voce to Sally.)* Wait!

(Sally darts back upstairs.)

LOTTIE. *(To Eldon.)* Don't forget the windows in the dining room.

ELDON. *(Mumbled.)* What a bother.

(He goes. Sally sneaks down to the hall.)

LOTTIE. You call me here tomorrow and I want to hear that operator say I got a collect call for Charlotte Talley from Sally Friedman.

SALLY. Good-bye. *(She exits. Eldon comes into the hall and locks the front door with a loud click.)*

ELDON. You'll let Sally in?

LOTTIE. I'll be here.

ELDON. Someone has to tell her about her brother.

LOTTIE. I'll do that.

(Eldon stands for a long moment looking at his father, then—)

ELDON. Dad? I better help him to bed. Come on.

TALLEY. I'm fine, sir.

ELDON. Come on.

(They exit. Tim has entered the room.)

LOTTIE. *(To Tim.)* It's embarrassing how they've had to let the place go, isn't it? The house hasn't been painted in four years.

TIM. Yeah, it's beginning to show it. The garden's pretty bad.

LOTTIE. They had it cleared out a couple of times. Hoboes came looking for a handout, Eldon told them if they'd clear out the garden they could have supper. Then the last two years, everybody's got a job somewhere.

There's no one left to handle it. They just mow the lawn and let the rest of it go. It's no good to anybody, anyway.

TIM. It's a nice old house.

LOTTIE. *(In pain.)* It was, at one time.

TIM. *(Looks at Lottie who is holding her breath.)* You in pain?

LOTTIE. *(Through the pain.)* No, no, I got a phone call coming tomorrow, I got to be in good shape for that. A person could get from day to day for thirty years looking forward to a phone call. *(The pain goes away.)* Oh, lord. *(Beat.)* Oh, wonderful. *(Beat.)* Wonderful, wonderful. *(Curtain.)*

END OF PLAY